designs
for
persuasive
communication

Prentice-Hall Series in Speech Communication
Larry L. Barker and Robert J. Kibler, Consulting Editors

designs
for
persuasive
communication

OTTO LERBINGER

School of Public Communication
Boston University

PRENTICE-HALL, INC., Englewood Cliffs, New Jersey

© 1972 by
PRENTICE-HALL, INC.
Englewood Cliffs, New Jersey

ISBN: C 0-13-200220-5
      P 0-13-200212-4

Library of Congress Catalog Card Number: 75-38718

10 9 8 7 6 5 4 3

Printed in the United States of America

PRENTICE-HALL INTERNATIONAL, INC., London
PRENTICE-HALL OF AUSTRALIA, PTY. LTD., Sydney
PRENTICE-HALL OF CANADA, LTD., Toronto
PRENTICE-HALL OF INDIA PRIVATE LIMITED, New Delhi
PRENTICE-HALL OF JAPAN, INC., Tokyo

to Beth
and those we helped design,
Jan and Susan

preface

All of us have designs on other people and they on us. We are not independent isolates but social beings who need the cooperation of others. In society it is impossible or undesirable to undertake certain tasks by ourselves, and many things can be done better or more pleasurably with others.

Although the desire to persuade and be persuaded varies among individuals, human nature and dignity require each of us to be the persuader at least some of the time. Interest in persuasion is, therefore, universal. Even as targets rather than initiators of persuasion, we are curious about how people try to influence us, for it is part of the game of life.

When we look beyond our friendship and family relations, attempts to persuade become formal and professionalized. While authority and other power relationships can be used in formal organizations, persuasion has become a supplement or alternative because it is more acceptable and usually more effective. For this reason, seminars and workshops in persuasion have been popular among executives, government officials, military officers and heads of educational and social agencies. But just as it has become customary for politicians not to admit that they seek power, so has it become the rule to conceal the subject of persuasion under such euphemisms as human relations, sensitivity training, managerial psychology, leadership skills, or principles of human behavior. Whatever the title, the ability to influence others has become an essential and important attribute of leadership.

Persuasion has also become a specialized field in one form or another.

Advertising and public relations are the most prominent. Other "promotional" or "contact" specialties such as missionary work, health education, lobbying and salesmanship also draw heavily on persuasive skills. The field of mass communication, although ostensibly intended to inform and entertain, must be added to those which employ persuasion.

This book is written for both the part-time persuader whose other job is that of an executive or administrator and the full-time persuader whose main function is to shape and change other people's values, beliefs, attitudes, and behavior. To accomplish his objectives, he will likely use the tools of communication, for these are readily accessible in a free society. The persuader-communicator will carefully design his messages for specific media of communication which will reach his target audiences and have the maximum impact. Words and other communication symbols will, therefore, constitute his major stimuli, the instruments of change.

Stimuli are not aimed and discharged in a vacuum. They occur in spatial and temporal situations which combine with the stimuli and exert a joint force. The stimulus situation, as we should now call it, is further expanded by the representational power of the symbols used in communication. By their denotative power they may refer to critical policies, decisions and actions of the communicator (or his client) and thereby have the force of an event. By their connotative power words may evoke emotions, needs, aspirations and ideals to the same extent as the actual presence of friends, loved ones, cherished objects, heroes and prominent men.

When, therefore, we speak of persuasion through communication we refer to the usual modes through which forms of influence are exerted. Persuasive communication in the title of this book thus combines the intent with the medium; the two words—persuasion and communication—become inseparable.

Many people have directly or indirectly helped to write this book. I am indebted to Earle Barcus, Robert W. Hawkes, Robert R. Smith, and David Manning White who have shared the teaching of Theory and Process of Communication, a course on which this book is partly based. My thanks also go to the many students whose comments in this course have helped to clarify some ideas in this book. Special appreciation goes to my several research assistants whose patient and diligent efforts facilitated my work: Laurie Antonik, Sarah Cowan, Donna McLellan, and Kathy Cummings.

OTTO LERBINGER

contents

designs
for
persuasive
communication

ONE

the nature
and strategy
of
persuasive
communication

1

the nature of persuasive communication

We know that some form of control or influence over one another is an inescapable part of human living. That's part of Saturday night dates, marriage, and the rearing of children; the supervision of employees, the making of group decisions, and the sale of products; the running of political campaigns, and any other human effort that involves the actions of others. That's why we can't live and work unless we learn how to design human communications that will get others to think and act in conformity with our wishes.

The term persuasion properly describes symbol manipulation designed to produce action in others. An appeal to both intellect and feeling is used to obtain some kind of psychological consent from the person who is being persuaded.

When it appears that unfair advantage is taken by a persuader because his motives are not in the best interests of the other person or group, the term propaganda is generally invoked. Objectively speaking, however, the distinction between the two terms is slight. Both rely on communication tools to achieve results which are predetermined. Rather than attempt to soften the meaning of persuasion, it is more instructive to categorize this process under the heading of attempts to control human behavior. Limitations concerning persuasion can be discussed separately.

Let us at the start be honest with ourselves and admit that while we defend human freedom and dignity we are not uninterested in how that freedom is used or what values produce self-respect.

Our central concern with actual control of behavior is evident in the way we deal with things rather than persons.[1] If we want a table in a different place, we simply move it; if we find a room too small and confining, we knock down a wall; if we don't like a view from the window, we plant trees or bushes or, occasionally, have the whole house moved.

This attitude of determined execution of our designs is easily carried over to people. We lift unwilling children into their baths and "boot the drunk out of the saloon." [2] The line between person and thing becomes indistinct. No wonder we sometimes think of persuasion as the ability to "move others."

Our tendency to think of persuasion as moving people reveals its link to force. The motive of force remains but the method of force is replaced by persuasion. Before proceeding to consider the basic design of persuasive communication, we should recognize this ancestry of persuasion in force and consider the general transition of civilization away from force toward techniques of persuasion.

Force, the primitive and ultimate means of guiding or controlling behavior, is now reserved for exceptional situations: war, crime, industrial strife, civil disorder, and relapses of individuals into violent rage. Its use implies a breakdown of normal processes, a failure of law and order. And the persons affected are mostly the military, police, criminals, immature or desperate persons, and innocent victims.

Even when force is employed, people don't actually have to be pushed around. Certain signs that represent the potential of force are sufficient stimuli: the bayonet, the uniformed soldier or guard, the armored vehicle, the prison camp or jail, and the hangman's noose. These symbols of force don't even have to be visibly present; the mere knowledge of their existence somewhere serves the purpose. In police states for example, only an occasional show of force is necessary to give the appearance of potency and ubiquity.

Most men of power realize that force is the worst instrument of control. It guarantees results but usually of a negative kind; people are prevented from performing certain acts. Positive results are difficult, if not impossible to attain, and then only at minimum and perfunctory levels of performance.

The successful use of force also depends on two conditions: there must be enough force available to apply, and those subject to force must remain weak. A feature of our highly structured and interconnected world is that the application of force can seldom be confined to one location. Furthermore, the weak often become powerful or enlist outside support. For these reasons, even those men of power who have no scruples about freedom and a democratic way of life have been willing to abandon force when an alternative was present.

The abandonment of force is especially pronounced in work situations. Here the equivalent of force is authority, for the ultimate consequence of disobedience is the dismissal—forceful, if necessary—of the offending person from the organization.

Traditionally, officers, managers, and supervisors have relied on authority as their chief instrument for coordinating the activities of their subordinates. These leaders legitimatize their exercise of authority on several grounds: as an adjunct of property ownership, as the reciprocal of being burdened with responsibility, or the claim to superior intelligence, or at least privileged information.

Men in management positions now generally agree that the more authority is pushed into the background and made invisible, the better.[3] Among the reasons for this modern view are rising egalitarian attitudes, the changing nature of work, and the redefinition of the role of the manager.

The superiority of one man to another is increasingly rejected as opportunities for higher education and access to information are made available to a wider spectrum of the population. Work consists less and less of mechanical tasks that can be specified and programmed by managers; these types of operations are increasingly taken over by automated equipment. The jobs left require judgment and creativity—requirements that authority cannot transmit. The role of the manager is thus less that of a coordinator and more that of a leader who is able to inspire others with a sense of mission, a set of values or "moral code," and a spirit of cooperation. In short, the modern manager relies less on authority and more on skills of persuasion.

Persuasion possesses a feature that other forms of power lack. It has the psychological property of freedom: "persuadees" feel they are acting of their own accord within the goals and guidelines set for them. Hence they use their capabilities more and achieve higher levels of productivity. As democratic values spread from the political sphere to the offices and shops where people work, this feature of consent of those governed will grow in importance. We can expect to see greater use of persuasion in the future, not less.

THE REACHES AND LIMITS OF PERSUASION

As the number of fields that employ persuasion expands, a deep-rooted fear of being manipulated by powers beyond a person's control has been aroused. The possibilities and limitations inherent in persuasion and related means of controlling human behavior must, therefore, be explored.

Herbert C. Kelman, a psychologist who has specialized in attitude change, compares the situation of the social scientist to that of the nuclear physicist. Both are amassing formidable knowledge that is "beset with enormous ethical ambiguities" for which social responsibility must be accepted. These ethical problems concerning human behavior are causing increasing concern for several reasons: "knowledge about the control of human behavior is increasing steadily and systematically"; "there is an increasing readiness and eagerness within our society to use whatever systematic information (or misinformation) about the control of human behavior [that] can be made available"; social scientists are becoming increasingly respected and therefore solicited for their contributions; and the availability of powerful mass media aids in the "extensive manipulation and control of the behavior of masses." [4]

What is even more frightening to some is not the mere possibility of manipulation, but the fact that persuasion has become the primary function of new specialized fields. The most prominent of these are advertising and public relations. Both are multibillion dollar fields—about $15 billion was spent in advertising in 1965 and about $2 billion on public relations. The one specializes in the sale of products, the other in ideas, people, and organizations. Both make heavy use of the mass media: advertising pays for the use of space and time while the publicists connected with public relations manage to get free space by preparing their messages in newsworthy form and thereby partially duplicating the function of the journalist.

What disturbs many people about these efforts is not necessarily the actuality of being manipulated, but the idea that a group of persuaders openly say that it is possible and consciously set out to do so. There is nothing new about the anxieties that are thereby aroused. In his article "Limits of Persuasion," Raymond Bauer, a social psychologist, says that "the specter of 'manipulation' and 'hidden persuasion' has stalked all the lands that man has ever inhabited." Reviewing the past, Bauer reminds us that black magic is found among most nonliterate people, that being "possessed by the devil" was a curse in the Middle Ages, and that witches are a part of our own colonial past. Turning to modern times, he recognizes the role of the mass media and public relations: "Remember how during the 1920's and 30's we worried about the mysterious powers of the mass media, particularly as manipulated by such [public relations] practitioners as George Creel and Ivy L. Lee?" [5]

Another pioneer in the field of public relations, Edward L. Bernays, is frequently referred to in controversies about manipulation because he coined the term "the enginering of consent" to describe the planning process used in public relations. Furthermore, in his autobiography he says: "I find it easier to change the viewpoint of millions than one man's," and "Age-old customs, I learned, could be broken down by a dramatic appeal, disseminated by the network of media." [6]

Social science findings support Bernays. Bernard Berelson and Gary Steiner in their *Human Behavior—An Inventory of Scientific Findings* characterized the image of man produced by the behavioral sciences as: "a creature who adapts reality to his own ends, who transforms reality into a congenial form, who makes his own reality." They go on to say that "man is not just a seeker of truth, but of deception, of himself as well as others." [7] These are general comments that can easily be misunderstood, just as Bernays' comments have been.

does the power to control human behavior exist?

This book will deal with many techniques of persuasion: the use of motivation research to determine the wellsprings of human behavior; the use of symbols that have pleasant, rewarding associations; the reference to ostensible communication sources that have high credibility and thus tend to be believed; the careful selection of opinion leaders as channels of communication to the public; and references to cultural value symbols such as our flag and American heritage which arouse emotional support. These techniques are expected to make a message more convincing, more persuasive, more likely to affect behavior.

But to say that these techniques of social science enable a person to *control* someone else's behavior is too extreme. The critical factor is whether an individual can be influenced against his will. Here is what Raymond Bauer concludes:

> People have manipulated each other since the beginning of time, and it seems inevitable that—for the highest as well as the lowest of ethical motives —each of us will, and will want to, have some influence on our fellow human beings. However, the social scientists have not developed theories or techniques which make it possible for one man to control another man's behavior against his will and without his knowledge; and, as far as I know, no such possibility is on the immediate horizon. If it does exist, it is in the fields of pharmacology and physiology rather than in psychology.[8]

This conclusion does not mean that under exceptionally controlled conditions a single individual might not be induced to do something against his will. Berelson and Steiner agree, for example, that some people can be hypnotized against their will.[9] Our concern, however, is over the possibility that omnipotent control might be exercised over large numbers of people, especially by means of communication techniques.

Subliminal advertising, or what Arthur J. Bachrach, a behavioral scientist, simply called the "invisible sell," is often mentioned as an example that concealed mass persuasion is possible through communication.[10] James Vicary's experiment in a New Jersey theater over a six-week period is cited as evidence. Two messages were flashed on the movie screen for a fraction of a second: "Eat Popcorn" and "Drink Coca-Cola." The exposure was so brief (less than 1/100 of a second) that the audience was not consciously aware of the messages even though they were perceived. Proof that they were perceived is that during the test period, Vicary claims, the sales of popcorn rose 57.8 percent and the sales of Coca-Cola rose 18 percent.

The study has since been discredited because there is insufficient evidence that proper experimental controls were observed. However, there seems to be agreement among psychologists that subliminal projection is technically possible in the restricted sense that a stimulus can be perceived without the subject's awareness. But that possibility does not make control over behavior possible. As Berelson and Steiner summarize the situation: "There is no scientific evidence that subliminal stimulation can initiate subsequent action, to say nothing of commercially or politically significant action. And there is nothing to suggest that such action can be produced 'against the subject's will,' or more effectively than through normal, recognized messages." [11]

The great amount of attention given by communicators to audience research can be explained in part as an attempt to determine the limits of persuasion. Or, expressed another way, communicators try to predict how people will react to different ideas because they recognize the limits of persuasion. As teachers, executives, and others who try to inform and influence people often sadly conclude, perhaps the problem is that people cannot be changed enough.

are there some possible long-run consequences?

What is true in the short run may not be true in the long run. Summarizing the effects of mass communication, Wilbur Schramm says that it does not work like an atom bomb or like a hypodermic, "moving swiftly through biologic channels to bring about the predicted result." In other words, there is no sudden, appreciable impact. But he does suggest that there is a slow, steady effect. Mass communication, he says, works like a creek: "It feeds the ground it touches, following the lines of existing contours but preparing the way for change over a long period of time." [12]

The change that should be feared is that communicators, with the help of social science which they are avidly seeking, may create the type of person who will respond to their stimuli. This type of person has been described by C. Wright Mills as the psychologically illiterate, by Andrew Hacker as the predictable man, and by Berelson and Steiner as the social man.[13]

The psychologically illiterate man has forgotten how to learn through firsthand experience. Like descriptions of mass man, he has his standards of reality created by the media. Occasionally he craves crime news and sports news because these are the few spontaneous events left in the planned world of pseudo-events.[14] What haunts us about the predictable man is that he seems to be robbed of his individuality and free will. For example, it strikes many people as uncanny and evil to hear someone make statistical or actuarial predictions of such human events as the number of fatalities to be expected on a holiday weekend. And what bothers us about social man is that he seeks approval from people much more than truth from reason or conviction from principle.

The drip-drip-drip of the mass media and other contrived pseudo-experiences which take up more than a quarter of the average person's wakeful hours may indeed be conditioning human beings, who in the future can more easily be manipulated than in the past. Awareness of this possibility probably accounts for the recent interest by psychologists in studies aimed at increasing people's resistance to persuasion.[15]

Responsibility for offsetting these possible undesirable long-run effects is not exclusively that of communicators or psychologists. The individual has a responsibility for personal development and discovery of identity; schools have a responsibility to transmit our cultural traditions and values and to strengthen man's critical ability; religious institutions have a responsibility to offset the excessively materialistic values of the marketplace. The value of living in a pluralistic society is that no single communicator monopolizes our attention, our thoughts, and our values. But this potentiality of a pluralistic society is realized only when all segments of society speak up and engage in the process of mutual persuasion.

2 designing the communication strategy— objectives and audiences

The intention to persuade must be followed up with a design. In everyday life we prepare designs unconsciously and are thus unaware of their elements. A professional persuasive communicator, however, must prepare an explicit overall design, a master plan, which identifies and describes all the essential elements of a communication situation.

We call our master plan a communication strategy. It outlines and coordinates all steps and aspects of communication to achieve a desired change in attitudes and behavior. Edward L. Bernays, in talking about public relations, defines strategy as "the broad lines of action along which one carries on." He cites such decisions as "whether to conduct speeded-up action or a long-time cumulative activity," and "whether to concentrate effort on direct contact with group leaders or to conduct a general effort aimed at the general public." [1]

Similarly, in his "Clues for Advertising Strategists" Donald F. Cox in effect says: "If you want to cause certain things to happen, here is how to do it." [2] He then virtually reviews the literature on mass communication to identify such variables as credibility, rational and emotional appeals, and selective exposure—all of which he considers important.

Of enormous help in outlining a strategy is the communication model. The purpose of a model is to isolate those basic elements that all communication situations have in common and to show their inter-relationships. [3] Although the communication literature contains a profusion of models, [4] there is agreement on fundamentals.

The modern source of most models is the Shannon-Weaver model which shows (1) a source, (2) a transmitter, (3) a signal, (4) a receiver, and (5) a destination. In a speech situation the source is the speaker, the signal the speech, and the destination the listener.[5] The transmitter and receiver refer to the physical means of producing and reproducing a message. In electronic communication these might refer to a microphone and an earphone. In human terms, the transmitter refers to the "encoding" process and the receiver to the "decoding" process.[6] Encoding means putting information and feelings into a form that can be transmitted; decoding means the opposite: translating the signal back into meaning.

More useful for designing a communication strategy is a model which is conveniently described by the statement: who, says what, through what channel, with what effect.[7] Its typical expression in diagram form is as follows:

Some models omit the fifth element, but for our purposes it is essential because as persuasive communicators we are keenly interested in the results of our efforts.

Because the success of a strategy hinges on the achievement of results, we design the steps of our strategic plan in somewhat reverse order to the communication model. First we consider the effects—that is, the behavior we seek from the receiver. Then we consider the characteristics of the receiver, also known as the audience, so we can proceed with the last phase—the preparation of appropriate messages to send through channels that reach our audience.

The resulting steps in designing a communication strategy are to:
1. Determine objectives.
   a. Study the client's problem
   b. Decide and agree on communication objectives
2. Analyze the audience.
   a. Identify the audience
   b. Measure and interpret audience attitudes
3. Design the program.
   a. Source
   b. Message
   c. Media
   d. Context

DETERMINE OBJECTIVES—THE FIRST STEP

All strategy formulation begins with a determination of objectives—that is, the desired effects of communication efforts. These objectives relate a communicator—and his employer or client—with his audience, which is embedded in the larger society. Objectives indicate the changes that the communicator hopes to achieve in his social environment. As indicated in the diagram below, the relationship between a client and his social environment is two-way. The inward direction consists of informational intelligence about the outside environment; the outward direction represents communication and other efforts to influence what goes on in the social environment.

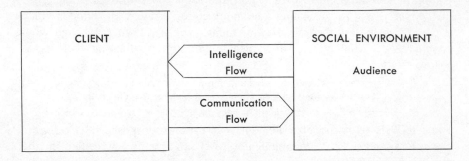

To determine objectives, two tasks are necessary: The client's problem must be studied and there must be a decision and agreement on communication objectives.

study the client's problem

A problem in persuasive communication is by definition one in which a person, group, or organization does not think and act the way a communicator would like them to. We shall use the term "client" to represent the sender, for in most situations the communicator works for an employer or client. Our initial task as communicators is to determine the nature and extent of the deviation between the "sender" and "receiver" of the communication network. We must then decide whether communication efforts can produce the changes desired by the client and what specific persuasive designs to use.

Beginning with the client, we must listen with attention and understanding to his explanation of a problem. Not only facts but personal beliefs, feelings, and values must be considered. Some of the listening and interviewing skills associated with the field of counseling are thus highly valuable. These will be reviewed in the next chapter after we have completed our strategy design steps.

When the client is a group or organization the problem may focus on the conflict of its social norms or policies with those of outside groups. These norms and policies must thus be understood. Furthermore, the client's readiness to reconsider them must be ascertained if it appears that the outside groups—our audience—will not change their position.

To analyze attitudes and policies pertaining to a problem, meetings must be held with all key client people who either are in communication with the audience involved or determine the norms or policies that are at issue. These meetings must be supplemented with an examination of publications, news clippings, and other messages that relevant audiences receive. Furthermore, any literature dealing with a group or organization's history, purposes, personnel, physical plant, financial situation, and prospects should be reviewed prior and as a supplement to client meetings. This research phase is excellently described by a public relations counselor, George Hammond:

> The counselor will analyze not only the existing attitudes and policies affecting each public but also the economic, social, and political developments that are likely to change these relationships. He will likewise research and evaluate existing communications policies, their objectives and effectiveness, and will dig deeply into the client's history, present operations, industry, and potentials.
>
> This research may very well begin with searching conversations with key people until a clear picture emerges—one that tends to be repeated with succeeding interviews. It may involve analysis of news stories and editorials, of market letters, books, radio or television programs, or magazine articles that have previously appeared. Or it may involve comprehensive, formal opinion surveys covering thousands of people and a wide range of topics.[8]

When the position of the client is sufficiently understood, preliminary research must be undertaken on the audience side of the communications network. Enough must be known about the identity and attitudes of the audience to enable the communicator to determine the extent and intensity of deviation from the client's position. More complete audience identification and analysis is the second step, which is discussed in the next section of our communication strategy design. At this point, however, when the communicator is satisfied that he understands the client's problem, he is ready to formulate objectives and obtain client approval for them.

decide and agree on communication objectives

The information obtained from interviewing the client, examining the literature, and investigating the problem externally are an admixture of facts and sentiments. They must be sorted out and analyzed for the purpose of defining the objectives of the communication strategy. The process of defining a problem and deciding upon objectives involves the kind of judgment associated with counseling. As Ronald Lippitt in "Dimensions of the Consultant's Job" points out, "every consultant has a cluster of ideas, or a set of concepts, which guide his perception of 'what exists' and 'what is going on' when he comes in contact with a particular group or organization or other social unit." Consultants who lack theory, Lippitt says, will have a harder time organizing and comprehending what they see.[9]

Objectives should ultimately be expressed in terms of a three-part question: What actions are sought, from whom, and when? Specific and concrete answers must be obtained, for objectives should not be so vague that they merely restate the problem. To say, for example, that the objective is to remove the misunderstanding that exists between a client and someone else or to create harmony between them is inadequate. The statement must go further and indicate what the specific subjects of misunderstanding are, to what attitudes they relate, and how these attitudes will affect the audience behavior in which the client is ultimately interested. In other words, the focus must be on "terminal behavior."

In deciding upon objectives, the communicator should observe two kinds of distinctions: between manifest and latent objectives, and between short-run and long-run objectives. The manifest purpose is one that is openly mentioned by the client, and the latent purpose is one that is not mentioned but is the more important.[10] For example, an optometrists' professional organization may state its objective as getting the community to know more about the optometrists' services. But this manifest purpose has a latent one—namely, to increase sales. Furthermore, the officers who seek a publicity program may simply be interested in justifying holding an annual meeting and want to do so by showing how much community attention it received.

Another distinction is between short-run and long-run objectives. For the optometric association a short-run objective might be to gain recognition for individual optometrists in their communities so that their business might improve. A long-run objective might be to bolster the professional status of optometry so that people with the usual eye care problems will first visit an optometrist rather than an optician or an ophthalmologist for an examination that involves refractive problems.

The two distinctions discussed—the manifest versus the latent purpose and the short-run versus the long-run—must be considered, for they help in defining communication objectives.

Once the objectives are clearly stated, the analytical phase is over and a diplomatic one begins. Edward L. Bernays considers this phase so important that the leading chapter of his book, *The Engineering of Consent,* starts with it. He says: "The first step in defining objectives is to bring about a meeting of minds of the policy makers, to get them to agree on specific objectives." [11]

In a follow-up chapter appearing in the same book, Howard Cutler offers three suggestions. The first is that the objectives must be practical and attainable. The main considerations are whether "an existing or a creatable community of interest between the client and the different publics whose support is essential" is present.[12] Cutler is asking for realism in the setting of objectives when he says that consideration should be given to "generally prevailing public opinion on broad economic and sociological trends, as exemplified by government action, current folkways, and philosophical convictions." [13] This statement can be viewed from the perspective of the short-run and long-run, for unless objectives are in harmony with the cultural patterns of society, no short-run attempt will work.

The only possible solution would be a long-run campaign to change impeding cultural patterns. But then Cutler's second suggestion becomes urgent. Objectives, he says, "must make sense in relation to the money, effort, and personnel available to pursue them." [14] Long-run efforts are usually more costly than short-run ones.

Cutler's third suggestion is to draw up a written statement of objectives for client approval. The discussions leading up to this point are sometimes as important as the final product. They assure two things. One is that the counselor is acting within the policy directives of the client and the limits of authority that are established. The second is that the counselor may have an unusual opportunity to influence the establishment or interpretation of such policy. Such policy may be in writing or it may simply be a reflection of the basic counselor-client pattern that is being established.

The Carl Byoir & Associates' *Account Executive's Manual* provides some useful advice for this stage of obtainng client approval. Both statements below remind the account executive to play his role as a professional courageously, faithfully, and responsibly:

> Stand your ground in opposition to the client when you possess the experience and knowledge to state positively that one course of action in the field of public relations is in the client's interest . . .
>
> Don't give the client a certain answer just because that's the one he wants to hear, if experience and judgment and honest conviction dictate a different answer.[15]

These suggestions should be followed if the public relations man is ever to make headway in the policy-making arena. Here is an opportunity to remove some of the dissatisfaction and frustration often felt when there is no room for "upward influence."

After the client has approved the communication objectives, the long process of studying the client reaches its climax. Now attention must be switched to the middle of the communication model: the audience that is the target of the communication strategy.

ANALYZE THE AUDIENCE—THE SECOND STEP

Once the objectives of a communication strategy are clearly known and have received client approval, strategy planning can proceed to audience analysis. The relevant audience has already been identified, for objectives must be stated in terms of what actions are wanted by whom. But such reference to the audience is likely to have been imprecise and incomplete. An audience analysis step is thus required to more closely pinpoint the audience and to measure and interpret its attitudes.

identify the audience

The aim of audience identification is to prepare an exact list of persons, groups, organizations, and geographical areas that are relevant to communication objectives. This task can be simple or complex. It is simple when the audience is a distinct group with a membership list, for example, the employees of a company who receive a company newspaper, or stockholders who receive an annual report. Most clients have lists of publics with whom they regularly communicate because these publics are important to their welfare. Audience determination is also easy if the client simply wants to reach as many persons constituting the general public as possible in a given geographical area; a review of the coverage of the various mass media is all that is needed.

The identification of a relevant audience becomes complex, however, with nonroutine, special campaigns. Discovering the right people to reach with a message is often the key to its success. In fact, a client sometimes selects a public relations or advertising agency on the basis of its familiarity with persons or groups relevant to given industries or fields. The past experience of these agencies serves as a guide to audience identification.

When such personal or agency experience is lacking, systematic procedures must be used. All of these procedures are involved in one form or another of an audience identification study. Such a study identifies who the decision makers are with regard to a particular policy, issue, or decision; it may also describe how the decisions are made and how much weight is given to different sources of information, staff members, counselors, public opinion surveys, and so on.

Decision making in some areas has been intensively studied and library references are available. This is particularly true of consumer behavior and voter behavior. In other areas, relevant data about decision making must be collected.

One illustration of a decision-making study again refers to the professional organization of optometrists whose goal is to increase public use of their services. In considering the problem of what audience they should try to reach, the first fact is that not everyone has a visual defect. Hence there is no need to try to communicate to the entire public if a way can be found to identify those people who can most benefit from optometric services.

One way to do this is to interview people who have used the services of an optometrist and to find out how they arrived at the decision to use optometric services. We would probably find a progressive screening process starting with the total population; this is then narrowed down to persons who recognize or admit that they have a visual defect; these are then pruned to persons who are willing to take some action; and the group can be further limited to persons who actually visit optometrists or their competitors, the ophthalmologists and opticians; and finally the audience is distilled to persons who elect initially to visit optometrists rather than ophthalmologists and opticians. Those persons and groups that are discovered to be particularly influential in committing people to action—choosing optometrists when they are appropriate—obviously become the targets of communication efforts.

Information from such audience identification studies then serves as the initial input in the process of media selection. Effective and economical ways of reaching the target audience must be found. This subject is discussed in Chapter 19, "Media Selection and Placement."

measure and interpret audience attitudes

Step two—audience analysis—is only half completed with the identification of the target audience. Information is needed about the attitudes held by a particular audience. The next part of the book which considers five designs for influencing attitudes provides the basis for studying the attitudes of audiences. As both a preview and a summary of some of the main points of these chapters, the following five questions are listed. They show what is needed for audience analysis.

1. *How interested are specific groups of people in the issue?* Specific target audiences may be referred to in the statement of objectives, but in this stage of analysis the communicator must leave no doubt about who the people are that he is trying to reach. These groups may have identified themselves by having taken the initiative in creating a labor dispute, asking

for government action, or otherwise creating a public controversy that involves the client. In other situations, the client wants to take the initiative in soliciting the cooperation of a public. He may, for example, want to build a plant in a community where zoning laws first have to be modified, or want to seek public support for legislation. Some railroads, for example, have sought state subsidies to keep them from bankruptcy.

Here the problem becomes one of deciding on target audiences whose opinions count and then interesting them in an issue.

This first question about the audience's expressed or potential interest in an issue will help determine to what extent the motivational design has application. Furthermore, depending on the analysis made, decisions on at least two principles of persuasion dealing with the attention factor can be made. If expected interest in a topic is low, the principle of primacy—stating the important or climatic material first—should be used. Second, if there is no way to obtain voluntarily and maintain interest, various kinds of captive audience procedures should be explored. Military officers and teachers do this in insisting upon attendance; employers sometimes do it in making attendance at certain meetings highly attractive for workers by letting them attend during working hours.

2. *How complex is the issue?* Some objectives, like the marketing one of getting people to eat soup along with sandwiches, are so simple that they are not issues at all. Other objectives like achieving racial integration, justifying the size of the military budget, or defending a wage proposal are so complex that even experts are confounded.

If an issue is complex, simple learning techniques such as described under the stimulus-response design should not be used. Usually this also means that advertising is an inappropriate tool, for the information load that it can carry is too limited. People cannot be sold on the virtues of the free enterprise system, for example, by merchandising it on transit ads as one would soap or soup.

A complex issue usually requires some application of the cognitive design. And along with this model, such principles of persuasion as whether explicitly to state conclusions should be considered.

3. *How controversial is the issue?* An issue can be controversial in two senses. The main way is that different people and groups hold different views. A second way is that an issue is based on opinion rather than fact. If people differ sharply in their opinions about an issue and if they are in a position to have their opinions felt because they are organized into pressure groups, the client must expect opposition in his communication attempts. One implication is that the client should probably present both sides of an issue rather than only his own side.

If an issue is controversial but its resolution is based on factual evidence, there is an opportunity to apply the cognitive design. How large the opportunity is depends upon people's willingness to surrender their opinions in the face of facts. On such issues as fluoridation some people are unwilling to allow any factual information to interfere with their cherished views and others are willing to allow a limited scope to facts. Most issues are an admixture of fact and opinion, so care must be exercised in not oversubscribing to the rational approach.

Drawing a distinction between the factual and opinionated aspects of an issue is also relevant to the kind of source credibility or social endorsement that is drawn upon. The more an issue is based on fact, the greater the advantage is of using the credibility of an expert in the relevant field. And the more an issue is based on opinion, the greater the need is to obtain the support of a person or group that a particular target audience feels it can trust.

4. *How deep-seated or ego-involving is the issue?* People may feel relatively indifferent about many issues but they may get deeply involved with others. Some attitudes, such as political ones, are built up over a lifetime of social learning and personal experience with the result that they cannot be changed easily by a single new influence; other attitudes are closely linked to underlying motives and cannot be changed without consideration of these motives; still other attitudes are so diffuse and related to personality traits that changes must consider people's ego ideals and defense mechanisms.

Deep-seated or ego-involving issues require the application of the sophisticated models of attitude change. Furthermore, the way certain principles of persuasion should be used is affected by this consideration. For example, if a topic is highly personal, conclusions should not be made explicit.

5. *To what extent is the issue socially anchored?* Some issues are mostly of personal concern—thus an appeal can be made to a person as an individual. Most issues, however, involve the actual or implied presence of other people. The discussion of the social model illustrated how many attitudes and actions, such as the purchase of products or production output levels, are influenced by others. Other matters, such as what forms of entertainment or kinds of food are preferred, are influenced by the cultural tastes of a social or ethnic group, but tolerance is allowed for individual variations.

The extent to which the social design is applicable is answered primarily by whether or not an issue is group anchored. If so, the various factors that facilitate the use of the social model should be studied carefully.

3

designing the
communication
strategy—
the program

The design of a communication strategy is completed with a program, which is a presentation of stimuli to a selected audience. These stimuli serve as the communicator's instruments of change, for his aim is to shape or steer behavior in a particular direction. They therefore become the culminating point of his strategy. He hopes he can have maximum control over the stimuli but unlike the psychologist in a laboratory setting he deals in a real life context where the situation contains distracting and competing stimuli.

This chapter outlines the major elements that constitute a stimulus situation or program. The second section of the chapter is an enlargement of the first step of strategy design, for it discusses some helpful counseling techniques.

DESIGN THE PROGRAM—THE THIRD STEP

The stimulus situation is the raw material for perception that the communicator hopes will command the attention of his audience. To the member of the audience, the stimulus situation is only one part of the environment to which he tries to adjust. But to the communicator it is the part of the environment he tries to construct for the purpose of informing and influencing his audience.

The stimulus situation encompasses the "who says what through what channel" part of the communication model and whatever context—part of the larger environment—is present during communication. For example, Roger Blough's defense on television of U.S. Steel's price increase in the face of federal opposition could be analyzed as follows: The chairman of the board of directors of the U.S. Steel Corporation is the communicator who presents a message consisting of selected information and ideas over the medium of television to a viewer who is in the context of his home (where group discussion may follow). Each of these elements—the source, message, channel, and context—must be considered in designing the stimulus situation.

consider source credibility

The source and channels of communication are considered briefly here in one of their aspects: the extent to which people rely on others and upon the mass media for contact with most events. Except for the events that people themselves attend, they rely on a professional group of people —gatekeepers—who select, interpret, and transmit information, ideas, and entertainment to them.[1] As expressed by Walter Lippmann, what people are exposed to is an image of reality or a pseudo-environment which can to some extent be manipulated.[2]

If a gatekeeper stands between the events of reality and the audience, the question of whether this communicator can be believed and trusted is important. It is in this connection that the concept of source credibility becomes important. This quality of the speaker was called *ethos* by Aristotle. He said that a speaker "worthy of belief . . . is the most potent of all the means to persuasion."[3] Modern psychological studies support the contention that "the effectiveness of a communication is commonly assumed to depend to a considerable extent upon who delivers it."[4]

Distinctions are made among several bases of credibility. The major distinction is between trustworthiness and expertness. A person who is perceived as sincere and as showing no intention to persuade is likely seen as trustworthy, while a person seen as skilled, informed, and technically qualified is likely to be judged as expert. The advantage of credibility based on expertness is that nearly all people in a given society will ascribe high credibility to such a source regardless of the informal groups to which they belong. Such credibility thus can be used by communicators with a certain disregard for audience characteristics.

These two components of credibility—trust and competence—are relevant in situations in which the audience is relatively autonomous and engaged in a kind of problem-solving or decision-making task. For example, this happens when the citizens of a community are asked to vote on a school bond issue. They will vote for the bond issue only if they are convinced it is desirable, for the vote is private. Another kind of situation, however, may demand compliance. The audience is under some kind of authority or social pressure to conform to the communicator's wishes. Where this is the case, two additional bases of credibility may be relevant: the likability and the prestige of the communicator. Raymond Bauer offers this explanation of how these components work:

> . . . a member of the audience may 'go along with' a communicator who is likable or prestigious without really being influenced to change his mind. What you get in this case is what we have called 'compliance,' indicating a change in overt behavior unaccompanied by any internal restructuring.[5]

Psychologists who have studied forced compliance situations in connection with cognitive dissonance studies report some paradoxical results of what we normally consider high credibility based on likability. A communicator who is disliked can get better results than one who is liked. Suppose that a person has overtly taken a position he doesn't really believe in. If the source is pleasant, the act of compliance can be rationalized as doing him a favor. An unpleasant source, however, puts more pressure on the individual to reduce the dissonance caused by compliance by telling himself that he really does believe what his overt behavior indicated.

The credibility factor becomes crucial when national loyalties and group beliefs are involved and are known to be in conflict. In such situations it is advisable to diminish the gatekeeping role or to make it more invisible. The use of pictures, slides, films, and television scenes that seem to bring the events directly to people without overt interpretation is one way to short-circuit gatekeeping. Another way to minimize gatekeeping is to reverse the process by taking the audience to the events. When a person has direct access to events he generally trusts his own impression more than somebody else's report of what happened. This is one reason why open houses, invitations for foreigners to visit us, and educators' conferences held by some corporations are highly persuasive instruments. Such direct access does not remove the possibility of other influences operating, for if a person is confounded by what he sees, he tends to rely on others —perhaps someone with relevant specialized skill or knowledge—for interpretation.

message

The message is the core of the stimulus situation and the part over which the communicator has the greatest control. Message preparation is theoretically approached on many different levels and by diverse specialists. For example, the mathematician studies how signals can most readily be transmitted and how each signal can carry the highest load of information; the semanticist studies how signs and other language codes are related to objects and other referents of meaning; and the social psychologist studies how people react to language codes.[6]

From the viewpoint of persuasive communication, our main interest is in the meanings that people attach to stimuli, and thus we are interested in the relationship between language and behavior. These aspects of messages fall mainly in the province of semantics. Books by Stuart Chase, Samuel I. Hayakawa, Benjamin L. Whorf, Charles E. Morris, Roger Brown, and A. Korzybski have provided valuable insights, especially in avoidance of the pitfalls of miscommunication.[7] In the future the field of psycholinguistics will make important contributions.

In this book semantical aspects of communication and message preparation are not discussed separately but as parts of other topics. The power of words is particularly discussed in the stimulus-response design, the order of presentation of arguments in the cognitive design, and the influence of linguistic habits on what is seen is discussed under the section on perception.

media and context

The least controllable aspect of the stimulus situation is the context in which the message appears. Gestalt psychologists in their studies of "figure and ground" have demonstrated what can be observed in everyday life; namely, that the meaning of anything depends on its surroundings. A news story (the "figure") appearing on the front page (the "ground") is given more attention and attributed with greater importance than one appearing on the back pages. If we focus on the words alone as the message, then we must also consider the size of the headline, the position of the story on the page, the other stories or ads on the page, and the kind of newspaper in which the message appears. If the medium is radio, the quality of the voice is part of the context.

Also part of the context are other space and time factors. Whether an employee newspaper or magazine is received at work or at home influences whether the social pressure of the family or one's co-workers are apt to be present and dominant. The time of day, week, and year that a message is received affects its motivational power and meaning. A radio commercial about the attractiveness of an outdoor museum will have more impact on a bright Sunday morning in spring than on a rainy or sunny work day.

The communicator tries to control as many of the factors we have discussed as possible. Sometimes he does this by relying less on the public media and on free publicity; he may, for example, decide to start his own stockholder's newsletter or pay for an advertisement and thereby control some gross physical and time features.

Two additional context factors have received major attention by the persuasive communicator because these factors heavily determine the outcome of his efforts. One is the extent to which he monopolizes the persuasive situation, and the other is the presence of deeds and events that support his words.

Persuasive monopoly.   It is seldom that a communicator with a given point of view monopolizes a persuasive situation. There are other communicators who present their viewpoints, and there are friends and relatives who will echo the various themes of the accumulated culture of society.

Over the long run, only the government of a closed society can approach a complete monopoly situation in which the thought patterns of all the people in a communication network could be changed. Every person in such a society would have to be controlled because each is a potential competitor to the state. Such a situation could only exist in a totalitarian state completely sealed off from the outside world. Only when no other communication systems exist in a closed society can there be a monopoly situation.

But where sealed borders can be crossed by radio and television waves as well as by such propaganda devices as leaflets dropped from balloons, a communication monopoly cannot be maintained. Totalitarian governments also realize that the attainment of a communication monopoly requires the supplement of force. People who disagree must be coerced into changing their views; they must at least learn to keep their thoughts private or face isolation through imprisonment or death.

Despite the example of Nazi Germany, the above description of a long-run communication monopoly is so extreme as to appear abstract. Not so abstract, however, are many short-run attempts at monopoly control over parts of people's lives. Moral judgment tends to differ in these situations because the overall context is one of freedom.

Roger Brown, in describing a monopoly situation, cites the parent's control over the child as an apt illustration.[8] The combination of force with communications is still typical. This is the manner in which the basic orientation of a child into our society is handled. Not dissimilar is the typical basic training in monasteries and military life. A young recruit is cut off from the outside world for a given period of time so that the indoctrination can proceed under the most favorable circumstances.

Without going into further examples, it is apparent that in the upbringing of a child and in various other forms of indoctrination, parents and others in positions of command seek a temporary monopoly situation. The principle that these attempts illustrate is that a communicator is most effective in gaining support of this message when he has a large measure of control over the audience's total environment.

Coordinate words and events. A communicator who works in the interests of a client cannot seek to control the environment of his audiences. All he can possibly do is to have maximum influence over that portion of the environment which his client controls and which is relevant to his objectives.

The communicator realizes that what he says must correspond to the realities of a given situation. The management he represents cannot be doing one thing while he is saying something else. If, for example, the information officer of an Air Force base says that the Air Force is doing all it can to reduce jet noise, but the base command refuses to build a blast barrier or properly instruct pilots on noise-reducing approaches, these words appear empty. Communicators should reflect actual decisions made. This is why they must work closely with chief executives.

It is necessary for an organization to coordinate its communications and actions as closely as possible. Failure to do so will result in loss of credibility whenever the incongruity between words and deeds is recognized by people. On the other hand, assuring the coincidence of words and deeds will tend to heighten the effectiveness of communications. When Khrushchev boasted of Soviet scientific progress and military power at a time when Sputnik was launched, even his enemies were inclined to admit the plausibility of his assertion. Likewise, when during a recession a company tells people to maintain confidence, its words become magnified if at the same time it announces a continuation of its capital spending program.

There are some areas of communication in which management has greater control over the environment than others. The field of employee relations is an example. Not only is there a captive audience in a sense, but the property belongs to management and it, therefore, controls a large part of the daily work environment. The way workers are treated by their supervisors will eclipse any written communications intended to produce a cooperative attitude toward management or to increase output; furthermore, any personal observation and experiences that are not in accord with what management says will triumph at the sacrifice of management's credibility.

In summary, parts of the environment of an audience that relate to the substance of a communication program can be seen in two ways: first, as the context in which a message will be perceived and therefore judged;

second, as events which in themselves serve as the main stimulus for influencing behavior. Both aspects are apt to be overlooked by communicators who don't also see themselves as management counselors.

COMMUNICATION COUNSELING:
ASPECTS OF STRATEGY DESIGN

In designing a communication strategy, the persuasive communicator serves as a counselor to his client. He must be able to give sound advice based on broad knowledge and experience. With reference to public relations counseling, for example, George Hammond says that he must have the "ability to interpret the forces of public opinion in terms of the interests of his client and to provide the means of communicating to important 'publics'. " [9]

As stated in the previous chapter, the determination of objectives begins with a face-to-face meeting with a client where his problem is explored. If the meeting between the counselor and the client is the first, more than an exchange of information takes place, for first impressions are formed that determine the quality of the future relationship.

It is obvious that interviewing and listening skills play a predominant role, and for that reason we begin with a review of these skills.

interviewing and listening skills

Information about the client's problems and objectives is mainly obtained from the client himself, at least initially. Interviewing and listening techniques must, however, be used skillfully to obtain information that is relevant and accurate.

The communication counselor can benefit a great deal by borrowing some techniques used in psychological counseling. The client-centered therapy approach developed by Carl Rogers provides a good start.[10] The main idea is to establish a productive counseling atmosphere by following such rules as these:

1. Exhibit a genuine interest in the client.
2. Encourage the expression of feelings as well as facts.
3. Leave your own wishes, reactions, or biases out of the discussion.

Although the counselor should remain sufficiently open to allow the client to describe his situation and objectives fully, some probing and direction must eventually be undertaken. A technique known as the "controlled, nondirective interview," which was developed by Robert L. Kahn and

Charles F. Cannell is helpful.[11] The main characteristic of this technique is that the counselor maintains overall control over the topics that are discussed, but once they are specified the client-centered, neutral procedures of Carl Rogers are followed.

One of the reasons why the nondirective aspect of interviewing is here stressed is that many counselors succumb to the temptation to talk too much, listen too little, and give premature advice. For the same reasons, the underdeveloped skill of listening is also given attention by counselors.

Ralph Nichols, a leading authority on the art of listening, proves how poor our listening habits are. He estimates that the average person remembers only about 50 percent of a short talk ten minutes after hearing it, and only about 25 percent after two months.[12] He concludes that people are highly inefficient listeners and the reason for this is that they are taught in school to read but not to listen.

People can listen at the rate of about 400 words a minute. The average speaker, however, delivers at the rate of 100 words. The time represented by that difference is usually wasted by poor habits. The recommendations for improved listening are largely based on using this extra time to increase listening efficiency. Nichols lists four processes used by good listeners:

1. The listener thinks ahead of the talker, trying to anticipate what the oral discourse is leading to and what conclusions will be drawn from the words spoken at the moment.

2. The listener weighs the evidence used by the talker to support the points that he makes. "Is this evidence valid?" the listener asks himself. "Is it the complete evidence?"

3. Periodically the listener reviews and mentally summarizes the points of the talk completed thus far.

4. Throughout the talk, the listener "listens between the lines" in search of meaning that is not necessarily put into spoken words. He pays attention to nonverbal communication (facial expressions, gestures, tone of voice) to see if it adds meaning to the spoken words. He asks himself, "Is the talker purposely skirting some area of the subject? Why is he doing so?" [13]

The fourth point refers to another advantage of the nondirective counseling technique. Learning to read between the lines is one of the main skills taught by clinical psychologists, psychiatrists, and human relations experts. People sometimes can't or won't tell us exactly what is on their minds. They may not know themselves or are unconsciously guarding their egos with rationalizations and other defenses. Furthermore, sometimes a client hints at things rather than stating them outright, so the burden of drawing a certain conclusion falls on the counselor.

In nondirective counseling, the counselor tries to encourage the client to speak by responding with a variety of neutral expressions. The favorite response is to say "Uh-huh" in about twenty different ways; other variations are "I see" and "I understand." In order to probe a particular point, such expressions as "You think that . . ." or "You feel that . . . ," followed by the appropriate summary idea or feeling can be used. The point is to keep the flow going—and in the desired direction—by showing interest and by priming the pump from time to time. There is also an assumption that any statement of judgment on the counselor's (listener's) part would jeopardize the flow.

Reading between the lines can be improved by remembering that language is expressive as well as cognitive. In nondirective counseling the distinction between the two kinds of language is exaggerated to a point where facts and logical details are allowed to pass by while sentiments and feeling are elicited by the counselor.[14] A counselor soon learns that a tremulous voice may be symptomatic of fear even if the client says that he is not afraid. The counselor may also infer by the late arrival of a client for an appointment that the client is trying to avoid him or holds him in low esteem. The various symptoms and signs of expressive or "silent" language must be learned.[15]

It is not being suggested that the communication counselor give greater weight to feelings, sentiments and attitudes than to factual, logical, and cognitive aspects. The former have been emphasized here because they are too often neglected. Actually, both must be attended to and combined so as to derive maximum meaning from a meeting with the client.

execution and evaluation of the communication strategy

Our discussion of the design of a communication strategy ended with the preparation of a program. But a communicator should look beyond the strategy to its execution and evaluation. A design must be skillfully executed if it is to fulfill its purpose. This calls for organizational skill in breaking the total design into tasks that can be performed by specific people at the right time. This skill is basically not any different from that required to organize other management activities. But communication counselors are likely to lack aptitude and training in principles of organization and management.

Chester Burger, a public relations man who has written on this subject, said: "A major weakness of the public relations profession, a weakness that gives rise to so many criticisms by the business community, is failure to manage properly public relations activity." [16] He suggests that the biggest opportunity for the improvement of public relations work as well as the enhancement of professional prestige lies in better management of public relations operations.

There is general agreement among counselors that they should report regularly to their managements even though there is little agreement as to the form, content, and method. The simple routine of scheduling meetings with management on a regular basis, perhaps monthly, as suggested by the Carl Byoir and Associates' *Account Executive's Manual,* should at least be followed. The Manual also recommends annual review and planning meetings. The habit of holding such meetings helps to develop an attitude of responsibility in the practitioner. Furthermore, by combining planning and evaluation in these conferences, practitioners are more likely to gear their activites to the achievement of objectives.

Evaluation should be seen as the control aspect of executing a communication strategy. There are three levels of evaluation that should be considered: the instrumental, the client-centered, and the societal.

The instrumental consists of various kinds of research to check the validity of important premises made in communication design. For example, circulation figures, readership figures, readability scores, and so forth, may be compiled to see how adequately a target audience is being reached.

Client-centered evaluation is the most typical administrative practice in business. Actual results are compared with expected results, and these results must advance the purposes of the client. In this way the benefits of a program can be appraised against the costs of maintaining a staff, consultant, or specific program.

Evaluation on the societal level is concerned with the impact of a communication strategy upon the interests of third parties and upon the overall welfare of society. A strategy, for example, that constantly uses opinion leaders as target audiences may have the unintentional effect of reinforcing or forming a stratified society that jeopardizes democratic values. As a part of a societal evaluation, the communications counselor should consider the impact of his choice of themes, slogans, and language upon the cultural symbols of society. For example, the excessive use of high value symbols, such as referring to every claim as a scientific fact, debases the meaning of words and destroys some of the foundations of faith in man's communication with man. A societal evaluation involves obvious professional interests.

In summary, the evaluational phase is an extension of communication strategy design which serves as feedback information that can be used in the determination of objectives. The intelligent use of feedback information assures the communicator that he is constantly learning from his current and past performance and that each job will be done better than before.

4

attitudes
and
behavior

Underlying the communication strategy is a central concern with people's attitudes and behavior. We say that we want to change someone's attitude or mind about something with the hope that at some appropriate time he'll behave in accordance with our wishes.

In speaking this way we recognize the importance of understanding human behavior. Not surprisingly, therefore, one of our major frames of reference in planning persuasive communications is psychology. Our starting point is the basic S-O-R formula of behavior. As shown in the following diagram, the formula indicates that a *stimulus* is presented to an *organism* which produces a certain *response*.

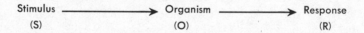

Stimulus ⟶ Organism ⟶ Response
(S)   (O)   (R)

We can relate this diagram to the communication model we reviewed in Chapter 2. The stimulus refers to the source, the message, and the channel; the organism, to the receiver; and the response, to the effects. By understanding these relationships we can infuse psychology into the process of communication.

The S-O-R formula reflects the basic concern of psychology, namely, "observing what goes into the organism (stimulus) and what comes out (response)." [1] Incidentally, the psychologist uses the term "organism" because he is interested in animal as well as human behavior. Furthermore, many experiments with rats, dogs, and monkeys provide valuable insight into how persons behave.

As persuasive communicators our focus is on the response that our message stimuli elicit. But we know that the person who produces an output in response to our input is not just a push-button gadget. His nature and background interact with the stimulus to determine his reaction.

Communication involves all three components of the S-O-R psychological formula. As stated by Colin Cherry, ". . . communication is not the response itself, but is essentially the relationship set up by the transmission of stimuli and the evocation of responses." [2] The person who is in the middle of this relationship serves as the connective or the "intervening variable." We dramatize his role by making him the "black box" in our new diagram:

ATTITUDES: THE WIRES INSIDE THE BLACK BOX

When an electrical engineer constructs an electrical gadget, he often puts a black box around it to conceal its messy and complicated wiring. To test the performance of the black box, he then introduces an electrical input at one end and records the output at the other. For example, if the gadget is a transformer, he may plug in four different inputs, 400, 300, 200, and 100 volts. If the outputs are recorded as 200, 150, 100, and 50 volts respectively, then he knows that the action of the black box is to divide the voltage in half.

The psychologist does very much the same thing. He is considerably more awed by the complexity of human behavior than the engineer by his gadgets. Thus he tends to view a person as an inscrutable black box whose behavior is usually understood only by observing how he responds to different stimuli. For example, if a psychologist wants to know the decibel level at which a person hears, he may introduce different levels of sound and ask the person to indicate when he hears sound. Similarly, we are all used to taking exams of all sorts in which we are asked to demonstrate what is inside of us: our ability to drive a car, our knowledge of the Bill of Rights, our grasp of calculus.

These responses measure physiological abilities, skills, and storage of facts. When the psychologist's attention turns to our evaluation of objects, ideas, and people, he enters the domain of attitudes. His interest now is whether we like or dislike something or someone, whether our reaction is favorable or unfavorable—in short, what our predisposition is to behave in a particular way toward a given object.

The lover wants to know how positively and strongly his mistress feels toward him; the military officer, how loyal his troops are to him; and the company executive, how obedient or cooperative his men are toward supervisors and the company. The sales manager wants to know similar things about his company's products: do customers like them? more than his competitor's products? enough to pay a slightly higher price? The politician mainly wants to know whether a citizen will vote for him, and his campaign manager will try to predict this behavior by measuring voter attitudes, namely to determine whether the client's candidate is preferred over others. The list of human behavior situations in which attitudes are relevant is enormous because choices must be made, relationships maintained, and the battle for men's minds won.

Psychologists and sociologists have generally accepted the view of Gordon Allport that the concept of attitudes ". . . is probably the most distinctive and indispensable concept in contemporary American social psychology."[3] For the persuasive communicator this conclusion is doubly true. His aim is to influence people, and attitudes are the part of a person that sum up, store, and organize his past experience as he approaches any new situation.[4]

a closer look at attitudes

To change attitudes, we must know a great deal about them. We shall first examine some formal definitions of attitudes, then describe their properties, and finally distinguish them from related concepts such as opinions, beliefs, and values.

A review of two definitions of attitudes is instructive. The first is the classic Murchison *Handbook* definition in which Gordon Allport in 1935 brought together the divergent prior usages of attitude and proposed the following definition:

> An attitude is a mental and neural state of readiness, organized through experience, exerting a directive or dynamic influence upon the individual's response to all objects and situations with which it is related.[5]

The second definition is that of D. Krech, R. S. Crutchfield, and E. L. Ballachey:

> . . . attitudes [are] enduring systems of positive or negative evaluations, emotional feelings, and pro or con action tendencies with respect to social objects.[6]

These definitions help us to understand the nature of attitudes better by examining some of their major attributes:

1. Attitudes relate a person to objects and are formed by a person's contact with his environment. Thus we can mold an attitude and, under certain conditions which we shall explore, change it. We also infer that perceptual processes—the ways the outside world is seen—are important in the primary stage of attitude formation.

2. Attitudes are a more or less enduring state of readiness. The second definition of attitudes by Krech, Crutchfield and Ballachey particularly notes this characteristic. Attitudes are not a momentary state of the organism such as sexual tension, nor are they absolute, fixed, or permanent; rather they range between these two extremes. One of our tasks is to learn how volatile or stable different attitudes are, for then we know how difficult our task is and whether persuasion is indeed possible. We also know that any new experiences, such as exposure to persuasive communication, is simply an increment to an existing body of stored experience. We cannot claim that in one speech we can change such basic attitudes as prejudice.

3. Attitudes have attributes of direction, degree, and intensity. These are typically the dimensions that opinion surveys attempt to measure. Direction tells us whether a person is for or against something, whether he is favorably or unfavorably inclined, whether he likes or dislikes something. Allport's definition refers to this attribute by saying that an attitude exerts a directive or dynamic influence upon an individual's response. With regard to anti-Semitism, for example, an attitude determines that the channel of expression—the target—consists of Jews and that the energy level of the individual is affected; that is, he will show signs of hostility, of aggressive acts against Jews.[7] The dynamic aspect tells us that a successful attitude change would involve more than redirection of hostility toward some other group but a decline in the level of aggression toward minority groups.

Beyond measuring the general direction of an individual's attitude we must assess variations in degree. For example, how hostile is the above anti-Semitic person toward Jews? Would he simply prefer not to socialize with them or would he go so far as Hitler and exterminate them? Questions which ask how favorably or unfavorably inclined a person is toward something measure degree. Is it very favorable, fairly favorable, about 50–50, fairly unfavorable, very unfavorable?

Intensity measures the degree of conviction with which an attitude is held. A typical question in an opinion survey which measures this attribute is: "How strongly do you feel about this?—not at all strongly, not so strongly, fairly strongly, very strongly, no answer." The relationship of intensity and degree is obviously close, for the more extreme an opinion, in either direction, the more strongly a person will feel about it.

When Allport refers to an attitude as a neural as well as a mental state of readiness, he implies that intensity has a physiological as well as a phenomenological basis. Such indices as galvanic skin response (GSR)— more popularly associated with the lie detector—circulatory measures as the heart rate, and changes in pupil diameter can be used.[8]

4. Attitudes are organized and vary in the degree of organization. Many different meanings have been assigned to Allport's assertion that an attitude is organized through experience. Robert E. Lane and David O. Sears refer to the "degree of integration or isolation of various opinions," their "breadth," and their "frame of reference." [9] The concern is with how narrow or wide a perspective an individual takes, how much of his cognitive structure is applied to an object or situation, and how consistent all the relationships are. The term "salience" is sometimes used to refer to the issues a person is concerned about or the extent to which an attitude is central or peripheral within a person's constellation of attitudes. More will be said about these considerations in the next chapter in connection with cognitive consistency theory.

The other main way in which the organization of attitudes is treated is by breaking down an attitude into three components: the cognitive, the affective, and the conative. Roughly speaking, these correspond with three existential stances that man can take with respect to the human condition: knowing, feeling, and acting.[10]

The cognitive component refers to how an attitude object is perceived—what the beliefs, information, or stereotypes are about the object. In explaining this component, Milton J. Rosenberg gives the example of a physician's negative attitude toward federal medical insurance. The physician believes "that federal medical insurance, if instituted, would lead to 'socialism' and 'debasement of medical standards,' which for him are negatively evaluated conditions, and that it would tend also to defeat, or reduce the likelihood of, such positively valued conditions as 'professional freedom' and 'maintenance of my income.' " [11]

The affective component refers to the feelings or emotions of an individual about the object of the attitude. Both the measures of direction and intensity, already discussed, are relevant here. When a person says, "I'm opposed to government subsidies of economic activities," he has made an affective response to the stimulus of government subsidies by showing his direction of feeling. If he adds, "And I feel very strongly about this," he has also indicated the intensity of his feeling.

The conative component is the action or behavioral dimension of an attitude. Krech, Crutchfield and Ballachey's definition of attitude refers specifically to "pro or con action tendencies." Observation of how a person behaves would be the most reliable way of measuring this attitude component, but the usual approach is to administer a paper and pencil inventory of how a person says he would act in the presence of a given object or situation. For example, a company trying to determine its employees' attitudes toward joining a union would specifically have to ask: "Would you vote for or against joining the union if it attempted to organize your shop?" More will be said later about the behavioral component of attitudes, in a discussion of the consistency of attitudes and behavior.

ATTITUDES AS A STORAGE AND TRANSMISSION MECHANISM

Attitudes serve as a storage and transmission mechanism. In one time direction, they link the present with the past; in another time direction, they link the present with the future. By reviewing this dual function of attitudes we can better understand the nature of attitudes and their attributes.

storage and transmission of the past to the present

When a communicator recognizes that preexisting attitudes of the audience must be considered, he is in effect saying that the past experiences of a person may influence his reception of new experiences. Attitudes serve to summarize the history of a person in the audience. They reflect his pattern of adjustment to the environment—including his reaction to communications. They serve as "mediators between the inner demands of the person and the outer environment. . . ."[12]

The communicator must ask several questions: What previous attitudes, if any, exist that might be salient to the present persuasive attempt? Are these previous attitudes for or against this attempt? How general or deeply rooted are these attitudes?

Answers to these questions are important because they determine the ease or difficulty of the attitude change campaign. There are some campaigns that should not be undertaken unless all the resources necessary for a prolonged and involved effort are available. On the other hand, some campaigns may be simplified and reduced in cost because existing attitudes serve as a foundation.

Attitude change problems might, therefore, be classified on the basis of the relationship between past attitudes and the ones desired by the communicator. Three categories may be used: (1) the origination or activation of an attitude; (2) the reinforcement of an existing attitude; and (3) the conversion of a previous attitude.

Origination or activation of an attitude. Some topics are likely to be entirely or almost entirely new to a person. This means that there is no fixed attitude from the past that bears on the subject. There is a void in the box we label "audience." Asking whether a housewife likes or dislikes a pan with a Teflon coating may result in a blank look (assuming she never heard of Teflon before). This is good from the communicator's viewpoint because at least his attempts are not resisted. On the other hand, he is not being assisted by an established interest in the subject. Neither can he build on specific previous knowledge. This means that an educational effort may have to be launched to provide the housewife with background information upon which the new attitude can be based.

Fortunately or unfortunately for the communicator, an isolated object can usually be categorized into some broader classification or put into a frame of reference which in one way or another makes sense. It is a property of both knowledge and attitudes that specific items are seldom in isolation. This is why the attribute of attitudes as being organized is important.

The relationship of one object or attitude to a family of items sometimes occurs naturally to a person; other times, it must be pointed out by the communicator. He may decide to label a Teflon pan as a *modern* household article and as a result transfer the feelings toward modern household things to the pan. Or he may decide to associate it with fat-free cooking, thereby activating certain favorable attitudes on the part of cholesterol-conscious people.

Word association tests and other projective and open-ended devices may be used to determine what stored concepts and feelings are linked to certain subjects. These will vary from person to person if the subject is really novel. If there is any cultural influence, certain uniformities will appear—at least in certain subgroupings of the population being studied.

Reinforcement of an attitude. When the audience is obviously aware of the existence of a certain subject and is favorably disposed toward it, the communicator's task is simply to reinforce the existing attitude. By drawing attention to the attitude and adding force to it, the likelihood of its translation into action is increased.

Reminders of all kinds fall under this category. When prior basic learning can be assumed, only a booster shot is needed. Such reinforcement is particularly effective when it occurs at the time and place certain behavior is wanted. A food commercial, for example, should appear just before mealtime.

The concept of canalization, which is much used by advertisers, is closely related to reinforcement. Canalization refers to the use of preexisting attitudes or behavioral patterns as ready-made launching vehicles for a specific message.[13] Most of the products advertised today are sufficiently known by people and related to existing needs and attitudes. Thus the advertiser can use this stored information and its accompanying attitudes as a base on which to build. What he typically wants to add is a preference for a specific brand.

A communication campaign becomes simplified and its results more predictable when existing attitudes and behavior work in favor of the communicator. There is not always, however, a void or a plus in the box labeled "audience." Sometimes there is a minus, which requires the conversion of an attitude.

Conversion of an attitude.   Conversion of an attitude is the most difficult situation a communicator faces because previous attitudes work against him rather than for him. To further compound the difficulty, attitudes are often deeply rooted in the history of a person and his value system.

A circular by a Midwestern supplier of educational booklets once boasted that any employer could change the socialistic thinking of his employees in as little as three hours. He could convert them into free-enterprisers that easily. The assumption was that if employees were given the correct information, their attitudes, which were based on inadequate and misleading information, would be converted.

Attitudes toward free enterprise are like political attitudes, however. A person acquires them through a long socialization process, through many experiences, and as a result of belonging to certain groups with whom he identifies. The problem of conversion is thus one of the most formidable facing any communicator.

An important factor that must be considered in such situations is how much control the communicator has over the total persuasive situation, for more than messages will be required. If he can influence other determinants of attitudes toward the free enterprise system such as people's income level, their place of residence, and their daily work experience, his chances of success are increased. Such a campaign would obviously be long-range and costly. More likely, since there is not sufficient control over all factors, the campaign would have to be abandoned unless other people cooperated in the total effort.

storage and transmission of the present to the future

Persuasive communicators usually talk about changing attitudes rather than changing behavior. The reason for this choice of expression is that the occasion of a communication and the occasion of acting on this influence are usually two different points in time and space. A driver listening to a television program is urged to drive safely, yet the place and time of applying this message is later that day or week. The postponement of action is a feature of our highly specialized, interdependent, mass society.

The communicator hopes that the stimuli he introduces into the black box will be stored there and transmitted to that time and place when a relevant decision is called for. A company that builds up a favorable corporate image hopes that this attitude toward the corporation will find expression when a person buys a product produced by it, when he is considering employment with them, or when he is about to invest in the stock market. The feature of attitudes that the persuader depends upon, therefore, is their more or less enduring states of readiness.

The consistency of attitudes and behavior. When attitudes serve in this transmission function from the present to the future, the basic assumption and meaning of attitudes is put to the test: Does the attitude predict the resultant behavior? Is the behavior consistent with the attitude?

Everybody knows of occasions when actual behavior contradicted the findings of an opinion or attitude survey. A candidate who was supposed to win didn't; a person who said he believed in fair employment practices never hired a Negro or a Jew; and so on. What accounts for this lack of consistency?

(1) *Opinions versus attitudes.* There are several explanations to show that the findings of surveys and actual behavior may be different. First, a distinction must be drawn between the expression of an opinion and the attitude or attitudes it supposedly represents. A simple definition of an opinion is that it is the verbal expresson of an attitude. A more complex one is that an opinion is a verbal answer to a question about a problematical situation; it refers to the cognitive response to a stimulus; it is "an implicit verbal response or 'answer' that an individual gives in response to a particular stimulus situation in which some general 'question' is raised." [14] These opinions are not always made public; they may be kept private, or they may be misrepresented when publicly stated.

Opinions may be used as a means of access to attitudes: for this reason, *opinion* and *attitude* are often used interchangeably. Keen interpretation must be exercised in drawing correct inferences about attitudes from opinions. An opinion may pertain not to a single attitude but to an attitude complex. For example, a negative opinion on the desirability of building fallout shelters may reflect an attitude of pacifism, of defeatism, of antiadministration sentiment, and of the unlikelihood of war.

(2) *Defining the stimulus situation.* The usual reason attitudes and behavior appear disparate is that the stimulus situation studied for the

determination of the attitude is not identical to the stimulus situation in which action is to take place. The usual way of assessing attitudes is through an opinion poll. The questions that are asked are abstractions of real situations. "Are you in favor of labor-saving machinery?" is only an abstract question; a worker confronted with real machines that might cause the loss of his job faces a real situation. The differences must be recognized.

There are at least three elements that may account for a dissimilarity in the attitude-measuring situation and that in which action later takes place. The first is that the question may refer to something on a higher level of abstraction than the concrete situation with which the attitude is compared. A general favorable attitude toward science, for example, does not necessarily mean that a person is in favor of scientific explorations of the moon. Masked by the favorable attitude toward science may be several negative attitudes, among them an attitude that problems on earth should first be tackled by science.

A second distorting element may be the presence of extraneous threats or rewards in the interview or action situation. Responses to some opinion surveys may be as much a reaction to the interviewer as to the questions asked. This is especially likely when repercussions are feared or when the interview is seen as a vehicle for obtaining something the interviewer wants. A management survey of attitudes toward foremen may not be valid if the worker fears that answers will be identified with him.

A third distorting element in the congruence of attitudes and behavior may be the person's general mental set, which is established by the interview situation. Opinions expressed about the Taft-Hartley law may be considerably different if the questions are asked in a union hall or in a worker's home. This raises not only the question of possible reprisals, but also that of the different social roles of the worker—which changes the stimulus situation.

These three factors must be kept in mind for more than purposes of measuring opinions and attitudes. They also create a greater awareness on the part of the communicator of factors other than the known or controlled ones which may be influential in a persuasive situation.

(3) *Conflicting intervening experience.* A communicator sometimes assumes that nothing happens to his audience between the time he delivers his message and the time action is taken. For example, an attitude survey taken immediately after the audience's exposure to the message is assumed to measure not only the present situation, but what will happen several days or weeks afterward. As both political parties know, however, a victory predicted by an election survey taken two weks before the election does not always materialize. The campaign may have been stepped up by the opposing party; an important event may have occurred that changes the

political content; one's candidate may have said something embarrassing; and so on. The point is that seldom—especially in a democracy—does a communicator have a monopoly over the persuasive situation that enables him to control the person's environment from the time he is influenced to the time he acts.

Inducing action. Since action is the ultimate aim of persuasion, attention must be given to the "action-evoking properties of events and situations." [15] The whole matter of implementation through reminders, personal influence, and the removal of action barriers must not be left to chance. Studies of voting behavior, for example, show the importance of telephone reminders, car pools, and other personal contacts in this connection.[16] Perhaps something can be learned from the motel operator who has long since discovered that the best signs and advertisements in the American Automobile Association will not lead to overnight guests unless the gateway to the motel is clearly marked and the roadway offers ease of entry. Banks have likewise learned the importance of the generous use of glass, especially in the doorway, as a way of helping some customers overcome their anxiety about banks and money matters.

Such efforts to induce action are necessary because many people are satisfied without translating attitudes into action. The pertinent question, as stated by the authors of *Opinions and Personality,* is: "To what extent are the functions served by a person's opinions fulfilled by the mere fact that he holds them, and to what extent does their fulfillment depend on some further action on his part?" [17] Merton and Lazarsfeld have advanced the view that one of the functions of the mass media is of a narcotizing nature.[18] No obligation is felt for taking action because the mere consideration of an issue, on television, for example, provides an exemption from further responsibility.

Finally, it must be remembered that attitudes are relevant not only to the "output" side of human behavior. Attitudes also serve to screen out incoming stimuli. This is a way of preventing the present from ever having an impact on the future.

As seen in the psychological formula, attitudes are the intervening variable in the middle that relate input to output—the stimulus to the response. This is why attitude change is considered the key to behavioral change.

5 psychological foundations of attitude change designs

Our understanding of attitudes and five basic designs for persuasive communication will be enhanced by reviewing some psychological theories that have contributed to the field of attitude change. Our premise is that when we change an attitude, we change a person's behavior in some way or another. Thus, the more we know about human behavior, the greater will be our understanding of how attitudes can be changed.

Psychologists in the field of attitude change differ in their beliefs about the number of theories they consider applicable and in their classification of the contributions of various schools of psychology. The editors of *Psychological Foundations of Attitudes,* for example, list two major theories: learning-behavior theory, which draws upon principles resulting from the study of human and animal learning, and cognitive integration theory, which is based on analyses of the individual's phenomenal representation of his world.[1] William J. McGuire in a key article on "The Nature of Attitudes and Attitude Change" in the second edition of *The Handbook of Social Psychology* lists four general theories: learning theory, perceptual theory, consistency theory, and functional theory.[2]

The needs of the persuasive communicator are pragmatic rather than theoretical. Hence our approach is mainly eclectic—to select ideas from any psychological theory that provides a principle or technique of attitude change. Secondarily, however, we want to reflect each idea faithfully and refer to its theoretical source. In this way our own applied principles and techniques can quickly be improved as advances are made in the field of psychology.

Since the two major theories are undoubtedly learning theory and cognitive consistency theory, these are reviewed in this chapter. They are expanded upon in the five chapters that present the basic designs for persuasive communication and in the two that review the subjects of perception and remembering. Other theories such as the perceptual and functional ones shall also be referred to in these later chapters.

LEARNING THEORY

Learning theory draws upon principles derived from the study of human and animal learning. It posits that learning an attitude is no different from acquiring motor skills, memorizing and reciting poetry, or reasoning in problem solving.

Carl Hovland, who was probably the foremost proponent of this approach, explicitly states in his book *Communication and Persuasion* that there are common principles that apply to all forms of learning.[3] And indeed, the experiments are reviewed in terms of such traditional psychological processes as the attention given to a stimulus, the degree to which it is comprehended, the role of practice, the rate of forgetting, and the ultimate impact on behavior.

four fundamental factors of learning [4]

A convenient way to review much that learning theory has to offer is to return to the S-O-R formula discussed in Chapter 4. This formula identifies three of four fundamental factors of learning: (1) the presence of an external stimulus which triggers learning behavior, (2) a motivated organism, and (3) a desired response, or repertoire of responses from which the desired one is elicited. We add a fourth factor, reward, to complete the list.

Stimulus. The aim of all learning is to produce and strengthen the connection between a stimulus and a desired response. A red traffic light should result in braking and stopping behavior; the sign of a restaurant should result in a stop for dinner by a hungry man; the sight of a favored brand of a product should lead to its purchase when shopping; and the reading of a preferred candidate's name on a ballot should lead to a vote for him. The aim of a persuasive communicator is to design a message (the stimulus) that will cause a person (the organism) to respond in a certain predictable and preferred manner.

If the communicator can control all four learning factors his chances of succeeding are high. But he mainly controls only the stimulus, possibly some of the rewards, and only occasionally or remotely a person and his responses. He therefore emphasizes the role of the stimulus and seeks to design one that is so powerful that a person will virtually be dominated by it.

Because he knows that learning is facilitated when his stimulus is presented without competition from other stimuli, the communicator seeks a persuasive monopoly. But only in what McGuire calls a "total institution" is such a situation present.[5] Most of the time he must remain satisfied in manipulating the distinctiveness and strength of the stimulus, which he hopes will capture the attention of his audience. His message then seeks to influence other aspects of learning such as comprehension and acceptance.

A Motivated Organism. Without motivation a person does not learn, for motivation creates a drive which impels him to respond to certain stimuli. The stronger the motivation, up to a certain point, the stronger will be the connection between a stimulus and response that satisfies the motive involved.

Many approaches have been taken to the subject of motivation. Charles Darwin, William McDougall, and Sigmund Freud claimed that human beings have certain instincts—built-in desires, wishes, or motives.[6] Darwin's doctrine of natural selection, for example, provided a foundation for believing that all behavior—animal and human, individual and social —lay in the evolutionary array of instincts that make for survival of the species. McDougall, one of America's first social psychologists, believed that all social behavior could be based on an urgelike view of instincts or propensities such as food-seeking, disgust, sex, fear, and gregariousness.[7] Freud, in turn, wrote about the opposing life and death instincts.

Although few psychologists accept instincts as a major explanation of motivation, they have no objection to the concept of drive.[8] An unfulfilled need on the part of a person is seen as creating a drive toward a goal— called an incentive—in the environment which is capable of satisfying that need. The advantage of this explanation over instincts is that it sidesteps the thorny question of innateness and simply refers to the existence of such needs as thirst, sex, and status. Behavior is then explained as a form of locomotion toward a goal that will satisfy a specific need or drive and thus reduce the tension of the organism until equilibrium is once again reached.[9]

Psychologists generally recognize two kinds of motives: primary or physiological motives, and secondary or learned motives.[10] A person is born with an urge to eat and drink and, at a certain maturational stage in life, to seek sex. However, one is socialized by one's family and culture to prefer certain kinds of food, drink, and mates. One also learns such motives as loyalty, cooperation, ambition, the need for approval, fear, and many others.

The motivational factor places several burdens upon the communicator. First, he must learn what classes of motives are relevant to certain communication programs. Second, he must use his knowledge of motivation by designing messages that arouse the needs and interests of his audience. Third, he must predict when given motives are operative in a given person or group and properly time the exposure of his messages.

Psychologists have provided many lists of human motives. Each field of application appears to have its own favorite source. In advertising, Martineau's *Motivation in Advertising* has been popular; [11] in employee relations, Maslow's hierarchy of needs has won wide acceptance; [12] in economic development, McClelland's *The Achievement Motive* is pre-eminent.[13] One of the best overall summaries, however, is provided by Krech and Crutchfield in their introductory psychology text and is reproduced below: [14]

	Survival and Security (deficiency motives)	Satisfaction and Stimulation (abundancy motives)
Pertaining to the body	Avoiding of hunger, thirst, oxygen lack, excess heat and cold, pain, overfull bladder and colon, fatigue, overtense muscles, illness and other disagreeable bodily states, etc.	Attaining pleasurable sensory experiences of tastes, smells, sounds, etc.; sexual pleasure; bodily comfort; exercise of muscles, rhythmical body movements, etc.
Pertaining to relations with environment	Avoiding of dangerous objects and horrible, ugly, and disgusting objects; seeking objects necessary to future survival and security; maintaining a stable, clear, certain environment, etc.	Attaining enjoyable possessions; constructing and inventing objects; understanding the environment; solving problems; playing games; seeking environmental novelty and change, etc.
Pertaining to relations with other people	Avoiding interpersonal conflict and hostility; maintaining group membership, prestige, and status; being taken care of by others; conforming to group standards and value; gaining power and dominance over others, etc.	Attaining love and positive identifications with people and groups; enjoying other people's company; helping and understanding other people; being independent, etc.
Pertaining to self	Avoiding feelings of inferiority and failure in comparing the self with others or with the ideal self; avoiding loss of identity; avoiding feelings of shame, guilt, fear, anxiety, sadness, etc.	Attaining feelings of self-respect and self-confidence; expressing oneself; feeling sense of achievement; feeling challenged; establishing moral and other values; discovering meaningful place of self in the universe.

How these motives are referred to in message appeals and appropriately timed shall be discussed in connection with the five basic designs.

Response. The output of an individual that is elicited by a particular stimulus is called the response. Some responses are automatic—for example, the reflex of the knee jerk or the dilation of the pupils to light. Other responses are innate in that they do not have to be learned but occur as a result of maturation—for example, when a child learns to crawl and walk. Most responses, however, are learned through life's everyday experiences and programs of formal training and education.

Many of the responses that a persuasive communicator seeks to elicit are already a part of a person's repertoire. In the marketing and political areas one assumes that shopping and voting behavior are established and must simply be channeled to the selections sought by a specific communicator. It is not so much the response that has to be learned but its association with a new stimulus—for example, the brand of the advertiser or the candidate promoted by the campaign manager. Response learning in marketing is usually limited to an ability to recall the brand, company names, and desirable product features. In politics, the task is similar unless a political issue becomes complex and the voter is politically active.

Our concern with the response factor in learning is, therefore, limited, for we use the storehouse of responses of our culture which most people have acquired. When we do teach new responses, they are usually of the "rote learning" type; that is, the individual in the audience is presented with the names of new persons, organizations, and products, which he is asked to commit to memory. Our communication task, therefore, is often to teach people new words. This kind of teaching has an honored place in psychology, for it is associated with the work of a German psychologist, Hermann Ebbinghaus, in the late nineteenth century.[15] His methods of learning are similar to the classical conditioning methods of Pavlov, which shall be discussed in connection with the stimulus-response design in Chapter 6.

Reward. Any event that strengthens a S-R connection may be called a reward.[16] A response that is rewarded is statistically more likely to be repeated than an unrewarded one. To have this effect the reward must ordinarily be satisfaction-yielding, which is another way of saying that the tension produced by an unfulfilled need is reduced. Drinking water when thirsty, eating food when hungry, and relaxing when tired are examples of such tension release.

Many situations are deliberately arranged to provide a reward for the successful performance of a task.[17] An animal may receive a food pellet when it depresses a certain lever, a human being receives a pay check after a week's work, a student receives a passing grade for successful completion of a course. These rewards obviously vary in kind. The food pellet is a primary reward that is immediately tension-reducing; the pay check is a secondary reward that can be converted into a primary one; and the grade is either a long delayed secondary reward or a symbolic one like praise which satisfies an acquired need.

The latter acquired needs often respond to rewards that are also learned rather than innate. For example, the reward value of relaxation is originally learned because the activity involved in reducing tension causes fatigue. The rest which follows is therefore rewarding. Certain verbal stimuli may then be associated with this relaxation and serve as rewards. The phrase "this is good" might acquire this capacity to elicit relaxing, rewarding responses; these responses are then transferred to any new situation the subject learns to label as "good." [18]

Thus an important aspect of the functioning of motivational factors "depends on the learned capacities of thoughts, words, and sentences to induce relief or relaxation and hence to function as rewards." [19] In mass communication situations these verbal rewards are particularly relevant because the ability to provide other kinds of rewards is limited.

Consideration of the response element, then, completes the inventory of the four fundamentals of learning. When all of them are present and appropriately related, the conditions for learning are optimized. But as we shall discuss in the next chapter, we are also interested in discovering whether some learning can take place without the presence of all four conditions.

COGNITIVE CONSISTENCY THEORY

The most active area of attitude theorization in the past decade has been cognitive consistency theory. We can take as a starting point Kurt Lewin's "general view of man as a cognitive mechanism reacting in an integrated fashion to the influences impinging upon him." [20] It is assumed that if we understand the organized set of cognitions he has about himself and the world around him, then a prediction can be made about how new information will affect a person. [21] Cognitive integration theory is based on this analysis of the individual's phenomenal representation of his world— the way he collects, processes, and stores information.

Taking a closer look at this cognitive mechanism we start by recognizing that a cognition serves as an image or map of the world and of a person's self—what Lewin calls his "life space." [22] Thus a cognition can refer to thoughts, beliefs, values, and actions. These cognitions are organized and integrated into a system which provides a person with meaning and stability. Thus he is able to go about his business in everyday life.

The need for consistency lies partly in our phylogenetic origins, for animals other than men operate according to consistency theory.[23] But further origins and reinforcement of this need can be found in child-rearing practices and role assignment. Although the motivation for consistency is not always considered an essential feature of consistency theories, the persuasive communicator can simply assume that a drive for consistency exists in all people.

It follows that cognitive inconsistency sets up psychological tension in a person. This is an uncomfortable state which a person tries to avoid. But if incurred, a drive to remove the tension is generated.

There are many modes of resolving cognitive inconsistencies and thereby removing the tension.[24] First, a person can put the inconsistency out of mind—to deny or repress the matter. Second, he can bolster the inconsistency by submerging it among a large body of consistencies so that it looms relatively less large. When a person is confronted by a contradiction between one of his beliefs and another, he can amass a great body of other beliefs that are consistent with the conflicting one. He drowns out the imbalance.

Two other modes stem from the process of Hegelian synthesis. One of them is differentiation whereby a distinction is drawn between two classes of the same concept. For example, if a person becomes aware of the inconsistency between believing in both the Bible and the theory of evolution, he can draw a distinction between the figurative Bible and the literal Bible. He can then tolerate the inconsistency between the literal Bible and the facts of evolution because he can still continue to believe in the figurative Bible which is not in conflict with evolutionary theory.

A second Hegelian mode is transcendence, whereby two concepts are built up and combined into a larger one organized on a superordinate level. If a person is in a science-religion dilemma, he can transcend the conflict by considering that both the rational man and the spiritual man may be jointly cultivated to reach a fuller life.

Three other modes of resolving cognitive inconsistency are possible. One is to change the object about which the opinion is held rather than the opinion about the given object. For example, if someone who dislikes politics accepts a political job he can always think of himself as a "statesman." Another mode is simply to devaluate an issue or task when an inconsistency is noted. In the previous example, a person could say that it doesn't matter what label is used to describe a field. Finally, there is the mode of simply bearing it and, indeed, making a virtue of it. A person could agree with Carlyle that consistency is the hobgoblin of little minds.

If the objective of the communicator is to prevent the weakening of an existing attitude he wishes to support, the above modes provide ideas for defensive action. But if his purpose is to advocate a change in attitude, the communicator should look for ways to magnify inconsistency and structure the alternatives for reducing it by making an attitude change the easiest solution. The following review of the development of consistency theories will be helpful in understanding these processes more fully.

balance and congruity theories

The beginning of cognitive consistency theories is usually traced to Fritz Heider's balance theory.[25] Among the systems he formulated was the triad composed of a person (P) who is the focus of analysis, another person (O), and one impersonal entity (X), which could be a physical object, an idea, an event, or the like. The relationship among these elements can either be balanced or unbalanced. If one person likes another (the relationship between P and O is positive) and both have the same view toward something, for example, a political issue, (the relationship of P and O to X is positive) then the system is in balance. But suppose P takes one view toward the issue and O another, then the system is unbalanced. P can restore balance by changing his attitude toward O or toward X. It is this kind of inconsistency in which Heider was interested—inconsistencies that explore ways in which people view their relations with other people and with the environment.

Osgood and Tannenbaum formulated a special case of balance theory known as the principle of congruity. Its main improvement over Heider's theory is that it deals specifically with the problem of direction of attitude change. As explained by Zajonc: "The authors assume that 'judgmental frames of reference tend toward maximal simplicity.' Thus, since extreme 'black-and-white,' 'all-or-nothing' judgments are simpler than refined ones, valuations tend to move toward extremes or, in the words of the authors, there is 'a continuing pressure toward polarization.' " [26]

Many of the examples of congruity theory refer to inconsistencies caused by statements about stands which are at odds with the evaluation of the source. Suppose that the *Daily Worker* is evaluated negatively and it comes out in favor of freedom of the press. Incongruity is the result.[27] Whether the source or the object is discredited depends on which of the two attitudes is the more polarized (extreme). Osgood and Tannenbaum have formulated the principle of congruity in quantitative terms which allow quite precise predictions as to which of these alternatives is the more likely.

cognitive dissonance theory

Leon Festinger's "cognitive dissonance theory" is based on the same assumptions as the two consistency theories just reviewed but goes further in several ways.[28] He uses the words consonance and dissonance in place of consistency and inconsistency so that more than a logical connotation is implied. Next, he measures the amount or level of dissonance aroused by the formula: [29]

$$\text{Dissonance} = \frac{\text{Importance x Number of Dissonant Cognitions}}{\text{Importance x Number of Consonant Cognitions}}$$

A cognition, as already stated, is defined as any knowledge, belief, attitude, or value that a person holds about himself, his behavior, or his environment. His cognitions are dissonant if they are not in accord with his expectations—which are acquired through his experiences, the mores of his culture, and his notions about logical relations between events. The meaning of importance varies but generally refers to the instrumentality of the cognition for the satisfaction of the individual's needs and values.

Brehm and Cohen in their book *Explorations in Cognitive Dissonance* list three types of situations in which the predictive value of the theory is demonstrated: (1) free choice among attractive alternatives; (2) forced compliance, in which an individual is induced to behave in a manner inconsistent with his attitudes; and (3) situations in which a person is exposed to information inconsistent with his existng attitudes or cognitions.[30]

As an example, let us consider the consequence of making a decision between two equally attractive alternatives. Suppose a person is torn between buying a Ford and a Chevrolet and he finally decides on the Ford. What will now happen to his reading of car ads? Will he still read them and if so, will he tend to read Ford ads or Chevrolet ads? The answers to these questions are that he will be more likely to read car ads after the purchase than before, and—this statement surprises most people—he will be more likely to read ads of the car he just bought than the car he almost, but didn't, buy.[31]

His behavior is explained by cognitive dissonance theory in this fashion: after he bought the Ford he was in a state of dissonance because he was aware of the attractive features of the Chevrolet which he relinquished. Hence he was in a state of tension which he reduced by increasing his reading of ads of the car he just bought, so that he could convince himself that he made the right decision. Of course, he could also try to discover the unattractive features of the foregone alternative, but an ad is not a good source of critical information.

There is an obvious communication implication in this discovery of cognitive dissonance. The best time to give people literature about a subject is right after they have made a decision pertaining to it. In this way we reward them for their act and reinforce their learning while at the same time taking advantage of the process of selective exposure that they will likely use to reduce dissonance.[32] Just as a consumer should be given brochures about his purchase, a new stockholder should be given a report of his company; a hard-to-get engineer who joined the company should be told of the advantages of being a member of the team; and a community that debated whether to change its zoning laws to allow a company to enter should be invited to an open house and informed about the company in the local newspaper.

The theory of cognitive dissonance explains a great deal of behavior. Its critics say that it too often does so in ex post facto rather than predictive terms. But combined with a broader knowledge of human behavior, the theory stimulates thinking about the different ways in which people's attitudes may be changed.

OTHER THEORIES

Learning theory and cognitive consistency theory provide the major foundations for the five designs that follow in the next chapters. References shall, however, be made to perceptual theory and functional theory, for these offer supplementary insights.

Several contributions are made by perceptual theory. One is a recognition that different persons differ in their perception of an object. For example, one person sees a speaker as having high credibility and another sees him as having low credibility.

Second, a persuasive communicator will sometimes find that attitude change involves not only the making of a new response to an old stimulus but redefining the stimulus to which the response is made. In other words, as stated by McGuire: "persuasion involves not so much changing the believer's opinion about a given object, but rather changing his perception of which object it is that he is giving his opinion about." [33] To change an attitude toward a person who is perceived as a "politician" it might be most effective to try to redefine him as a "statesman."

Third, perceptual theory has drawn attention to the role played by a person's frame of reference. In judging how big or heavy something is, the size and weight of other objects with which it is grouped may serve as a standard. For example, an American compact car appears larger on European highways where the typical car is small, than it does in the United States. The same kind of judgment process takes place with social objects and issues which are the usual focus of attitudes. Sherif, Sherif and Nebergall state that an individual likely categorizes the various alternative positions on an issue by comparing them with his own stand. This categorization is in terms of three "latitudes" of reaction in a total range of positions: a latitude of acceptance, a latitude of rejection, and a latitude of noncommitment.[34] For example, in asking businessmen whether they would attend a meeting with students, they might agree to it with liberal students (who are in their range of acceptance) but not with revolutionaries (who are in their range of rejection).

While perceptual theory focuses on the outside—namely, what is seen in the environment—functional theory turns inward. A person's attitudes are considered to be determined by his needs rather than the particular object toward which an attitude is directed. As stated by Daniel Katz, "the functional approach is the attempt to understand the reasons people hold the attitudes they do." He groups four functions which attitudes perform for the individual: [35]

1. The *instrumental, adjustive,* or *utilitarian* function upon which Jeremy Bentham and the utilitarians constructed their model of man. A modern expression of this approach can be found in behavioristic learning theory.

2. The *ego-defensive* function in which the person protects himself from acknowledging the basic truths about himself or the harsh realities in his external world. Freudian psychology and neo-Freudian thinking have been preoccupied with this type of motivation and its outcomes.

3. The *value-expressive* function in which the individual derives satisfactions from expressing attitudes appropriate to his personal values and to his concept of himself. This function is central to doctrines of ego psychology which stress the importance of self-expression, self-development, and self-realization.

4. The *knowledge* function based upon the individual's need to give adequate structure to his universe. The search for meaning, the need to understand, the trend toward better organization of perceptions and beliefs to provide clarity and consistency for the individual, are other description of this function. The development of principles about perceptual and cognitive structure have been the contribution of Gestalt psychology.

The perceptual and functional theories of attitude change supplement the two major ones discussed in this chapter. All of them shall be drawn upon in Part II where the five basic designs are presented. In these chapters the psychological foundations of attitude change shall be expanded upon and applied to practical situations.

TWO

five
basic
designs
of
persuasion

6

the stimulus-response design

The stimulus-response (S-R) design is the economy, stripped-down model of attitude change. Based on learning theory, it employs only two of the four elements of learning. Knowledge of a person's motives and the need to reward his behavior are considered unessential—although not necessarily undesirable. The connection between a stimulus and response, which is always the object of learning, can be made without these two factors.

THE PRINCIPLE OF ASSOCIATION

A simple but bold assertion is made by the S-R design—namely, that when two experiences occur simultaneously or in close succession, the recurrence of one of them tends to reinstate the other.[1] If a light goes on when a person flips a switch he learns the causal relationship between the switch and the light; if he repeatedly sees Crest associated with toothpaste, he'll likely pick up a tube in the supermarket or drug store; and if the opening of the refrigerator door is followed up with the appearance of his dog drooling for food, then he sees evidence of learning by association.

This type of learning is achieved by a process known as classical conditioning. It is exemplified by Pavlov's well-known experiment with dogs. He observed what all of us can—namely, that when a dog sees food, he salivates. The objective of one of Pavlov's experiments was to condition a dog to salivate not to the sight of food, but to a substitute stimulus—the ringing of a bell. This is what Berelson and Steiner mean when they define classical conditioning thus: "When a new stimulus is repeatedly paired with another stimulus that automatically elicits a certain response, the new one alone gradually becomes capable of eliciting the same or a similar response." [2] The procedure is as follows: a bell is rung, it is followed up instantaneously or almost so with the sight of food, and the result is that the dog salivates. The bell is called the conditioned stimulus and the food the unconditioned stimulus; salivation is the unconditioned response.[3]

What this experiment really accomplishes is that the natural response of salivating to the sight of food—the unconditioned stimulus—becomes associated with a new stimulus, the sound of a bell. Looked at in this manner, Pavlov's classical conditioning experiment can be seen as the fundamental process of learning.

The elegance of the S-R design is its simplicity. The basic law of association, according to psychologist Edwin R. Guthrie, is the only absolutely necessary factor in learning.[4] In order to condition a certain response, the only requirement is that the stimulus which has evoked it be learned by a person. Nothing is said about the existence of a need or drive in that person; neither is anything said about rewarding him for engaging in the proper responses. Let us examine whether the neglect of these two factors is justified.

Looking back on Pavlov's experiments, it is, of course, true that he could not completely ignore the problem of the need-state of the dogs. If a dog was satiated, his response to the sight of food or the ringing of the bell would not be the same. Optimum conditions for the experiment were, therefore, a normal or slightly above normal state of hunger. But even if we recognize the existence of a need-state as a condition of learning, the burden on the experimenter or persuader is still not heavy. The reason is that we are talking about needs that are so universal that they apply to animals as well as humans—that is, the biological needs. The typical cycle of these needs is of short duration, so that a state of satiation is soon followed by one of derivation. If a stimulus is frequently repeated, it is likely to coincide with a state of derivation within a short period of time, even on the basis of chance.

The neglect of the other condition of learning, that a response must be rewarded if it is to be repeated in the future, must also be examined. Pavlov's dogs were on occasion allowed to eat the food they saw. Without this consummatory act, the link between the stimulus and response would have been broken. Can one agree then with Guthrie, who sticks to his simple model by saying that such a reward is not absolutely required for all forms of learning?

In an article on the impact of television advertising, Herbert E. Krugman leads us to believe that Guthrie's simple S-R model is plausible. He points to the incontestable fact that television advertising messages have been learned by the public.[5] Such learning, he says, has much in common with classical experiments in the learning of nonsense material (a string of meaningless words) and unimportant material which does not evoke high ego-involvement. Materials classified as trivia by a person are learned in a different way from serious matters.

What happens with low involvement messages that are often repeated is that they are perceived by the public, remembered, and then injected into purchase behavior without first producing a change of attitude. In other words, the meaning of persuasion as the overcoming of a resistance attitude is not involved at all.

The theory of perception is central to this process. Television advertising changes a person's "frame of reference"; it shifts the "relative salience of attributes" suggested to a person by advertising as he organizes his perception of brands and products.[6] Krugman's example is a product first seen primarily as "reliable" which is then shifted to one seen primarily as "modern." The product is still seen as reliable but the new primary perceptual emphasis is "modern." The relative frames of reference have shifted in importance. This shift in salience is manifested in the purchase situation which serves as a catalyst: "The product or package is then suddenly seen in a new, 'somewhat different' light although nothing verbalizable may have changed *up to that point*."[7] Attitude change may occur after the act of purchase (and this is in line with the theory of cognitive dissonance discussed in the previous chapter).

Krugman's analysis of learning from television gives partial support to Guthrie's view that a reward is not an essential condition for learning. People do learn in a calm, relaxed, and almost passive way.

ESTABLISHING MEANING AND REPUTATION

A basic and important aim of persuasive communication is to identify persons, things, and ideas, and attach specific meanings, importance, and desirability to them. The S-R design is appropriate for these kinds of objectives because they fundamentally involve the forming of new associations in people's minds.

Most of the applications deal with the development of meaning in language.[8] Two kinds of meanings must be considered: denotative and connotative. Denotative meaning indicates the relationship between a word and the object or event to which the word refers. Connotative meaning associates affective qualities with the object and the symbols that represent it.

The formation of denotative meaning is at the heart of all forms of publicity and advertising programs which introduce a new product, person, organization, or idea to people. The public must be exposed to the new object in as concrete a fashion as possible and simultaneously, to the word, slogan, or symbol that will represent it.

Such efforts at establishing denotative meanings is usually combined with obtaining favorable connotative meanings. As will be discussed later, chief ways of doing this are (1) through the use of adjectives that elicit highly affective responses from the audience; (2) the substitution of emotionally neutral or moderate words with intensely emotional ones; and (3) the placement of an object in close physical or temporal position with positive symbols.[9] Let us now review some of the major applications of the S-R design.

new product advertising and publicity

Many new products appear on the market each year which have to be given names. Nylon, Teflon, and Corfam are just a few of the products introduced by DuPont in the past few decades. Each of them had to be shown to the public and paired with a name so they could be asked for in a store. Newspaper, magazine, and television advertising were used for this purpose, sometimes reinforced with special store displays, demonstrations, and the distribution of free samples. The S-R design with its underlying principle of association was the basic approach used, even when supplemented with lengthy copy and product publicity which are related to the cognitive design.

Sometimes a refinement of the S-R design is used in that the consumer must learn to distinguish the new product from an old one. All watches tell time, but when the first battery-operated watch was introduced it had to be differentiated from the usual spring-driven watch. Drawing on the conditioning process of "discrimination training," [10] the consumer is exposed to ads which show the battery-run watch side by side with a spring-driven one; he is also told that the new product is not a watch but an "electric timepiece." Thus the use of a new name hopefully creates a new conceptual category in the consumer's mind.

Most advertising uses the S-R design to attach favorable meanings to products, whether old or new. This is done through a variety of associational symbols shown along with the product: the brand name, the corporate name, popular or prestigious persons, distinctive and attractive surroundings, and positive sounding adjectives. These techniques are daily observed by all of us.

corporate identification and image programs

RCA, Chrysler, and Uniroyal are among the many companies that have undertaken deliberate corporate identification and image programs as a way of influencing the way they are seen by the public. Identification programs concentrate on "controlled visual and verbal communications to identify the corporation, its component units and its products." [11] These programs that emphasize denotative meaning usually overlap with the more widely used corporate image programs. The latter emphasize connotative meaning because they are designed to create favorable impressions and attitudes.

In identification programs the aim is to help the public to recognize the company in every possible way. For this reason, a "corporate identifier" or "signature" is used to encode the desired corporate image for precise and efficient communication with the public.[12] In the case of RCA, the logotype—the corporate name or trademark—was given major attention. The old circled initials and lightning bolt which first appeared in 1922 was replaced by a bold rendering of computerlike block letters. This new logotype was legible, distinctive, and visually pleasing. It had a wide range of applicability and was reproducible in many sizes and on many materials. It was placed on stationery, trucks, uniforms, electronic tubes, and atop the Rockefeller Center headquarters. Furthermore, it satisfied Robert Sarnoff's aim to "reflect the continuity between our achievements of the past and our progress in the future." [13]

The overlap of corporate identification with corporate image programs is obvious from the following statement by Peter Schladermundt:

> A company's corporate image—its insignia or trademark or colophon or logotype or imprint, by whatever name you choose to call it—symbolizes the company itself and is its most priceless asset. This is the visual device that should command instantaneous recognition signifying the quality of personality of the company it represents. In the public eye it must convey the strength, standards of service, and craftsmanship, integrity and reliability of the organization which it symbolizes. If it is a simple symbol, instead of a spelled out name or initials, it must immediately transfer the desired characteristics to the brand or corporation name, and to the product or services for which that name stands.[14]

Corporate image programs are more broadly concerned with what Erving Goffman, a sociologist, calls "impression management": the ways in which the impressions formed—whether of a person or corporation—are guided and controlled.[15] Besides becoming widely known, a company wants to be well liked and associated with certain unique characteristics that distinguish it from others. Chrysler, for example, wanted to be seen as progressive and contemporary, and as stable and strong; and it thought that its new pentastar symbol would help promote that image.[16]

According to A. J. Spector, the images that companies seek to project typically fall into five broad categories: *achievement* (strong or powerful, large company, stable, long tradition of reliability); *action* (progressive, active, forward-looking, scientific or research-minded); *product and customer* (consumer products, men customers, low prices); *personality* (warm and friendly, relaxed and informal, youthful, exciting, serene); *esthetic* (good taste, beautiful or attractive, modern).[17] A great deal of skill is required by designers and communicators to choose symbols that will produce the desired connotations for a company.

The corporate image provides the background for specific messages directed toward consumers, stockholders, and other groups. How these messages are evaluated depends in part, then, upon this image. Gestalt psychology tells us that a person acts not "in terms of a combination of separate responses to a combination of separate stimuli" but in terms of a "whole response to the whole situation." [18]

political image-building campaigns

As the title of Wyckoff's book *The Image Candidates* indicates, a major feature of modern election campaigns is image building.[19] Voters respond less to a reasoned discussion of issues than to the personalities of the candidates. And what they perceive in candidates is largely determined by the medium used: the print medium highlights reputation; radio provides clues to character through a candidate's voice, his reasoning ability, and eloquence; television, the newest political medium, focuses on how a candidate looks. Wasn't Nixon's five o'clock shadow in the 1960 television debate with Kennedy one of the acknowledged reasons for losing the election? Wyckoff's summary of the impact of television is that:

> . . . television apparently does more than just present political candidates. Television transfigures candidates into personal images of characterizations that can be quite unique to the medium. Thus, it is necessary to have a term to describe this unique image, a term such as "image candidate." [20]

Starting with the 1952 election, advertising agencies have played an increasingly important role in election campaigns. In that year Batten, Barton, Durstine and Osborn (BBDO) was given major credit in Dwight Eisenhower's election to the presidency.[21] In image campaigning, the candidate is not so much the projector of desired qualities as he is a suitable screen or receptacle for "elements of projection that reside in the viewer rather than the person viewed." [22] As summarized by Nimmo: "Ideally the candidate as a receptable will be pleasant, not abrasive; have a clear, but not too specific, personality; be self-assured, even cocky, but not pretentious; be articulate, but not erudite or glib; be courageous but also cautious; and appear handsome, but not too pretty." [23]

Many associational techniques which underlie the S-R design are used in political television commercials. These, incidentally, exploit short time periods (twenty-second and one-minute spots, perhaps five-minute trailers) so that they won't preempt popular television fare and cause resentment. Nimmo describes the following commercial prepared by Jack Tinker & Associates, the same agency that gave Alka Selzer its "fun image":

> Although Rockefeller was the product the agency merchandised, he never appeared in the spots. A typical sixty-second commercial, for example, gave the viewer a picture of a road as seen from the front end of a moving car, the broken white center line moving to the sound of the throbbing engine and a voice declaring, "If you took all the roads Governor Rockefeller has built, and all the road's he's widened and straightened and smoothed out; if you took all those roads and laid them end to end, they'd stretch all the way to Hawaii." The road ends as though on a Hawaiian beach, the car turns around to the strains of Hawaiian music and begins a return trip, and the voice adds, "All the way to Hawaii and all the way back." [24]

REPETITION, CAPTIVITY, AND CONTIGUITY

The S-R design works best under conditions that minimize the presence of the motivational and reward factors. Thus the principle of repetition and the technique of the captive audience are relevant here. The principle of contiguity is also discussed because it directly strengthens the operation of the S-R design.

repetition

The technique most closely connected with the S-R design is repetition. The stimulus is presented over and over again; just as blow after blow of a hammer finally drives a nail home, so the communicator hopes that this constant hammering will get the point of a message across. This concentration on the technique of repetition is excellently described by Leonard Doob, who writes:

> Many people worship at the altar of repetition when they think of human learning or of propaganda. They have observed that apparently repetition can accomplish psychological miracles and hence they deify

the process by ascribing to it sole efficacy in determining behavior. Repetition in truth is important, but its importance should not be exaggerated or misunderstood.[25]

One advantage of repetition is that it increases the statistical probability that people will be reached at a time when relevant motivation is operative. To some extent, this means that the problem of human motivation can be ignored. The price for this neglect is simply that more repetitions are required; also the cost of a given campaign rises.

In this connection, communicators would benefit by paying attention to the economist's law of diminishing returns. As applied to communication, this law states that each unit of increased effort leads to a smaller and smaller addition to the total effect, and might eventually lead to a decrease in the total effect. For example, if a budget of $100,000 is increased to $200,000, the total reach of a campaign will not double. The communicator must watch for a limit beyond which repetition will not add substantially to the desired results.

A communicator must also watch out for the possibility of repeating a message so often that it loses its discriminatory capability. There are many frequently mentioned examples to illustrate this: As early as the twenties "Victrola" no longer referred to a phonograph made by RCA Victor. Instead, the salesman would ask, "What brand victrola?" Similarly, in some parts of the world, "Gillette" refers to any brand of safety blade. What happened in these cases is that advertising was repeated so often that the word fell into common usage and became a generic term rather than a brand name that helped discriminate one company's product from that of another.

Another overuse of repetition is called connotative semantic satiation: an existing evaluative word is depolarized or neutralized of its connotative meaning.[26] For example, the phrase "brilliant white" evokes an increasingly less bright image with successive mention.[27] Where the intention is to arouse feelings, a similar diminution of arousal occurs with the repeated presentation of an emotionally provocative stimulus.

Such reductions in the impact of a repeated stimulus can in many cases be mitigated by varying the stimuli: using synonymous phrases, changing examples and illustrations, and alternating emotional cues. The attention arousal power of the successive stimuli would also thereby be kept at a high level. Were the identical stimulus to be repeated, especially with the typically low-motivated audience attending to advertisements, less careful examination of the stimulus would occur. Research shows that a "certain novelty within a familiar context seems to be the most attention-catching." [28]

captive audience

Pavlov's dogs were kept in a harness. Occasionally communicators want to achieve this effect with human beings by exposing them to messages in situations where physical escape is difficult or impossible. Thus the dependence upon motivation as a way of securing audience attention is lessened. Assuming that people do not escape psychologically, the communicator is assured that he has the attention of his audience. Another possible advantage is that he might be able to lock an audience in a situation where a persuasive element such as positive group pressures are present. Captivity may, however, lead to audience resentment if the communicator takes blatant advantage of a situation or if awareness of being captive becomes too obvious.

Airplanes, trains, trolley cars, and buses are ideal captive audience situations because passengers are literally enclosed in limited space. But perhaps because these situations are too imbalanced in favor of the communicator, laws in most cases prohibit the playing of sound tracks or radios over which individual passengers have no control. Visual communications, such as posters, however, are usually permitted. Natural settings provide another opportunity for the captive audience technique. A person or group is assembled for some primary reason such as working, attending class or some other regular meeting, or participating in some social, ceremonial, or entertainment function. These are suitable occasions for making announcements and associating with the goals and values of the group. Messages that run counter to the purposes of the primary occasion should, however, ordinarily be avoided or at least weighed against the likelihood of creating resentment.

contiguity

Because the S-R design uses words and symbols sparingly, they must be carefully selected, structured, and presented. The key consideration is the principle of contiguity, for if objects or events are to be linked together they must be similar or close to each other in space or time.[29]

The coupling of favorable adjectives with nouns, which is a well-known practice, makes the most obvious use of contiguity in space; grammar demands that adjectives are placed next to or close to the nouns they modify. Referring to a "superb first novel," or a "delightful comedy" is intended to influence us. Similarly, those communicators who want their message to relate to a propitious event must take advantage of contiguity in time. For example those manufacturers whose space-related advertisements appear on the same day that the event of the United States' first successful orbit was announced probably gained more prestige than those who waited a few days or weeks.

The S-R design is a simple model of influencing attitudes and behavior. Little or nothing has to be known about a particular audience and the elements of motivation and reward can virtually be ignored. The emphasis in communication can, therefore, be placed upon the stimuli used. Advertising men in particular have preferred this S-R design but they have recognized its limitations.

We next turn to the cognitive design, which builds on the S-R approach in learning theory but also draws heavily on cognitive consistency theory.

7

the
cognitive
design

When the aim of persuasive communication goes beyond the presentation of new words and favorable associations into longer, more complex messages, the cognitive design is demonstrated. In part we can think of this model as an extension of the S-R design. Some psychologists would say that higher-order classical conditioning is all that is involved. This refers to the building of a chain of further conditioned responses based upon a previously established one. But other theoretical approaches provide more satisfactory explanations of the cognitive design.

Cognitive consistency theory contributes most significantly to this design because it sees man as a rational being trying to construct a meaningful picture of himself and the world around him. He is an information-processing creature who in various degrees actively seeks information, relates it to his existing cognitive maps, and attempts to achieve consistency and stability in these informational transactions with his environment.

Functional theory also makes a contribution by asserting that this need for cognitive clarity and consistency has a motivational base. For example, Daniel Katz refers to the "knowledge function." [1] He states: "Individuals not only acquire beliefs in the interest of satisfying various specific needs, they also seek knowledge to give meaning to what would otherwise be an unorganized chaotic universe." [2] Without attitudes in the form of stereotypes that simplify the rich, complex world around him, a person would feel incompetent to cope with present and future experiences.

65

Hence the purpose of the knowledge function of attitudes is to build economical constructs—cognitive maps—that make it easy for a person to understand his environment.

Perceptual theory also contributes to the cognitive design, because the way a person sees a stimulus may be more influential in forming an attitude than his opinion about it. Gestalt psychologists, whose approach is mainly perceptual, corroborate what we have already said—namely, that "every person has a need to explore, to know about the external world." [3] Furthermore, he wants to organize what he sees into complete and stable patterns. Most of the textbook examples deal with the perception of physical forms, for example, the tendency to see open figures closed, to reverse the figure and ground, or to see either an attractive young woman or an old hag in an ambiguous picture.[4] Similar verbal tendencies occur: a boy with long hair may be perceived as a girl, and a deeply tanned person as a Negro.

Despite the many theoretical inputs to the cognitive design, it shares the quality of simplicity with the S-R design. Not too much has to be known about man except that his verbal capacity exceeds an animal's and that he has the facility to manipulate verbal symbols in a process known as reasoning. Furthermore, in this age of the computer, many communicators want to imitate it and show that man can reason and arrive at logical conclusions if fed the same kind of informational food—facts.

"LET THE FACTS SPEAK FOR THEMSELVES"

The cognitive design is a message-oriented approach to persuasive communication. The tendency is to diagnose difficulties in human understanding as stemming from inadequate or wrong information held by a person or group. Hence the solution is to determine what corrective facts to present to an audience. That is why the slogan of this design is: "Let the facts speak for themselves."

Businessmen, administrators, and professional persons find this approach compatible with their way of thinking and making decisions. They know that the way to make a decision is to collect as much relevant information as possible, carefully consider the facts, and arrive at a solution.

This faith in the "facts approach" finds wide support in the business and behavioral science literature. For example, George D. Halsey writes:

> Attitudes can be changed only by changing the beliefs, allaying the suspicions, and removing fears which have caused them. This can be done best by giving employees the correct information about the company. In

addition to being given information regarding personnel rules and policies, they should be told as much as possible about the firm's business, and this should be in language the employee can understand.[5]

The Opinion Research Corporation is also an ardent supporter of the facts approach. In its report entitled *Collectivist Ideology in America,* it says: "The index has demonstrated over and over again that people try to be fair—that they come to reasonable conclusions when they have the facts." [6] Jerome Bruner in his *A Study of Thinking* comes to a similar conclusion: "Man is not a logic machine, but he is certainly capable of making decisions and gathering information in a manner that reflects better on his learning capacity than we have been as yet ready to grant." [7]

Faith in the facts approach was exemplified by the armed forces in World War II. The Army had inaugurated a series of "Why We Fight" orientation films. The objective of these films was to indoctrinate the American soldier for the explicit purpose of strengthening his convictions and promoting a stronger sense of personal commitment. Letting the facts speak for themselves was the approach decided upon by the Army as the best means of strengthening convictions about the war without the direct use of propaganda. This approach is described in the following policy, which was adopted by the Information and Education Division of the Army:

> In other words, the theory was that if the men had the facts about the war, they would draw the desired inference that the war had a meaning going far beyond the mere necessity of the militant answer to Pearl Harbor. This assumed (1) that the 'facts' were really such as to lead reasonable men to make the 'correct' inference and (2) that the rank and file of soldiers were capable of enough rationality to make the inference.[8]

Or, as stated by one group of authors, the basic idea behind the information or facts approach is that: "This approach emphasizes the fact that people seek to understand their world and to achieve a consistent picture of its complexities." [9] It assumes that people want to make an optimal adjustment to the environment, and in order to do this, they need adequate information. If people had wrong attitudes or behaved incorrectly, it might be due, as the many examples above illustrate, to false or limited information.

As related to the S-R design, the cognitive one is, in one sense, an enlargement on the stimuli. Not just a word or slogan is required, but an assemblage of facts and a line of reasoning that will convince an audience. Their cognitive maps must be organized or reorganized to support the communicator's position. Then the feeling and action components of attitudes will hopefully fall in line with the cognitive.

Scientific investigation calls for rational procedures in the search for facts and their objective measurement and assessment. Conclusions are based on statistical inference or other scientific evidence. The same procedures and values are applied to economic reasoning and rational decision-making processes in business and elsewhere.[10] In these situations information is the raw material out of which decisions are made. The communication of information is thus an important part of efficient and effective operations.

Facts and attitudes are not completely separate entities; they partially overlap. As Kenneth Boulding's book *The Image* illustrates, facts or knowledge usually consists of images: subjective knowledge or what people believe to be true.[11] As an example Boulding refers to a manufacturer who receives information that his sales expectations have not quite come up to what he expected. If the attitude toward the economy were optimistic, this information would lead to little more than a pep talk to his salesmen; but if the attitude were pessimistic he might order a cutback in output and the dismissal of labor.[12]

Two areas of application that emphasize the cognitive design are discussed below. The first, speech communication, helps to illustrate the nature of information and scientific evidence. The second, public information and organizational communication, shows how information serves as an integrative force in social systems.

speech communication

Speech is the ancient form of communication. In classical Greece it reached a zenith and occupied a prominent place in political life.[13] Since then, while the print media have sometimes replaced speech, many occasions remain where the primary mode of communication is oral. We are asked to deliver reports in church groups, Kiwanis-type clubs, P.T.A.s and public hearings; sometimes we are asked to give formal speeches at trade or professional meetings; and occasionally some of us give speeches that are transmitted to large audiences through the broadcast media.

In both the informal and formal situations the intention is to inform and, usually, to persuade. This means that skill in organizing facts and arguments is important. Message preparation, as Erwin Bettinghaus reminds us, involves more than a recital of statements of facts: "People do not necessarily learn 'plain, simple' facts. They have to be led from simple kinds of statements to the complex ones in which the communicator is more interested." [14] Bettinghaus defines proof as "the process of using evidence to secure belief in an idea or statement." [15] The presentation of evidence and the reasoning used to draw a conclusion are considered instrumental to persuasive communication.

An example used by Bettinghaus is a speaker who supports a school-bond campaign. Which of the following alternative ways of stating his case should be used?

Method 1: "We need more money for schools. This is a good proposal. Our children deserve the best, and this bond campaign will give it to them."

Method 2: "Last week our schools were visited by the State Department of Education. Officials from that department report that we will lose our state accreditation if we do not provide more classrooms and more teachers for our basic courses. If we lose our state accreditation, our children cannot be accepted at the state university. In order for them to have the same advantages as the children of other school systems, it is necessary for us to pass the proposed bond issue." [16]

Bettinghaus suggests that the second method is more effective, for it presents evidence to support beliefs. The subject of proof, which is an application of classical logic, is too complex to discuss here except to identify some of the elements. Bettinghaus uses the Toulmin model which employs three basic elements: (1) evidence, which is "any data that can be used to establish a conclusion"; (2) warrant, which is "the statement that shows the reasoning that must have gone on between finding the evidence and making the claim"; and (3) support for the warrant, which offers additional observations, further opinions, or clarifying statements for the warrant.[17] Three additional elements are introduced for complex situations: a qualifier, reservation, and support for the warrant.

The formal kind of speech preparation discussed here receives further support from psychologists who are concerned with the order of presentation of persuasive arguments.[18] Some principles derived from these studies are discussed later in this chapter.

public information and organizational communication

Public relations men and publicists are major users of the cognitive design. Both groups function as disseminators of information about a person, group, event, or product through various communication media to attract public notice.[19] They have an obligation to satisfy people's "right to know" about the operation of governmental units and the activities of corporation and nonprofit organizations that affect the public interest. There is also information that people "want to know" or that management feels the public "ought to know." The latter communication objective usually has a persuasive and propaganda intent.

Press releases are the favorite device used by public relations men to send information to newspapers, broadcast stations, and magazines.[20] When the information or event is highly newsworthy, press conferences are held in which spokesmen for an organization briefly talk about a subject and journalists and other writers have an opportunity to ask questions. Press kits containing background information, photographs, press releases, and other materials are usually presented. Although most of these materials are written in simple form and refer mainly to selected facts, the same principles used in the preparation of speeches are relevant.

When the public relations man serves as an editor of a company publication he might well be viewed as operating a miniature mass media system.[21] He does this with employee newspapers and magazines which are intended to satisfy the employee's need to know something about his fellow workers and his company. Controversial issues and attitude change materials are also included in some of these employee publications. Furthermore, some examples have been reported of unions that have withdrawn or reduced demands for wage increases upon management's presentation of evidence of inability to pay or the possibility of loss of jobs resulting from a worsened competitive position.

Economic education and other public affairs materials are also sometimes contained in employee publications. A word of caution must, however, be added, because the facts approach has generally been overused. Deeply held attitudes are not only a function of what a person knows about a certain issue; other factors are also involved. Attitudes may be held because they conform with those held by the groups to which one belongs, or they may be held in the face of conflicting facts. Businessmen should expect that an attitude toward the free enterprise system, for example, is not something that can quickly be changed through a series of articles in the company newspaper or in the reading of several pamphlets in the company book rack. The military should likewise have learned that motivation to fight is not brought about by telling the men why a war is being fought. Information plays a role in each of these situations; but it might be better to conclude that facts are not enough.

RATIONAL MESSAGE PREPARATION

Because the cognitive design is message-oriented the techniques and considerations that facilitate the operation of this design are related to the rational design of messages. They deal with the role of education and intelligence in understanding messages, the structure of messages, their context, and the arousal of cognitive inconsistencies.

consider difference in audience rationality

Because the cognitive design places such heavy emphasis on the rationality of man, it seems logical that human beings who are highly rational are more susceptible to this method than the less rational. Rationality is defined and measured by means of the usual intelligence tests or level of education.

The earlier mentioned studies of the U.S. Army documentary films supports this surmise in that: "The general effects of the films on opinion tended to increase with higher intellectual ability." However, the authors of these studies also pointed out that general intelligence should be broken down into three components: (1) learning ability, (2) critical ability, (3) ability to draw inferences.[22]

Thus, an intelligent person's ability to learn makes him more susceptible to propaganda because he can comprehend it, while a less bright person might not. As cleverly stated by Doob, "An anxious genius may be more susceptible to some propaganda than a happy highgrade moron." [23] Because of an intelligent person's ability to draw inferences, he is able to interpret and see implications that others might not. When facts are accurately and logically presented, their impact on a more intelligent person is greater than on a less intelligent one. If, on the other hand, a propagandist uses unsound or irrational arguments, an intelligent person's greater ability will make him suspicious and less persuasible than a less intelligent person.

Explicit or implicit conclusion-drawing. A consideration connected with the concept of rationality is whether conclusions to an argument should be explicitly drawn or whether the audience should be left to draw its own conclusions.[24] If the audience is intelligent, it is probably safe to let it draw its own conclusions. The advantage in so doing is that the possibility of being seen as a propagandist—somebody with an axe to grind— is presumed to be sharply reduced. Karlins and Abelson suggest that reducing the chances of being seen as a propagandist might be an important factor when the audience is hostile or suspicious.[25]

However, if there is any danger that the audience might not understand the point of a message, the safest thing to do is to draw the conclusion. The more complicated an issue is, the safer the latter procedure would seem to be. About the only word of caution that needs to be added comes from work done by psychotherapists. Their use of nondirective counseling suggests the inadvisability of giving advice to a client when personal issues are involved, that is, when there is high ego involvement.[26] For this reason, a reservation is often added to the explicit stating of conclusions—namely, that it should apply only to impersonal issues.

Emotional and rational appeals. The use of the cognitive design implies a preference for rational appeals over emotional ones. In the classic Hartmann experiment one group of voters was given a rational leaflet urging them to vote for Socialist Party candidates and another group was given an emotional leaflet.[27] Based on election returns, the author concluded that the emotional appeal was superior. Other studies sometimes support this conclusion but others do not.

Perhaps a conclusive statement about the relative superiority of one approach over the other is impossible because of the unreasonable nature of the topic. As Hovland points out, "the classification of different contents as 'emotional' or 'rational' appeals has not been based on clear-cut operational definitions." [28] In the Hartmann study, the emotional leaflet used "highly sentimentalized language to play up various threats (war, economic depressions, and so forth) and emphasized the satisfactions to be derived if the Socialist program were put into effect." [29] Bettinghaus, in describing emotional appeals, refers to the use of metaphors such as "Passing this bill means the *rape* of our woodlands." [30] Robert T. Oliver includes humor and laughter as emotions and says: "The successful persuasive speaker knows how to get his audience to laugh with him in full-bodied approval of his mood, attitude, or point of view; and to join him in laughing at some object, person, or point of view toward which he wishes to direct scorn." [31]

These various emotional approaches are intended to arouse feelings and to "energize the audience's support." [32] But to assume the opposite for rational appeals—that they do not contain motivational force—would be an error. Our conclusion must be that we not only talk about a matter of degree in distinguishing these two kinds of appeals, but that which is the superior depends on the issue under discussion and the composition of the audience.

plan the order of presentation

Decide on a one- or two-sided approach. Whether people are influenced more by hearing both sides of an argument or one side only involves another technique that refers to rationality.[33] It follows from what has been said above that when an audience is highly educated or intelligent the presentation of both sides is more effective. When the educational level of the audience is low, one side may be more effective.

However, more than the educational level must be considered. If the audience is initially opposed to the point of view being presented, even if the educational level is not high, the argument will appear biased. For this reason, it is recommended that two sides of an argument be presented to an audience that is hostile to the view being advocated.

The likelihood of counter-propaganda must also be considered. If the chances are high that the audience will subsequently be exposed to other viewpoints, it is advantageous to present both sides of an argument. The rationale behind this technique is that the negative side of the argument will be presented in the context of the positive conclusion. It is then assumed that this conclusion that takes both sides of the argument into account, because it has been learned first, will cancel out any subsequent conclusion drawn by the other side.

Appearing first or last. When there are two sides to an issue, does the communicator who reaches people before his rivals do have an advantage? [34] Does "smearing" a political opponent work despite the subsequent presentation of refutable evidence? For greater impact should the favored side be presented first or last?

All these questions concern the laws of primacy and recency. In 1925, F. H. Lund posited that the law of primacy dominated: that "the side of an issue presented first will have greater effectiveness than the side presented subsequently." [35] But this simple conclusion was challenged, for other evidence showed that sometimes a recency effect prevailed. About the only unequivocal conclusion that can be drawn at this time is that a speaker should avoid appearing in the middle of a program and should not place his important arguments in the middle of his message.

More can be said, however, about some conditions that favor appearing first. Hovland lists five:

1. when cues as to the incompatibility of different items of information are absent,
2. when the contradictory information is presented by the same communicator,
3. when committing actions are taken only after only one side of the issue has been presented,
4. when the issue is an unfamiliar one,
5. when the recipient has only a superficial interest in the issue (low cognitive need).[36]

When a communicator enjoys a persuasive monopoly, these conditions are more likely to exist than in an open marketplace of ideas. The audience may lack prior knowledge about an issue and thus not be alerted to the possibility of a conflicting point of view. The communicator might also be in a position to "freeze" the audience's viewpoint, for example, by "requiring persons attending political meetings to make public expressions of their views." [37] Furthermore, having a persuasive monopoly reduces the likelihood that the audience will be warned not to say "yes" or "no" until both sides are heard.

refer to the receiver's frame of reference

The cognitive design often involves the making of a judgment by a person. Judgments involve a comparison of two or more items—ideas, standards, or beliefs.[38] When the task is a simple one such as selecting the heavier of two weights, the standard of reference is built into the situation. If a person is asked whether a particular weight is extremely heavy, very heavy, moderately heavy, and so on, he will implicitly use some frame of reference provided by prior experience. Such experiences may reach far back in his lifetime or reflect the impressions of a few moments ago. In either case, the task of the communicator who asks a person to make a judgment is to become aware of the frame of reference the person is likely to use. Depending on the issue or activity involved, the communicator may be able to influence this frame of reference.

Take the example of a rally observed by the author. The rally was staged for the purpose of supporting a certain cause. The master of ceremonies asked the audience to show its support with dollars, as well as by paying attention to what the speakers had to say. The master of ceremonies asked who in the audience was ready to give $100 to fight for the cause. Nobody moved. But something did happen: people now had a frame of reference. What subsequently happened was that two people on the platform whipped out their checkbooks and wrote out the suggested amount. (This was a form of social influence that will be discussed later.) Next, the audience was asked who was willing to give $50. The audience began to participate. A few hands were raised. The speaker then asked who was willing to give $25, $10, $5, $1, or any small amount.

Isn't it reasonable to conclude that more money was collected this way than would have been if the master of ceremonies started by asking who would give $5? The frame of reference that had been established was the giving of $100. Hence, the many people who gave $5 contributed only one-twentieth of that amount, which seems rather small. Five dollars would have been given more reluctantly, however, if the frame of reference were $25, since $5 is one-fifth this amount.

Where ideas rather than dollars are involved, the same process takes place, but with greater complexity. One consideration concerns "assimilation contrast effects" caused by a person's own attitudes toward an issue which act as an established anchorage or frame of reference.[39] As previously stated in discussing the nature of attitudes (see Chapter 4), it is sometimes necessary to consider not only a person's position on an issue but his range of acceptances, rejections, and noncommitments with regard to alternative positions. This expanded knowledge of a person's attitude allows certain predictions to be made about the acceptance of a communication based on the discrepancy between the advocated position and the person's attitude of acceptance. As stated by Sherif, Sherif, and Nebergall:

> If a message or communication does not fall appreciably beyond the range of acceptances, the discrepancy will be minimized in placing the communication. Hence, the communication is likely to be *assimilated* into his range of acceptances.
>
> If the message falls well beyond the range of acceptances, the individual will appraise it as more discrepant than it actually is. Its position will be displaced away from his acceptable range, and the extent of the *contrast effect* will be in proportion to the divergence of the communication from his acceptable range.[40]

A second and related consideration is the degree of the receiver's personal involvement in an issue. If it is high, his latitude of rejection is greater than those of acceptance and noncommitment. Hence the likelihood that the contrast effect will occur is also greater.

arouse cognitive inconsistency

We know from the discussion of cognitive consistency theory in Chapter 5 that various kinds of imbalances, incongruities, and dissonances which a person recognizes produce forces that can change his attitudes. Persuasive communicators can, therefore, use the approach of arousing cognitive inconsistency in the audience.

From our previous discussion of source credibility and our reference to Osgood and Tannenbaum's incongruity principle, we know that one technique is to get a source credible to an audience to take a stand different from it. The source can denounce ideas the audience is for and support ideas it is against. Another technique with which we are already familiar is to get a person to recognize that his "conceptual baggage" is no longer in accord with reality.[41] Giving a person new information, either through communications or direct experience, that will make him more aware of this discrepancy is a general approach implied by the cognitive design.

Now, however, two additional techniques require fuller discussion. Both relate to the internal organization of attitudes as reviewed in Chapter 4. Attitudes were described as having three components: beliefs, feelings, and actions. The internal structure and interplay of these components become vehicles for attitude change.

Obtaining audience commitment. If a person can be made to say or do something publicly that he knows does not reflect his true beliefs, then cognitive dissonance is created. Pressure would arise to bring the two components in line. Among the ways to do this are for a person either to retract or deny the public statement and action or to change his belief to conform with what he did.

The "weakest link" hypothesis explains that the alternative which is "easiest" to follow will be chosen.[42] If there were some convenient explanation for having made a statement or if he could say he was misunderstood, the person would retract the statement. But if the original belief lacked affective support (emotional commitment) and if there were no strong justification for having made the public statement, he would be more likely to shift his beliefs to conform with the act.

Whether or not justification for action exists is often related to the reward factor. A person may act contrary to his beliefs for a variety of reasons: he may feel intimidated, he may like the communicator and not want to let him down, or he may receive some tangible or monetary reward.

Minimize justification for discrepant behavior. The size of the reward is a critical consideration, and one in which learning theory and cognitive consistency theory sometimes conflict. Learning theory usually states that a larger reward will serve as a greater reinforcement to learning than a small one. Cognitive consistency studies demonstrate, however, that in certain situations the opposite is true.[43]

In the classic Festinger-Carlsmith study, college students were asked to perform a boring task. Two groups of these students were then asked by the experimenter to tell the next group of subjects that the task was interesting and enjoyable—a statement clearly not true. The members of one group were paid one dollar each for this attitude-discrepant behavior, and members of the other group were paid twenty dollars.[44] Translating these rewards into dissonance-reducing terms, we now realize that for the one dollar group there was considerably less monetary justification for complying with the experimenter's request than for the twenty dollar group. Thus the one dollar group is more likely to reduce the dissonance caused by the discrepant behavior by revising its judgment of the task—truly believing it was pleasant—than the twenty dollar group. The latter can justify their "lying" by the large size of the reward.

Further features of rewards should also be recognized. One is that a low reward seems to prod a person to look more closely at what he is doing and to discover satisfying features that have previously gone unnoticed. Another is that the cognition of a high reward may increase the feeling of coercion and thus produce a stubborn unwillingness to perform the task.[45]

Change feelings. The usual sequence of attitude dynamics between the cognitive and affective factors is that after a person acquires a belief he links it to affective responses. This sequence can, however, be reversed if some means is found for a person first to acquire an affective disposition toward a belief object.[46] A boy who falls in love with a girl presumably starts with the affective component but soon constructs cognitive beliefs about that girl to support his feelings. Similarly, other attitudes can be formed or changed through this reversed process.

In a study of this process, Rosenberg hypnotized his subjects in order to induce change in their feelings toward Negroes moving into white neighborhoods; [47] attitude change on the cognitive level was subsequently proven. Other methods that lend themselves better to real life situations can be used. Reinforcement of feelings through the use of rewards, psychodrama—the improvised enactment of certain roles or incidents—and other techniques associated with the motivational and social designs next to be discussed can be used.

Use "socratic method." A person forms a belief for a variety of reasons—because it is held by a prestigeful person, by a positive reference group, by "everyone," or when labeled with some respected term such as "democratic," "fair," and so forth.[48] As a result, the internal consistency among beliefs on logically related issues is usually not maintained even though the need to bring this about exists. One reason a person is unaware of this lack of consistency is that he tends to maintain logic-tight compartmentalization among his isolated beliefs. A communicator may, if it serves his interests, create pressures toward consistency by making "permeable" the barriers between the isolated cognitions.[49]

William McGuire states that "a person's beliefs on logically related propositions can be modified by the Socratic method of merely asking him to verbalize his beliefs, and thus inducing changes toward greater internal consistency." [50] There has to be some degree of temporal contiguity in the eliciting of the inconsistent beliefs. But the person does not have to be conscious that his beliefs are inconsistent. In addition, McGuire found that the opinions listed earlier in a series are shifted more than those elicited later and that there is an impact on unmentioned but logically related issues as well as on the explicit issue.[51]

8

the motivational design

The previous two designs, the S-R and cognitive, were message-centered approaches to communication which virtually ignored the middle element of the S-O-R formula of behavior. Only general characteristics of the audience such as a responsiveness to stimuli and some variations in rationality were considered. The motivational design acknowledges the importance of this audience variable and examines the function of motives and rewards.

Thus the title of Raymond Bauer's article, "The Obstinate Audience," introduces the major orientation of the motivational design. He rejects the assumption so often made about advertising and propaganda that "the communicator *does* something to the audience" and that he has "considerable latitude and power to do what he pleases to the audience." [1] Communication is instead seen as a transactional process where both the communicator and receiver give and take something of value. As expressed by a sociologist, W. Phillips Davison:

> . . . the communicator's audience is not a passive recipient—it cannot be regarded as a lump of clay to be molded by the master propagandist. Rather the audience is made up of individuals who demand something from the communications to which they are exposed, and who select those that are likely to be useful to them. In other words, they must get something from the manipulator if he is to get something from them. A bargain is involved. [2]

How the audience exerts an influence on the communicator is illustrated in an experiment by Raymond Bauer and Claire Zimmerman.[3] Four groups of university students were asked to write sample speeches on the topic of teachers' pay. One week before, all the groups were read short passages on this topic—two groups were given arguments supporting a pay increase and the other two were given opposing arguments. Within each of the two halves, one group was told that their audience was the American Taxpayers Economy League and the other, the National Council of Teachers (both were fictitious organizations).

The question was whether the number of arguments each group remembered in its speeches was influenced by the audience it anticipated. The arguments were indeed influenced. For example, of the two groups listening to arguments in favor of raising teachers' pay, the group that anticipated a favorable audience (The National Council of Teachers) remembered more arguments than the group anticipating the audience interested in saving the taxpayers' money.

Public speakers are not surprised by these finding for they always ask what kinds of persons will be in their audience—what their interests and attitudes are. Furthermore, as Bauer points out, a speaker also considers his secondary audiences or reference groups—that is, persons important to the speaker who might indirectly receive the message.[4]

The motivational design does more than recognize the influence of the audience on the persuasive communicator. It takes this as a starting point to examine the function of the final two fundamentals of learning: motives and rewards. In doing this we accept the premise of psychology that "all behavior is caused."[5] We therefore look behind the attitudes of a member of an audience and find the reason why he holds them. This reason is a motive. Then we examine how the satisfaction of a motive through rewards enhances the learning process.

THE CLASSIC DRIVE MODEL

The study of motivation has been defined as "the analysis of the various factors which incite and direct an individual's actions."[6] Of the several approaches used in such studies the most prominent is the classic drive model.[7] In this model a motive is defined as an internal stimulus which impels a person to act in a way that reduces the tension that originally created the motive.[8] A person is thus viewed as someone who experiences a deficiency or disruption in himself or his surroundings and as a consequence seeks to correct this disequilibrium. For example, a hungry person who feels stomach pangs is activated to look for food to reduce this inner tension. The hunger serves as the drive—the energy—to look for the food (stimulus) that will elicit eating (the response). The consummatory act of eating is the reward.

a closer look at motives

The motivational design assumes that little or no learning can take place in the absence of some unfulfilled need or desire which serves as a drive. Man is seen as a goal-seeking animal constantly striving to reduce the tensions within him. In this manner he successfully adjusts to his environment.

Once our audience member is aware of an internal stimulus, the need, he will scan his environment to locate objects that have valence relative to his motivational priorities. (Chapter 11 on perception will further discuss this relationship.) These objects in the environment serve as incentives to propel our audience member toward them. For example, if we are engaged in a college recruiting campaign and have created attention to job openings in our organization by including some of the motives discussed above, then we have succeeded in this first step. We must, however, go further by showing the audience member the best path to the goal. We provide him with a "cognitive map" by telling him when a recruiter will be visiting the campus, to whom to write, or how else to act in order to apply for the job.

Another assumption of the motivational design is that motives can be influenced from the outside. A communicator does not have to view motives as biologically innate and fixed entities. He can create new higher-level motives and build around them. Hunger is a biological need, but a restaurant manager obviously doesn't stop at satisfying stomach pangs. An appetite for special cuisine is aroused and various other satisfactions summarized under "atmosphere" are built into the experience of dining out. These other satisfactions may appeal to a person's social status, his need for relaxation and escape, and so on.

It seems that the hedonistic model of men is accepted. The maximization of gratification and the minimization of deprivation becomes the formula that explains human behavior.

Obtaining the maximum amount of positive reward with the least expenditure of effort or at the lowest possible cost does not, however, explain all behavior.[9] Events and stimuli that are typically classified as unpleasant or are avoided may be sought out. J. Loeb, for example, discovered that preschool-age children chose smiling and frowning faces more frequently than neutral faces or a blank space.[10] If one agrees that the sight of someone frowning is relatively unpleasant because it indicates disapproval, the choice of the frowning face is not explained by a tension-reduction drive.

As Berkowitz suggests, a person's exposure to unpleasant stimuli might be seen as intermediary behavior to achieve a sense of control over dangers or to learn how more realistically to appraise a danger so as not to exaggerate it.[11] He points out that clinical psychologists explain these phenomena in such terms as "undoing," "belated mastery," "drive for competence," and "identification with the aggressor."[12] The ultimate goals might still be to achieve security and internal tension reduction.

William McGuire offers another explanation for behavior that in classical theory is considered irrational and inconsistent. He says that we may be seeing the end of classic theories of behavior and the beginning of what he calls "complexity theories."[13] In place of the classic organism's penchant for "stability, redundancy, familiarity, confirmation of expectance, avoidance of the new, the unpredictable," the new "romantic" organism operates differently: "It has a stimulus hunger, an exploratory drive, a need curiosity. It takes pleasure in the unexpected, at least in intermediate levels of unpredictability. It wants to experience everything; it shows alternation behavior; it finds novelty rewarding."[14]

The craving for excitement associated with the young generation does indeed appear to support such complexity theories. Persuasive communicators may have to consider a wider variety of motivational stimuli than they have in the past.

rewarded behavior is learned and repeated

The manner in which information refers to a person's needs and wants is an essential communications consideration. W. Phillips Davison makes this point and states that "communications serve as a link between man and his environment, and their effects may be explained in terms of the role they play in enabling people to bring about more satisfying relationships between themselves and the world around them."[15] In saying this, Davison attaches the motivational factor to the operation of the cognitive design previously discussed. He also refers to the function of rewards in the motivational process:

> The communicator can influence attitudes or behavior only when he is able to convey information that may be utilized by members of his audience to satisfy their wants or needs. If he has control of some significant aspect of his audience's environment, his task may be an easy one. All he must do is tell people about some environmental change or expected change that is important to them.[16]

Let us now examine the function of rewarded behavior more closely.

Why is it that children continue to love ice cream and hate castor oil? One tastes good and is rewarding; the other tastes bad and is punishing. Similarly rats can be taught to enter a box with a triangle drawing and avoid one with a circle. The box with the triangle has a piece of cheese behind the door panel and the one with the circle has an electrical shock device.

The secret behind both examples lies in what Edward L. Thorndike called the law of effect and B. F. Skinner calls operant conditioning.[17] The principle in both is that the satisfaction or annoyance to which behavior leads will modify the tendency to repeat that behavior. We repeat what is rewarded and avoid what is punished.

B. F. Skinner is credited for many experiments dealing with the process of operant conditioning.[18] Working with pigeons, he points out that pecking is an innate response and that a pigeon in a cage wanders around pecking everywhere. Suppose then that the psychologist wants it to learn to peck at a round red target. All he does is wait until the pigeon happens to peck at it. When it does, the psychologist immediately feeds it grain. Evidence shows that the probability of the recurrence of this pecking at the target increases. We say that the behavior has been reinforced. As explained by Homans in his summary of Skinner's experiments, "the pigeon's behavior in pecking the target is an operant; the operant has been reinforced; grain is the reinforcer; and the pigeon has undergone operant conditioning. Should we prefer our language to be ordinary English, we may say that the pigeon has learned to peck the target by being rewarded for doing so." [19]

The challenging and creative task for the persuasive communicator is to think of the kinds of "grain" that can serve as rewards for his audiences. If the communicator is himself a member of line management or has influence with those who decide policy and command resources, his task will be easier. Furthermore, as we shall see in the next chapter, many human motives are of a social nature.

MOBILIZING SUPPORT

When the communicator's problem is to stir people into action or to encourage greater effort, the motivational design is appropriate. Every politician knows that by using shrewd guesswork, keeping an ear attuned to the grass roots, and by employing professional pollsters he can discover what issues are uppermost in the voters' minds and thereby engage their attention and support. Fundraisers also know that in addition to appealing to people's general sense of social responsibility, it is helpful to identify a specific motive for giving. Recruiters for high-talent scientific and engineering personnel have discovered that besides an attractive salary, they have to offer an opportunity to write and publish professional papers, sponsor attendance at professional meetings, provide a choice of research projects, and offer other inducements.[20]

Two additional problems have received particular attention and are described below. These are the stimulation of consumer demand in an affluent economy and the improvement of employee performance.

stimulating consumer demand

Because of books like Pierre Martineau's *Motivation in Advertising* [21] and Vance Packard's *The Hidden Persuaders,*[22] the best-known application of motivation research is in the field of marketing. Marketing men seek to increase the demand for their client's products and services by dropping the assumption that people would, without prompting, be aware of their needs and know how a given product or service would satisfy them. The purpose of motivation research is to investigate people's motives thoroughly and clarify the relationship between these motives and specific products and services.

Motivation research applied to marketing usually involves two operations: (1) to discover consumer motives that might be related to a product; (2) to reshape a product—actually or psychologically—so that its ability to satisfy the discovered needs are more obvious.

The first operation involves the attempt to discover people's preconscious or unconscious needs. By definition, the person is not aware of them, but they can, nonetheless, have dynamic effects on his conscious behavior. The needs are temporarily dormant, but they can be put to work to help sell products; a new frontier is opened up.

The usual result of the first operation is that a single, "easily describable reason" for the purchase of a particular product is found.[23] Buying a car is linked with springtime sexual rejuvenation; soup is seen as satisfying some repressed incestuous desire for mother; soap becomes a path to beauty rather than cleanliness alone. Such explanations are appealing because presumably they apply to a major portion of the population. However, these explanations are sometimes criticized for ignoring simpler explanations, or considering the possibility that several motives may be operating at the same time.

The second operation in motivation research calls for the reshaping of a product so that it will stimulate the motives that have been discovered. A product is assigned a suitable personality and status, so to speak. For example, tea is given a bisexual personality so that men can be added to its consumers. Thus, truck drivers and athletes—real men—are pictured drinking tea.

The same process of creating psychological associations can be used to create brand differences for products that are fundamentally similar. Different brands cater to different personality types. A thinking man smokes Brand A, while a person interested in that quarter of an inch in life that really counts smokes Brand B. A consumer chooses the brand that matches his self-image.

Products have also been reshaped semantically. A man who already owns eight pairs of shoes is not likely to get terribly excited at the prospect of a ninth pair. This reaction simply reflects the law of diminishing marginal utility—that the addition of each additional unit leads to a smaller and smaller increment of satisfaction. To the marketing man, this law is more easily explained by saying that people tend to get satiated. Therefore, the demand for a product grows more slowly or becomes arrested.

Semantic redefinition of a product is one way of overcoming the consumer's feeling of satiation. The ninth shoe becomes the "carefree shoe"; it is not really a shoe at all, but a blending of a slipper and a shoe. With these or similar words, the marketing expert hopes to get the consumer as excited about this new concept of a "shoe-slipper" as he was about the first pair of shoes he ever owned. He hopes thereby to beat the law of diminishing marginal utility.

Motivation research makes obvious sense in the field of product promotion where the aim is to increase sales by satisfying people's needs. Increased sales are highly correlated with an increased knowledge of people's motives.

improving employee performance

When employee communications goes beyond the provision of simple job and company information to the improvement of employee attitudes and performance, reference to motivation supplies a great deal of insight. The formal goal of providing employees with job satisfaction was added to that of producing products and services for a profit with the publication of Roethlisberger and Dickson's classic study, *Management and the Worker*.[24] At a later date, Lemuel Boulware of General Electric reflects this goal in his semantical reformulation of an employee as a "job customer." [25] Through this designation, the same kind of motivation research thinking that we above applied to marketing has been applied to employee relations.

Employee morale surveys have long been a standard diagnostic tool used by management to discover employee motives and measure their satisfaction. Surveys such as the well-known Science Research Associates' Employee Morale Inventory ask questions about satisfaction with hours of work, working conditions, supervisory relations, pay scales, credit and praise for work well done, and so on.[26] Advantage has also been taken of theoretical contributions by psychologists. Abraham Maslow's hierarchy of needs approach has been found to be particularly useful.[27] Starting from the bottom, most basic level of needs, Maslow identified five levels: [28]

1. *Physiological:* the needs for food, water, air, shelter, rest, and exercise required to satisfy the biological demands of the human organism.

2. *Safety:* needs to be free from fear of deprivation, danger, and threat, on the job and off.

3. *Social:* the needs people have for gregariousness and social interaction. People like to group together for many purposes of life. They need to associate, to belong, to accept, and to be accepted, to love and to be loved. In the human relations literature this is usually expressed as "the need to belong." The informal group is a major way to satisfy this need.

4. *Ego:* needs for reputation, self-respect, and self-esteem. Man needs to feel competent and knowledgeable. He needs respect, recognition and status.

5. *Self-actualization:* the needs for the realization of individual potential, the liberation of creative talents, the widest possible use of abilities, and, in short, for personal fulfillment.

These surveys and studies of motivation have helped to correct the many wrong assumptions that management—and, indirectly, those responsible for employee communications—have made about the way employees should be supervised. Douglas McGregor's *The Human Side of Enterprise* distinguished between two leadership styles: Theory X, an authoritarian, bureaucratic style, and Theory Y, a participatory style.[29] Among the assumptions concerning employee motivation made by Theory X are that "the average man is by nature indolent—he works as little as possible; he lacks ambition, dislikes responsibility, prefers to be led; he is inherently self-centered, indifferent to organizational needs; he is by nature resistant to change, and he is gullible, not very bright, the ready dupe of the charlatan and the demagogue." [30] These assumptions have been replaced by almost opposite ones as suggested by Maslow's formulation.

These findings are important to the communicator because he directly or indirectly makes references to rewards the organization provides. The distinctive feature of employee communications is that the communicator or the management for which he works has control over many of the rewards that employees seek.

With regard to rewards, Daniel Katz makes an important distinction between "instrumental system rewards and instrumental individual rewards." [31] System rewards accrue to an employee because he is a member of the organization, while individual rewards accrue to him because of his superior effort and performance. A fringe benefit or cost of living raise applies to all employees, while piece-rate incentive, a promotion, or special recognition apply to specific individuals for differential performance. System rewards are effective for attracting and holding employees in the system—that is, keeping turnover and absenteeism low; but they are not effective for securing high quality or quantity of work, nor in eliciting innovative behavior and spontaneous activity needed for the survival of the organization.

Communicators must make this distinction clear. Furthermore, if individual rewards are expected to motivate employees, attention must be paid to the size of the reward, its relationship to performance (so that the principle of operant conditioning can work), and the fairness of the reward.[32] Many rewards are of a social nature, so we shall return to this subject in the next chapter dealing with the social design.

MOTIVATION RESEARCH AND STRUCTURE OF APPEALS

The motivational design is based on the premise that a knowledge of people's motives will provide a bond between the communicator and his audience. The primary facilitating technique, therefore, involves the study of people's motives—human motivation in general, and the specific motives of a particular audience. Another technique is to use motive-arousal stimuli.

motivation research

The subject of human motivation is included in virtually every introductory text in psychology and is treated in several specialized books.[33] The amount of material is too extensive to summarize here. What has already been said about the motivation shows, however, that human motives range from the biological to the social, from the unlearned to the learned, from the emotional to the rational, and from the unconscious to the conscious. If a communicator at least opens his mind and imagination to the richness of human motives, he may become aware of human dimensions formerly ignored or treated lightly.

Information about the specific motives of a particular audience can be obtained in several ways. One way is to examine books on such specialized subjects as employee relations, advertising, stockholder relations, and voting behavior.[34] Many of these books contain sections that specifically treat the subject of motivation as applied to behavior in certain arenas of life; or, to put it another way, these books are an index to the motives of different publics.

A second way to study the motives of specific publics is to make a survey that tries to discover the reasons for people's opinions, attitudes, and behavior. Such surveys are often called motivation research studies, although other in-depth attitude studies also contain similar information.[35] The subject of human motivation is complex and the number of motives and their interrelationship complex.

Clinical psychologists are best trained to offer deep insight into motives. But they must be cautioned to look at the right level of motivation. One might discover that milk is indeed related to some repressed incestuous desire and recommend that milk sold in round glass bottles would sell better. But the consumer might be operating on a different level of motivation and find that a squared cardboard carton fits more easily into the refrigerator.[36]

Many techniques are used in motivation research studies. Use of the depth interview which allows the respondent to answer open-ended questions and to associate freely is almost standard. This technique is supplemented by various kinds of projective tests: word association, sentence completion, Rorschach and thematic apperception drawings. In this manner the motives behind purchase behavior, philanthropy, voting, and other forms of behavior can be identified and better understood.

use of motive-arousal stimuli

Once an audience's motives are discovered, use should be made of this knowledge. The most obvious way is to build appeals into a message that will link up with people's motives. If the stockholders of a company have been dissatisfied with the size of dividends, then a dissenter engaged in a proxy fight should mention inadequate dividend payments and state what he plans to do about it. If management knows that union demands will lead to some layoffs, then management should alert employees to the implications of these demands to job security.

A communicator should consider a technique of persuasion in relation to creating interest. The question is whether the beginning or the end of a message should contain the most motivating material.[37] Although the overall answer is inconclusive, a message should start out with motivating material if there is any suspicion that the initial interest of the audience is low. At least the audience's attention is obtained. What may be sacrificed is its continuing attention. But this will be lost only if the communicator has no conclusion to reach. If he can specify how a need can be gratified, then the audience's attention and interest should be maintained.

The choice of which appeals to use requires a further consideration. It is usually easier and more efficient to ride upon existing needs than to try to create new ones. This idea is called canalization in the mass media literature and has been mentioned earlier.[38] The communicator makes use of the audience's natural needs or previous learning. Motivation research is insurance against overlooking such hidden assets.

Motives do not remain constant over time. They change in kind and in the intensity with which they are held. There is thus an obvious advantage for messages to reach people at a time when relevant needs are present and intense. This means, for example, that a talk on the virtues of a company by an employer will usually have a greater impact on prospective college graduates in May or June than it would in September or October. It means that a bread-and-butter issue in a political campaign will have a greater impact during a recession or depression than during prosperous times.

9

the
social
design

The existence of customs, traditions, standards, rules, values, fashions, and other criteria of conduct demonstrates that influences operate on individual attitudes and behavior. Muzafer Sherif called these socially sanctioned modes of behavior social norms.[1] They are both the product of social interaction and social stimuli to which members of a group having these norms are subjected.

In an intensive study of about 250 Bennington College girls, Theodore Newcomb used the concept of social norms to explain why entering students who came predominately from conservative homes turned out to be liberals in their senior year. His study showed that the attitudes of individuals are strongly rooted in the groups to which they belong. Those students who conformed to the liberal political norms of the college were in various ways rewarded by their fellow students.[2]

Studies like Newcomb's show that social approval, like money, serves as a generalized reinforcer of a wide variety of attitudes and human activities.[3] We know that a smile leads to a repetition of the behavior which instigated it and a frown leads to a cessation. Social approval takes many forms, for as Homans humorously observed, "some men find some of the damnedest things valuable—or so it seems to the rest of us." [4] Psychiatrists know that even such "secondary reinforcers" as "Hmm" in response to certain words spoken by someone will increase the use of the reinforced words. Hence they wear poker faces so as not to influence the answers they get.[5]

The function of rewards is not new to this social design, for the motivational design also referred to it. But the social design is chiefly characterized by the role that other persons—either individually or in groups—play in rewarding or punishing a person's actions. B. F. Skinner's principle of operant conditioning applies. When a person engages in a desired activity (the operant), this activity is reinforced (rewarded) by social approval in the same way that a pigeon's peck at the right spot is rewarded with grain.[6]

SOCIAL INFLUENCE: SOURCES AND IMPACT

The social design begins with the everyday observation that one of the characteristics of human beings is their high sensitivity to the reactions and opinions of others. This sensitivity is the cornerstone of the field of social psychology. We shall first demonstrate that social influence exists and why a person is dependent on others, and then examine the impact of this social influence and dependence on attitudes and behavior.

sources of social influence

Robert B. Zajonc's article "Social Facilitation" serves as a useful introduction.[7] He says that the main efforts of social psychology are explicitly or implicitly committed to the problem of "how and why the *behavior* of one individual affects the behavior of another." [8]

Two types of reactions are observable: audience effects and co-action effects. In the first, the mere presence of one or several onlookers affects the behavior of a person. This effect is positive or negative depending on the nature of the task. If what a person is doing is a well-learned response then his performance likely improves, but if he is learning something new —for example, nonsense syllables, his performance is impaired. In co-action effects individuals are "all simultaneously engaged in the same activity and in full view of each other." [9] The classic example is that a chicken who has eaten to full satisfaction immediately continues to eat more when a companion chicken who has not eaten for twenty-four hours is brought in. The experiments of Floyd Allport on human beings showed that in a wide variety of tasks, such as chain word association and multiplication, performance improved in a group situation, but in problem-solving and judgment tests, solo performance was better.

Zajonc concludes that in the presence of others, either as spectators or as co-actors, the emission of dominant responses is enhanced, but if "strong (and many) incorrect response tendencies prevail, then the presence of others can only be detrimental to performance." [10] His explanation is that in social situations an individual's general arousal or drive state is increased and that other people provide cues as to which responses are appropriate or inappropriate.

A person's dependence on others is greater than is often realized. Leon Festinger makes this clear in examining pressures toward uniformity in a group—pressures that also increase the need to communicate.[11]

One source of pressure is that physical reality can not always serve as the basis for the validity of opinions, attitudes, and beliefs. If there is a difference of opinion over which of two cars is faster, a simple race can decide the issue. But there are many other matters in which "reality" for the individual is to a high degree determined by what is socially accepted as reality.[12] Deciding whether economic conditions will change with a newly elected president is less a scientific conclusion than a consensus among members of a group who share similar beliefs, opinions, and attitudes.

But the famous "line experiment" by Solomon Asch shows that even the perception of a physical object is subject to group pressure—even when members of a group are previously unacquainted and no overt effort is made to influence one another's behavior.[13] A group of eight individuals is instructed to match the length of a given line with one of three unequal lines. Each individual is in turn asked for his answer. Because this is a simple judgment of perceptual relations, most groups succeed by making few errors. But what happens if all the participants except one are previously instructed to give wrong answers? Will the naive individual trust his senses or conform to the judgment of the group?

Asch reports that there was a marked movement toward the unanimous majority by "the minority of one": one-third of all the estimates in these groups "were errors identical with or in the direction of the distorted estimates of the majority." [14] Asch's explanation is instructive:

> The individual comes to experience a world that he shares with others. He perceives that the surroundings include him, as well as others, and that he is in the same relation to the surroundings as others. He notes that he, as well as others is converging upon the same object and responding to its identical properties. Joint action and mutual understanding require this relation of intelligibility and structural simplicity. In these terms the "pull" toward the group becomes understandable.[15]

Thus belonging to a group, even a temporary one, makes a person sensitive to his relations with others to a point where much of reality is defined for him.

Group locomotion is a second source of pressure for uniformity among members of a group. Once a group has decided on a goal—which is itself sometimes a formidable task—it must determine how to reach it. Since a group consists of individual members, tasks must be assigned to each one so that the activities necessary for group locomotion are carried out. Festinger predicts that the magnitude of pressures for uniformity is greater under two conditions: (1) when "members perceive that group movement would be facilitated by uniformity," and (2) "the more dependent the various members are on the group in order to reach their goals." [16]

While communications to establish social reality or gain group loco-motion are instrumental in nature, Festinger also recognizes "consumma-tory communications"—communication which is an end in itself because its expression is satisfying.[17] This kind of communication serves as a reward and as such serves to tie a person closer to those who provide it.

The review of the ideas of Zajonc and Festinger clearly demonstrates that a person is dependent on others for several reasons: to establish social reality, accomplish group goals, and enjoy interpersonal rewards. We must now examine the impact of this social influence on attitudes and behavior.

social impact on attitudes

In studying the impact of social influence, a useful distinction to draw is between two different types of influence as suggested by Herbert C. Kelman: the kind that results in public conformity and the kind that results in private acceptance.[18] In the former there may be superficial changes on a verbal or overt level without the accompanying changes in belief that characterize private acceptance.

This consideration led Kelman to propose three processes of social influence: (1) compliance, which occurs "when an individual accepts in-fluence from another person or from a group because he hopes to achieve a favorable reaction from the other"; (2) identification, which occurs "when an individual adopts behavior derived from another person or a group because this behavior is associated with a satisfying self-defining relationship to this person or group"; and (3) internalization, which oc-curs "when an individual accepts influence because the induced behavior is congruent with his value system." [19]

The social aspects of these processes vary considerably. In the case of compliance, the relationship is less social than instrumental. The re-ceiver of communication realizes that the other person can supply or withhold the means needed by him to achieve his goals. Thus he will publicly express opinions in which he doesn't believe when his behavior is observable by the influencing agent. Identification is more deeply rooted in social relations because it is based on the attractiveness of another person or group to an individual. So long as this attractiveness exists the individual seeks to maintain his relationship by meeting the expectations of the influencing agent.

In the case of internalization, the role of the influencing agent is defined by his credibility as a source of information. The concept of credibility is related to the social design because in a sense the receiver of information anticipates social rewards and punishments. When he listens to someone whom he trusts, he expects the recommended action to be a rewarding one. The expectation of a reward adds this fourth learning factor to whatever equation is being used. The effect of such source credibility is, therefore, to reinforce learning.

It should be noted that source credibility can have at least two bases.[20] One of these is respect for the communicator's expertness about a specific subject, which leads to a belief in what he says. This type of credibility is closely related to the cognitive design and simply means that what is heard is perceived as being the truth. The second basis of credibility is trustworthiness. This results not only in believing the message, but also in expecting a reward. Source credibility based on trustworthiness is essentially a social concept, since a communicator who is considered trustworthy by one group may appear otherwise to another. Generally speaking, a communicator is trusted if he is seen by the audience as belonging to their group or class, or in some way upholds the interests of the groups.

At the heart of the social design, then, is the dependence of a person upon others—for information, a sense of reality, and moving ahead on tasks that require cooperation. As a consequence of this dependence, he is sensitive and vulnerable to their positive or negative social approval. He may thus simply comply publicly without really changing his opinions, or he may truly change his attitudes—but even then, sometimes only in the context of certain social situations. So while the communicator can benefit from the potency of the social design, he should also realize that the changes may be superficial.

ESTABLISHING SOCIAL NORMS AND LEADERSHIP PATTERNS IN INDUSTRY AND EDUCATION

The applications of the social design are so widespread that virtually every attitude and area of behavior is touched. In previous chapters where applications of other designs were discussed, further reference was made to the social design. For example, the reason soldiers are willing to fight on the front lines is that they don't want to let their buddies down. This means that efforts to create group cohesion are more effective than the showing of "Why We Fight" films.[21] Similarly with advertising and product publicity, high use is made of social status motives. Furthermore, there are occasional consumer boycotts that are organized by unions and, more recently, by Blacks and protest groups to punish companies and stores whose social policies are considered unfair.

Among the areas where the operation of the social design has been most recognized are the fields of industrial relations and education. The discovery of the informal group in the Western Electric Hawthorne studies accounted for the rising attention given to social pressures in the work group.[22] These informal groups consist of people who are in one's work group, or with whom one drives to work, chats, or relaxes. A feature of the informal group is that its reaction is usually immediate and its pressure constant. Thus the omnipresence of social rewards and punishments results in a powerful behavioral influence. This influence has been most felt with regard to social norms on levels of output, union activity, and the degree of resistance to change.

In the field of education, the close relationship to the larger process of socialization was recognized. "How to rear children so that they will become adequate adult members of the society to which they belong"[23] is one of the contexts of education. As pointed out by Lee J. Cronbach, the learning of attitudes is an important part of the educational process. Such attitude-learning, he states, is "based on an emotional relation between teacher and pupil. . . ."[24] The student imitates the teacher whom he holds in high regard. In other words, the teacher serves as an identification figure. However, not only his attitudes and values are imitated, but also his personal idiosyncracies.

In both industrial relations and education, attention has been given to the nature of leadership. An important aspect of these studies is how much use a leader should make of group decision-making processes. The early study by Ralph White and Ronald Lippitt on children's groups demonstrated that the same group of people will behave in markedly different ways under leaders who create an "authoritarian," "democratic," or "laissez-faire" atmosphere.[25] An idea of the difference in leadership styles is reflected in how general policy is determined. In the authoritarian situation all determination of policy is made by the leader; in the democratic situation all policies are a matter of group discussion and decision, encouraged and assisted by the leader; and in the laissez-faire situation the group is given complete freedom for group or individual decision, with a minimum of leader participation.

The results differed substantially. Under autocracy the quantity of work done was somewhat greater than under democracy, but it created much hostility and aggression, including aggression against scapegoats. Under democracy, which makes greatest use of the social design, the work motivation was stronger than under autocracy, even when the leader left the room; originality was also greater. Under laissez-faire the group did less and poorer work than in other situations, and it was more characterized by play. As can be expected, these results gave much impetus to notions of progressive education and democratic leadership styles in industry.

Other applications of the social design are reserved for Part III, where a broader sociological context is presented. There the major emphasis will be on the influence of social class on sociopolitical attitudes and on the role of personal influence in mass communication.

ELEVATING THE SOCIAL NATURE
OF THE INDIVIDUAL

The essence of the social design is that a person is no longer appealed to as an isolated individual, but as a member of a social group. Practically all the techniques associated with the social design are variations of this theme.

social saliency

The first factor to consider is the extent to which a given issue in attitude change is of a group-anchored nature. A broad knowledge of motivation, especially social motivation, is highly helpful. Such knowledge helps to determine the extent to which an opinion has been molded by social influences and the extent to which it is still dependent upon them. It is probably safe to say that whenever an issue has the potential power of influencing a person's group membership or affecting his status in the eyes of others, the issue has a social dimension. How people vote, for example, has a social dimension to the extent that it shows loyalty to a given group. Identification with a given party may also have status meanings for a person. Many Democrats who move from the city to the suburbs switch from the Democratic to the Republican party as a sign of higher status.

A consideration associated with the social nature of an attitude concerns the extent to which a communicator can make his audience aware or unaware of the connection between a given issue and his group memberships. The more salient—prominent in a person's awareness—the group-anchored nature of a message, the greater will be its influence on the relevant group norms.[26] A demographer speaking to a predominantly Catholic audience on the subject of birth control would, therefore, increase his chances of changing attitudes if he avoided reference to Catholicism. Such a tactic assumes, however, that the audience would not of its own accord associate their religion with the issue of birth control.

Another way of looking at saliency is to picture a psychological frame of reference in which the specific issue is at the center. Other attitudes and group norms which could be related to this specific attitude can then be seen as outer fields around the central issue. Depending on the strength of association, a related attitude may fall inside or outside an audience's psychological field. Those that fall within the field are obviously not under the control of the communicator, for they occur more or less automatically to an audience. But those that fall outside this part of the psychological field become a variable for the communicator. He can choose to bring or not to bring certain related attitudes and group norms into the psychological field.

Take the fluoridation issue as an example. The communicator can consciously try to keep this issue in a scientific or health context; to the extent that science is credible to a given audience, his chances of success are maximized. If, on the other hand, the fluoridation issue is put in the context of religious beliefs or government control over individual rights, certain negative attitudes will be aroused in some people, thereby weakening the chances of success.

To summarize, we are concerned with the relationship of a part to the whole. This whole or context is not fixed, but may vary according to the references made by the communicator. The communicator must be highly sensitive to any cues he inserts into his message that might bring unwanted group norms into the audiences' psychological field.

cohesiveness

Whenever an attitude is anchored to a given group, the factor of cohesiveness must be considered. This is defined as "the total field of forces acting on members to stay in the group." [27] The strength of any group attachment varies from individual to individual. Depending on the person, some groups will be highly valued and others will not. Thus, recommended attitude changes that conflict with the norms of a highly valued group will be resisted more strongly than those related to a less valued group. As a result of this, certain long-run attitude change campaigns require more than just communicating a message. The communicator must also try to influence the group that has a hold over an individual.

There are many variables which influence an individual's attachment to a group.[28] The number and type of needs satisfied by a group, the existence of alternate ways of satisfying these same needs, the degree of power or even force which can be potentially exercised by the group over its members, and the particular status of a person within the total group are some of the variables that might be involved.

A good example of the application of these considerations can be found in the public relations campaigns associated with union-management relations. The attempt by the steel industries in 1959 to influence the outcome of collective bargaining was particularly instructive. When the public relations theme was based on fighting inflation, *Business Week* reported that management was meeting with some success.[29] When, however, management introduced a second issue—a change in work rules—it had the effect of strengthening the workers' loyalty to the union. Any shift of allegiance to management was immediately arrested, and the union members became more dependent upon the union for protection against management.

ambiguity of situation

The degree of group influence is affected by a third factor—the extent to which a situation, whose description a communicator is trying to influence, is ambiguous.[30] We said earlier that the more unstructured the stimulus situation, the greater will be the dependence upon either stereotypes, which are socially derived, or current social influences.

The classic experiment by Muzafer Sherif that demonstrates the power of group influence in an ambiguous situation is the so-called autokinetic effect.[31] A person is placed in a completely dark room and asked to observe a pinpoint of light. What he doesn't know is that the light source is fixed, but because of the physiological features of visual perception, the light will appear to be moving. He is asked to report on the direction and distance the light moves—which varies idiosyncratically among different individuals. Suppose he establishes a personal norm in approximately the six o'clock direction for a distance of three feet. What happens if he then overhears persons in other experimental rooms report observations around the norm of a 12 o'clock direction and a distance of one foot? As you might guess, he begins to modify his subsequent reports in the direction of the group norm. He does this because he has a need for a stable frame of reference but can't find it in his visually-deprived and, therefore, ambiguous environment. Hence he becomes dependent on "social reality"—the views that others have.

A communicator can use this ambiguity factor either to strengthen or weaken group attachments. If he wants to strengthen membership loyalty to a group, he may want to remain somewhat vague about a situation facing it. This technique is used by totalitarian organizations and nations, and is especially effective under conditions in which there is a communication monopoly. It will not work when members have independent access to information. When the opposite result is desired—a decrease in group influences—the obvious technique is to supply as much information about a situation as possible. This approach is implied in the "rumor clinics" conducted by various organizations. Rumors spread when people are concerned about a situation and have little reliable information about it.[32] When information is available, rumors are not needed.

group decision making

A fourth factor is group decision making. If an individual cannot be persuaded to change his attitude independently because he is attached to a larger social body, we must try to change the entire group. This is the basic idea behind group decision making. It is one of the human relations techniques used in many supervisory and executive development programs.[33]

Kurt Lewin's studies during World War II on changing the food habits of housewives gave impetus to the group decision-making technique.[34] The objective of the program was to increase the use of beef hearts, sweetbread, and kidneys—"intestinal" foods toward which most housewives had a rather deep-seated aversion. Two kinds of groups ranging in size from thirteen to seventeen members were compared for results. The lecture-type groups were told of the nutritional value of the meats, their economy and relationship to the war effort, and recipes that might be used to prepare delicious dishes. The group-decision-type of groups were given the same message but in discussion format. Furthermore, they were asked by a show of hands who was willing to try one of the meats within the next week. A subsequent follow-up showed that only 3 percent of the women in the lecture group served one of the meats never served before, whereas 32 percent of the women in the group-discussion groups did.[35]

In his discussion of the factors that led to the superiority of the group-discussion technique, Lewin highlighted the higher degree of involvement, the psychological impact of making a decision, and approaching the housewife not as a quasi-private, psychologically isolated person but a member of a group—even though the housewives never saw each other again. No wonder a certain mystique developed around the group-discussion technique.

There are many variations, of course, in the extent to which such participation in group decision making is authentic and when it is merely contrived. When it is authentic, members get an opportunity to influence the group's decision, and in this sense it is a reflection of a democratic process. On the other hand, when the decision has been predetermined by the communicator or moderator, participation is mere manipulation. This does not mean that the manipulative approach may not be effective in the short run, but it is likely that a sustained campaign or relationship requires an authentic approach.

Other group processes can also be applied. In addition to the group-decision method, there are various forms of multiple role-playing.[36] These are ways of putting individuals in interaction with other members of the group and they are capable of producing attitude changes on both the individual and group levels. Encouraging or forcing a person to make a public commitment regarding his opinion on an issue is another popular technique. This exposes an individual to group sanctions and moves an opinion which may have remained private into the public domain. The use of campaign buttons is a popular example. The raising of hands at a meeting showing how people stand on issues is another example. These techniques not only invoke group sanctions, they also force the individual to complete his thinking and arrive at a decision.

10

the personality design

The designs of influencing attitudes and behavior considered so far have been enlarging on the personality factors that might effect results. The cognitive design considered a person's intelligence level; the motivational design considered his needs and desires; and the social design considered the rewards obtained from social conformity. The final method—the personality design—seeks to provide the most comprehensive treatment of a member of the audience as a total person.

The extension of influence processes into the realm of the psychology of personality is not surprising. One reason is that communicators, particularly public relations men, have been reaching into difficult problem areas. When attempts are made to produce significant changes in people's social prejudices and political stereotypes, for example, an extraordinarily high degree of psychological resistance is encountered. Such resistances are usually more deeply rooted in people's personalities than the motives and social forces discussed so far. The second reason for the increased importance of the personality design is that opinions and attitudes are in the last analysis an integral part of personality.

EXPRESSIVE AND DEFENSIVE FUNCTIONS OF ATTITUDES

Attitudes were earlier described as an intervening variable between stimulus and response. They represented a convenient concept that stood for the person or receiver in the process of communication. Attitudes were the wiring inside the "black box" and as such explained the relationship between a person and his environment.

This approach is in accord with the viewpoint of M. B. Smith, J. S. Bruner, and R. W. White in *Opinions and Personality*. The authors state that at the most general level: "One's opinions or attitudes serve as mediators betwen the inner demands of the person and the outer environment. . . ." [1] They suggest that if the reasons behind attitudes are understood then these could serve as helpful guides in changing people's attitudes and behavior. This was done in the motivational design where motives were identified as the reasons underlying attitudes. Now, however, we are concerned with a broader approach that relates to a person's identity.

personal identification

The personality design adopts the view of Smith, Bruner, and White that some attitudes express an individual's personal style and identity. They say that social influence must be viewed not as a simple matter of conformity needs or prestige suggestion but "the resultant of a deeply complex process of attempting to find and proclaim one's social identity." Underscoring the notion of a personal signature, the authors continue by saying: "Our opinions are as much a badge of social membership as anything else: a badge worn for informing others who we are and for confirming identity to ourselves." [2]

In this study of the relationship between opinions and personality, the authors selected ten normal men and examined what function was served in each of their lives by holding a particular set of opinions about Russia and Communism. For example, among the processes they considered was "externalization"—the way a person's response to an external event is "colored by unresolved inner conflicts." [3] The approach the authors take reflects the functional theory we briefly introduced in Chapter 5.

Daniel Katz examines four functions performed by attitudes for the individual—the functions of adjustment, ego defense, value expression, and knowledge.[4] Some of these functions are new names for designs that have already been discussed. The adjustment function essentially combines the motivational and social designs, and the knowledge function is similar to the cognitive design. The other two functions—value expression and ego defense—are treated here under the personality design.

As described by Katz, the value expression function for a person gives "positive expression to his central values and to the type of person he conceives himself to be." [5] Some reference was made earlier to marketing techniques that relate a product to a person's self-image. Value-expressive attitudes are also important in connection with voting behavior and ideological campaigns involving a person's beliefs.

The ego defense function of attitudes involves the individual's attempt to protect himself from internal conflict and external dangers. This function centers largely on the reduction of anxiety created either through his own unacceptable impulses or through threatening forces from without.[6] Issues dealing with prejudice, deviant types of personalities, public health measures, and political apathy are often related to the ego defense function.[7]

The functional approach to attitudes, then, provides us with our major orientation to the personality design. We next consider some special topics that have been associated with the study of personality and persuasion.

vulnerability to persuasion

Three topics have been closely associated with the study of personality and persuasion. Their common denominator is that they determine an individual's vulnerability to persuasion. The first examines the Freudian concept of ego defense mechanism; the second reviews variations among people with regard to general persuasibility irrespective of the issue involved; and the third deals with the likely reactions of certain personality types, particularly the authoritarian, to certain issues.[8]

Ego Defense Mechanisms. The Freudians and neo-Freudians have probably authored the most widely accepted explanations underlying the personality model. Basically, the three-level house of Freud is used, with the id in the basement reflecting the blind impersonal instinctual impulses; the ego on the main floor representing the "controlling self which holds back the impulsiveness of the id in the effort to delay gratification until it can be found in socially approved ways," and the superego in the attic, which represents the conscience or the inner control by way of moral scruples.[9]

The function of ego defense is to eliminate any stimuli from conscious awareness which threatens the ego.[10] Some of these stimuli are internal and refer to the impulses that must be controlled. Three mechanisms describe this control process: inhibition, repression, and denial.

The method of inhibition means that a particular motive is accepted but it is put on a waiting list, so to speak, until such time that an overt response can be made in connection with it. The priorities underlying the waiting list may represent a conscious decision to postpone a gratification or may represent a person's scale of values.

A second method of controlling internal stimuli is the method of repression. This is the most basic ego defense because the motive is so well-guarded the person forgets it exists. Although conscious awareness of the motive is lost, the motive itself continues to live and manifest itself in other ways. These other ways include the mechanisms of projection, the attribution of the motives to someone else; reaction formation, giving strong expression to the motive which is opposite to the disapproved one; displacement, in which the existence of any aggression which is consciously unacceptable to a person is rerouted from the real target to a weaker one. These defense mechanisms are often seen as the causes of certain attitudes and behavior. A person who suspects all kinds of evil doings on the part of young people, whom he is apt to call juvenile delinquents, may be reading his own repressed motives into others.

The ego protects itself from threatening external stimuli as well as internal ones. The basic method is one of denial, in which a person will obliterate the perception of fearful aspects of his environment. If the person cannot control the exposure to the stimuli, it is distorted. The person simply doesn't get the message. This was dramatically illustrated in an experiment in which prejudiced persons were involuntarily confronted with anti-prejudice propaganda. Cartoons were used to lampoon a character dubbed Mr. Biggott. As stated by the authors of the study, the intention of the cartoon was roughly this:

> The prejudiced reader would perceive that Mr. Biggott was an absurd character; that it was absurd to have such ideas—that to have such ideas made one as ridiculous as Mr. Biggott. He would, then, as the final stage in this process, presumably reject his own prejudice, in order to avoid identification with Mr. Biggott.[11]

What actually happened was that the prejudiced respondents "went to such lengths to extricate themselves from their identification with Mr. Biggott that in the end they *misunderstood the point of the cartoon*."[12] The mechanisms of this propaganda evasion which are discussed point out the likelihood that in most cases they are unconscious. People are defending the integrity of their self-images without knowing it.

The general persuasibility of people. Much attention has been given in the literature to the question of whether certain personalities are more susceptible to propaganda than others "irrespective of what he knows about the communicator or what it is that the communicator is advocating."[13]

It may be argued with Daniel Katz that there is little practical value in this consideration.[14] This may be true of mass media audiences, but in interpersonal communication situations that deal with specific groups or individuals, "the predispositional factor of a person's general susceptibility to many different types of persuasion and social influence" may be relevant.[15]

Who are the people who can be persuaded most easily? Irving Janis in a summary chapter on "Personality as a Factor in Susceptibility to Persuasion" offers a three-item answer. The most persuasible men are those who: (1) "respond with rich imagery and strong empathic responses to symbolic representation"; (2) hold themselves in low self-esteem; (3) have an "other-directed orientation." [16] Having rich fantasy responses enables a person to imagine the benefits that would accrue from the communicator's premises. Being other-directed means that a person's value stresses "group conformity and adaptation to the social environment." [17] Holding oneself in low esteem appears to increase one's dependence upon approval from others, and this approval can be obtained by agreeing with others. Some of the typical indicators of low esteem are listed by Janis as follows: "feelings of shyness, lack of self-confidence in ability to deal with everyday social situations, high concern about the possibility of being rejected by one's friends, uneasiness at social gatherings, passive compliance to authority, excessive timidity in asserting personal wishes, periodic feelings of sadness, discouragement, and hopelessness." [18] In short, we may agree with Cohen that a person with low self-esteem does not place a high value upon himself.[19]

Who are the people unlikely to respond to persuasion? These are people, according to Janis, who display either of two characteristics: (1) "overt hostility toward people they encounter in their daily lives," or (2) social withdrawal tendencies. The first kind of person may have paranoid tendencies that encourage antisocial behavior, and he may have a need to be aggressive and to demonstrate his power over others. The second kind of person, according to Janis, shows schizoid or narcissistic tendencies as characterized by such indicators as: "aloofness, weak and unreliable emotional attachments to love objects, marked preference for seclusive activities, and few affiliations with formal or informal groups within the community." [20] To oversimplify, such people can be seen as being more concerned with warding off people than in dealing with issues; as being emotionally unable to react to other people; and, in some cases, of being less capable of responding to external symbols. In short, these people's energies are mostly inward directed so that little energy is left to respond to the social environment.

In the above answers, Janis speaks only of men because the results for women have not been as clear as for men. More research is necessary, but until then, Janis concludes that "all available evidence supports the popular belief that in impersonal matters [social, political, and intellectual issues] girls are more persuasible than boys." [21] The explanation typically offered is that women are more yielding, perhaps as a result of cultural training in conformity. It is also likely that the greater influenceability of females may be due to their more effective message reception rather than to their greater yielding, for there is evidence that females are in general more verbal, more likely to attend to and comprehend the spoken and written word.[22] The latter finding is sure to be applauded by the Women's Liberation movement.

The authoritarian personality. Psychologists have given much attention to a combination of traits—a syndrome—associated with the authoritarian personality. This syndrome is characterized by nine variables listed below:

1. *Conventionalism.* Rigid adherence to conventional, middle-class values.

2. *Authoritarian submission.* Submissive, uncritical attitude toward idealized moral authorities of the ingroup.

3. *Authoritarian aggression.* Tendency to be on the outlook for, and to condem, reject, and punish people who violate conventional values.

4. *Anti-intraception.* Opposition to the subjective, the imaginative, the tenderminded.

5. *Superstition and stereotype.* The belief in mystical determinants of the individual's fate; the disposition to think in rigid categories.

6. *Power and "toughness."* Preoccupation with the dominance–submission, strong–weak, leader–follower dimension; identification with power figures; overemphasis upon the conventionalized attributes of the ego; exaggerated assertion of strength and toughness.

7. *Destructiveness and cynicism.* Generalized hostility, vilification of the human.

8. *Projectivity.* The disposition to believe that wild and dangerous things go on in the world; the projection outwards of unconscious emotional impulses.

9. *Sex.* Exaggerated concern with sexual "goings-on."[23]

The authoritarian is often seen as someone who is rigid in his perceptions, absolutistic in his values, and compulsive in his behavior. He is contrasted with the "democratic" personality who is problem-centered and flexible in his approach to answers.[24] From this description of the authoritarian personality it is easy to see the application to problems of attitude change. Janis suggests that consideration of the authoritarian personality is particularly significant when dealing with certain issues: "so-called immoral behavior of people in foreign countries, or in other outgroups," and deviation from "conventional moral standards."[25]

Experiments by Walter Weiss and Bernard Fine have illustrated some of these applications. In one experiment they identified students who had authoritarian tendencies and discovered that this group responded more to aggressive, punitive appeals to get tough toward juvenile delinquents than did students without the aggressive needs associated with the authoritarian personality.[26] In another experiment a similar reaction was obtained by inducing an aggressive mood. This was done by severely criticizing students in one group for writing supposedly poor papers.[27]

A closely related personality syndrome is dogmatism. As studied by Rokeach in *The Open and Closed Mind,* the dogmatic or closed-minded person exhibits these characteristics: he tends to "compartmentalize" the various kinds of beliefs he holds; his mood of pessimism pervades his views about the future of the world; like the authoritarian, he is inclined to believe in the absolute correctness of various authorities and to reject the ideas of individuals who do not agree with them; and in general, he is inclined to take a very narrow view of the problems of the world.[28]

In dealing with the dogmatic personality, the persuasive communicator must stress the authorities who support a particular position and in whom the dogmatic person places trust rather than in the merits of a position. Since the dogmatic person "judges things on the basis of who is supporting the idea," a message relying solely on rational arguments is likely to be rejected.[29] Messages that relate to changes in the social order are particularly vulnerable to this personality characteristic of dogmatism.

CHANGING EGO-INVOLVED ATTITUDES

When an attitude relates to an individual's self-identification and is important to him we call it ego-involved. In the following applications of the personality design we have illustrations that refer to value-expressive and ego-defensive aspects of personality.

marketing, politics, and prejudice

The value-expressive aspect of the personality design has many important applications in the field of marketing. The studies of motives as related to the motivation research design often include the discovery of self-images that can conveniently be connected with certain products.[30] The sophisticated young man and woman who are listeners to good music on expensive "hi-fi" sets and who must, of course, sit on a rug and be dressed in suitable leisure clothes is but one example of such model images. These models for consumer behavior are similar in function to the identification figures used in education.

As mentioned earlier, much of modern political behavior by voters involves personality variables. Daniel Katz, particularly, supports this view when he states: "Perhaps the bulk of voting behavior, however, is the elicitation of value expressive attitudes. Voting is the symbolic expression of being a Republican or a Democrat." [31] For public relations purposes this idea might be applied to many ideological campaigns and pressure group activities of business, labor, and other institutions. A content analysis of the speeches made by leaders of these organizations would reveal a high frequency of statements supporting a particular creed and advocating a certain ideal way of life.[32]

Applications of the ego-defense aspect of the personality design have become particularly numerous in recent years. The classical application in Nazi Germany, involving the problem of prejudice (and related ones of minority groups, and anti-Semitism), was largely an expression of repressed motives through such mechanisms as projection and scapegoating. Similarly, the well-documented studies of lynching mobs in the South reveal economic frustrations and concern over status.[33]

Another problem closely related to prejudice concerns attitudes toward deviant types of personalities. Some examples are the treatment of juvenile delinquents, or, as during the McCarthy era, the treatment of so-called eggheads.

public health and safety

Some areas of application of ego-defense have concerned such issues as the use of seat belts in cars, the link between cigarette smoking and cancer, the contamination of cranberries with weed killers, the building of fallout shelters, and the highly controversial issue of fluoridated water. What these five issues have in common is that they concern public health and safety and have certain political overtones.

The question of whether or not to install seat belts (originally called safety belts!) involves ego-defense, because the driver and the occupants of a car do not like to admit the possibility of an auto accident. For this reason all kinds of rationalizations are used as reasons for not installing them. People claim that seat belts are dangerous, that they are a nuisance to install, that they are expensive, that they are uncomfortable, and that they will get awfully dirty after a while. Some people even bring in the value-expressive element by suggesting that they lose a degree of independence of movement. One girl of dating age who was interviewed even suggested a moral angle to this loss of freedom.

The issue of the possible link between cigarette smoking and cancer probably involves the ego-defenses of the largest number of people. Many smokers like to deceive themselves into thinking that the use of a filter cigarette will reduce the danger. People who have made no change in their smoking habits give such varied explanations as these: they just do not believe the findings; they consider statistical proof, which has long been accepted for vaccines, as unscientific when applied to smoking and cancer; they smoke for pleasure and the findings are not convincing enough to make them give up smoking. Finally, there are some fatalistic people who say that if you are going to get cancer you would get it anyway and that one's own actions wouldn't make much difference.

The case of the contaminated cranberries similarly involved ego-defense. Because of the cancer scare that was connected with it, the sale of cranberries dropped sharply after Arthur S. Flemming, Secretary of Health, Education and Welfare, issued a warning against tainted berries. Unfortunately for the cranberry growers, most people did not associate as much pleasure with eating cranberries as they did with smoking cigarettes. It is somewhat humorous to note, however, that many politicians who were giving Thanksgiving Day speeches were caught in the dilemma of recognizing people's ego-defenses and upholding patriotic values associated with eating cranberries. This is a rather interesting example of the occasional conflict between the value-expressive function and the ego-defense function of attitudes associated with the personality model.

The issuance by the Office of Civil Defense of the Department of Defense of the "Fallout Protection" booklet in December 1961, involved the highly political issue of "what to know and do about nuclear attack." The booklet dealt with survival topics: the possibility and danger of war, the holocaust that a nuclear attack would bring, the chance—not the certainty—of survival. The objective of the booklet was to tell people what they, as individuals and members of a community, could do to prepare for a possible nuclear attack. To achieve this objective, the writers had to maintain a delicate balance in the amount of anxiety to create. It had to be high enough to produce action but not so high as to produce defensive behavior, that is, of causing people to run away from the subject. A rational tone was maintained throughout, but the appeals used included some value-expressive themes: the duty to care for one's family and the patriotic duty to survive. A combination of approaches—the informational, social, and the personality—were employed.

The fluoridation issue might to some people be a simple question of whether fluorides in water do or do not reduce tooth decay and whether there are any undesirable side effects. If this were the case, a simple booklet such as the American Dental Association's "Fluoridation Facts— Answer to Criticisms" would suffice. But the issue was not so confined by many people. These people talked about moral values and democratic values. They felt that no one should have the right "to fool around with God's water" or to deprive the individual of freedom to get "uncontaminated water." The value-expressive function therefore became relevant and the personality design was drawn into the campaign.

These five examples of public health and safety issues underscore

Irving Janis' conclusion that there is a "need for systematic investigation of the apparently 'common sense' rules of thumb that so often enter into the calculations of public health experts and government officials who attempt to modify the public's belief and attitudes on matters related to the threat of illness, disaster, war, or other recurrent sources of danger." [34] The personality design is bound to receive more attention in the future.

APPEALING TO THE EGO

The most important lesson of the personality model is that the chain of communication between a communicator and his audience may be broken through the operation of ego-defenses. Since, as was pointed out, this is likely to happen when the stimuli from the outside are of a threatening nature, care must be taken not to scare people off. The use of fear appeals had been given particular attention in this regard.[35]

fear appeals

It is generally recommended that a mild or minimum, rather than moderate or strong appeal be used. As applied to a high school film on dental care, for example, a simple drawing showing cavities would be preferable to a photograph of badly decayed teeth. A strong fear appeal would create hostility toward the communicator or lead to all kinds of rationalizations for not following recommended dental care. But although the dangers in the use of stronger fear appeals must be recognized, there are times when a strong fear appeal is more effective than a weak one. Studies involving the use of auto seat belts or discouraging smoking show that great opinion change occurs with the higher fear appeal.[36] The rule that seems to operate is that if an audience seems unconcerned about a danger then a stronger "anxiety-producing" stimulus is needed to get through to them than if they are already worried about an issue.

Regardless of the strength of fear appeal used, it is important that it be followed by appropriate reassurances. The fallout shelter booklet serves as a useful illustration. The booklet might have contained a strong emotional appeal in the form of an actual photograph of the effects of the atomic explosion over Hiroshima. This approach was avoided, however, in favor of a minimum fear appeal. A convenient example of a five-megaton weapon was used even though the Soviets had exploded a fifty-megaton bomb. Furthermore, the booklet was written in a factual manner that had the effect of keeping emotional reactions to a minimum.

Another example of the prudent application of the fear appeal technique is the poster in Great Britain linking smoking with cancer. The poster contains only the two symbols, a lighted cigarette and the word "cancer." Because the message is mild, it will scare fewer people away and may influence the smoking behavior of some people.

timing

A second technique involves the question of timing. For some it is advisable to begin by making a person aware of his ego-defense attitudes.[37] They can sometimes be brought to the surface by waiting for frustrating situations to develop or by deliberately producing them.

These activated attitudes can then serve two purposes. One purpose is to direct the emotional drive behind these aroused attitudes toward the objectives desired by a propagandist. The classical example is mob behavior brought about by an agitator. Left-wing, revolutionary parties have also used this technique in winning political campaigns or in overthrowing governments. In the past, the organizing campaigns of labor were marked by such emotional drive.

A second purpose of activated ego-defense attitudes is to help individuals or groups to become aware of their feelings and thereby to develop the kind of self-insight that may herald a change. This is one of the advantages of the role-playing technique used in human relations training programs for supervisors.[38]

appealing to ego ideals

A third facilitating technique concerns the choice of appeals. With regard to the value-expressive function of attitudes, the aim is to find a counterpart of the personality in the selected appeals. Certain central values representing a person's self-image or ego ideal might thus become salient and influence a decision. The ego ideal concept is particularly important if the object is to change the existing values of the person. If a person becames dissatisfied with his self-concept or with the associated values, then he may do something about them.[39]

The matching of appeals with personalities was evident in the illustration of the authoritarian personality. The use of aggressive appeals was effective in convincing authoritarians that a tough attitude should be applied to juvenile delinquents. In other situations, such as antiprejudice propaganda, it has been found that the method of authoritarian suggestion was more effective with authoritarians than methods relying on the dissemination of information.[40]

In the personality design we have tried to relate attitudes to a person's conception of himself. Since communicators are not psychiatrists, we cannot adequately understand a person's need for expression and defense.

But the limited aspects of personality we reviewed in this chapter should help us in two ways: to reinforce our awareness of the limits of persuasion, and to indicate that with ego-involved attitudes—some of which are also deeply held—we must consider the functions that attitudes perform for the individual.

THREE

man's intake
and
storage
of
information

11

man's perceptual system

Man can be viewed as a cybernetics mechanism, one whose actions are governed by the information that reaches the guidance center of his brain. This information is almost always a combination of current and stored information. Current information allows man to adjust to his immediate environment. Were this the only information that guided him he would have absolutely no autonomy and simply drift with his environment. Stored information—memory—serves to evaluate current information and to steer man in accordance with his goals and values. But were man entirely guided by the past he would be like a mere projectile with no opportunity to change his destiny. Both information intakes and storage are required by man to function as a self-steering, cybernetics mechanism.

The persuasive communicator hopes that the information he prepares and transmits will shape the behavior of his audience. To have this power, the information transmitted must reach the senses of the receiver and be stored for future use. In this chapter we shall examine the intake of information, a process psychologists call perception. The next chapter shall examine the storage of information.

THE CLASSICAL PROCESS OF PERCEPTION

Perception is the "process of becoming aware of objects, qualities, or relations by way of the sense organs." [1] It tells us how a person forms percepts—the things of which he is aware. This connection between the outside and the inside is the most vulnerable and critical link in the chain of communication because it serves as a gate and functions in a "go, no go" manner. No wonder psychologists sometimes speak of perception in terms of "ports of entry." [2]

The process of perception is analogous to crossing an international border. Just as the immigration officials and customs officials determine whether or not persons and commodities are allowed to enter, so do the mechanisms of perception. Two sets of basic questions must be answered: (1) Is everything "out there" allowed to enter? What "entrance requirements" are demanded? (2) What happens to those things that are allowed to enter? What kind of a "naturalization" or "assimilation" process takes place? When communicators speak about barriers of communication, the above sets of questions are certainly included among them.

These questions are so important to communicators that every attempt is made to crash through these perceptual barriers. One is the device of source credibility. It is used to gain automatic admittance, just as a prominent national figure is automatically allowed to cross the border to reenter his own country. A second device is the use of strongly structured and intense stimuli. They would have a way of overpowering the receiver, just as a strong physical force or powerful loudspeaker would overcome or penetrate the sentinels on duty at the border. The third device is subliminal perception, a subject we have not previously discussed and therefore one that requires further explanation.

Subliminal perception is analagous to smuggling operations in the sense that something is brought into a territory without the awareness of customs or other officials. As applied to people's perception it means that something is put over on them without their being conscious of it. This is typically done by using weak stimuli. A well-publicized example, mentioned earlier, was the flashing of "Drink Coca-Cola" on a drive-in movie screen at such short exposures that the audience was not aware of it. During the refreshment break, purchases of this beverage were reported to be higher than would normally have been expected.[3]

encoding and decoding

The communicator tries to prepare and present stimuli that will penetrate the perceptual gateways of his audience. For this reason he needs to understand the set of perceptual variables that intervene between sensory stimulation and awareness.[4] A helpful approach is to add the encoding and decoding processes to the basic communication model as shown below: [5]

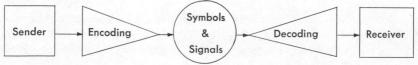

The purpose of communication is to reproduce the same information, idea, attitude, or other meaning in the receiver that is in the mind of the sender. As Schramm simply states, "When we communicate, we are trying to establish a 'commonness' with someone." [6] The sender does this by encoding something in his mind into a message by selecting appropriate and significant symbols. These are usually words but may also consist of other signs which represent something. The symbols of such a message are then, from a technical viewpoint, converted into signals that can be transmitted by means of sound waves, electrical impulses, or any other signal capable of "transporting" a message.

On the receiving end, the process is reversed. The signals are encoded into a message and message into meaning. If this "picture in the head" of the receiver is the same as that in the sender, then communication is perfect.

Because the field of experience of the receiver is never identical to that of the sender, perfection in human communication is seldom if ever achieved with more than simple messages. The connotations of words used, as well as the whole array of associated meanings based on the unique life history of each individual and group, varies from person to person. All that can be hoped for is that the sender will try to understand the background of his audience, to empathize with them, and to relate to these audience characteristics as much as possible.

A further reason why communication is seldom perfect lies in the nature of the symbols and signals needed to form and transmit a message. These constitute the stimuli that are part of the larger environment faced by the receiver. These stimuli excite the human senses and create what the psychologist calls sensations, distinguished from percepts—that of which we are aware. While we take it for granted that discrete sensations, like dots of a magnified newspaper photo, are readily transformed into meaningful patterns, this process involves complicated learning.

Gestalt psychologists particularly have been interested in the nature of sensation. They claim that a person does not consciously compound the sensations or impressions received from the several senses.[7] Instead there is a spontaneous fusing of sensations into symmetrical, connected, completed, and meaningful patterns—even when stimuli such as drawings presented to the observer are incomplete. We see a human face with all of its features even though a feature such as a nostril may be missing. We see correctly spelled words even though a letter or two are missing. Furthermore, we add a chimney to a house and a beard to Karl Marx to satisfy our need to make our mental pictures whole and, therefore, meaningful.

The Gestaltists use this kind of evidence to claim that there is a tendency for individuals to structure their experience. This leads to their belief that the learning process is rooted in the process of perception itself. They place great emphasis on outside factors (the environmental field) that were stressed in the cognitive design.[8]

These details concerning sensations can be overlooked by the average communicator. They may, however, be useful to and worthy of further exploration by the artist, the television producer, and the cinema photographer who increasingly tend to focus upon the raw material of perception. Pointillists like Seurat experimented with a kind of mosaic technique in which uniform patches of color were used to build up pictures. In a similar fashion, Marshall McLuhan points out how the alphabet is a technology that predisposes a child to think and act automatically in certain fragmented ways, and that modern electric technology fosters and encourages unification and involvement.[9] The message that gets through to us is shaped by the nature of the medium used and the kinds of symbols it is capable of transmitting.

external and internal factors in forming percepts

Another way of analyzing the process of perception is to view a percept as the compound of external and internal factors. The perceptual aim of a person is to form reliable mental pictures of the world outside with minimum effort. By constructing "cognitive maps" and other forms of stored experience, he is able to reduce his dependence on immediate external stimuli. He is also able to achieve stability or constancy in what he sees. Minor variations in sensory events or variations in the mood or mental context of a person does not alter the percept that is formed.[10]

To understand this constancy mechanism and the interplay of external and internal factors the "perceptual loaf" diagram below is helpful. It indicates the different proportions of outside and inside factors that constitute any single picture in our minds.

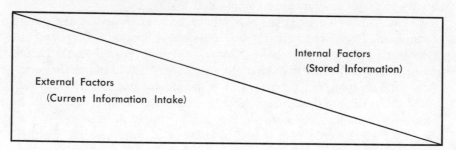

The perceptual slice on the left-hand side represents a percept so heavily based on current information that it lacks an internal frame of reference and excludes meaningful experience. A slice on the far right-hand side, on the other hand, depends so much on the perceiving person that a percept would lack validity and vary greatly from person to person.

The verb "to sense," he says, has a double meaning; to make us feel and to make us perceive.[12] In the first meaning, as channels of sensation, the senses are curious and interesting but they are not instruments of our contact with the world. They are simply passive receptors that respond each to its appropriate form of energy. Gibson advocates the second meaning where the senses are seen as active perceptual organs, better called systems, "that can search out the information in stimulus energy." [13]

In reviewing the various classifications of sense modalities, Gibson concludes that there is today no accepted list. His own preference is for the following list of perceptual systems:[14]

1. The basic orienting system—provides general orientation
2. The auditory system—listening
3. The haptic system—touching
4. The taste-smell system—tasting and smelling
5. The visual system—looking

Most of this book is devoted to a thorough examination of each of these systems from the viewpoint of their capabilities for useful perception and adaptive behavior.

From a communication viewpoint, our interest too is in the senses as receptors of information. We shall, therefore, examine the comparative advantages of the two main perceptual systems, the auditory and the visual, then consider man's limited channel capacity and ways of overcoming some of its limitations.

comparative advantages of the visual and auditory systems

The fact that media men classify media according to whether they are visual, aural, or audiovisual indicates that one problem of media selection concerns the choice of which of man's perceptual systems to reach. For this reason, the communication literature refers to studies which deal with the efficacy of one sense compared to the other, or combined senses over single senses. Joseph T. Klapper and Robert M. W. Travers have summarized many of these studies with the following conclusions: [15]

1. When the objective of the communicator is the retention of information which is "simple and brief," an aural presentation is superior to a visual one. The same is true of meaningful, familiar material. This suggests that for the purpose of getting people to retain simple advertising or public relations slogans, radio is superior to billboards, poster, or leaflets. A combined aural and visual presentation is, however, optional, so television would be superior to radio.

A slice from the middle region enriches the raw stmulus presented to our senses with a context provided by our stored experience and thus enables us to represent the external world accurately and faithfully, or to duplicate the message intended by a sender. In a sense, all perception is enriched.[11] This enrichment is the basis of stereotyping—drawing final impressions on the basis of limited information.

This view of perception as slices of external and internal factors is useful to both information gatherers and information disseminators, and helps to make them more sensitive to the part played by perception in the acceptance or rejection of their messages. For example, a much-used in-terview technique based on the Rorschach or inkblot test and to a slightly lesser extent the Thematic Apperception Test is to present a person with ambiguous stimuli and ask him to describe what is there. The description will be a projection of his personal attitudes and motives. This is the way he sees and interprets it. His percept is not stimulated by any structure, since there is none to speak of. Unfortunately, information disseminators sometimes unwittingly use the same technique. By providing too little information, they prepare the stage for misinformation and rumor-spreading. The antidote, of course, is more and clearer information.

The second technique suggested by the slices of internal and external factors approach is that a communicator must always provide a comprehensible context or frame of reference for any specific message he wishe to get across. If he can assume that relevant experience is already stored the past experience of the person, he must include cues in his messaᵍ that will activate and apply this stored experience to the present messaᵍ If, on the other hand, the communicator cannot make this assumptic his specific message must be preceded by suitable background mater The various background briefings given to newspaper reporters by gove ment officials is an application of this technique. News articles themsel reflect on an increased tendency to provide the reader with a context will make a particular news event meaningful. The difference betw providing a context and not providing it is, perhaps, the basis of a dis tion that some newspapermen like to draw between what is mere and what is the truth.

The classical approach to perception has been examined briefly will now examine another approach to the subject and consider specific features of man's perceptual system.

THE SENSES AS PERCEPTUAL SYS

The view that sensations are the basis of perception and th senses serve as channels of sensations is not accepted by all psycho James J. Gibson feels that sensations are mere byproducts of perc

2. When the objective is the retention of "lengthy" or "complex" material, visual presentation has a number of advantages. One is *referability,* which Travers defines as "the extent to which a display of information presents data for a relatively long duration so that the receiver can refer to it repeatedly to guide his external or internal behavior." [16] The visual system is also superior when the message is long, when it involves spatial orientation, or when the environment is noisy and an auditory message may be lost. The capacity of the eye to make spatial discriminations means that graphs, pictures, and other displays can be devised to code information. Storage of information is also easier because basically only paper and ink is required as against the complicated mechanical and electrical equipment needed to store auditory materials. Other generalizations are based on the ability of the receiver. When the reading skill of the audience is high—with educational level used as the main criterion—the visual, printed media are more effective; when reading skill is low, oral presentation is more effective. The cultural preferences of a particular group or society must also be considered. These preferences are usually established through the educational system, and in the United States definite preference is given to the visual mode. In societies where educational facilities are lacking and illiteracy exists, communications must, of course, rely more heavily on aural means.

3. When the immediate attention of the receiver must be obtained, the auditory system is superior. In the case of vision, the receiver's gaze may simply be oriented in the wrong direction. Such inattention is not likely with an auditory signal. Furthermore certain auditory signals, such as high-pitched sounds used in air raid signals, have the capacity of forcing themselves on the perceptual system so that they cannot be ignored.

4. When speed of transmission is important, vision has an edge over hearing. A reading speed of 300 words per minute is common but speakers rarely exceed 200 words per minute. Methods of speech compression can, however, be used by discarding very small segments of speech but without leaving any gaps in the sound. When this is done as much information can be communicated through the ear as through the eye in any given interval of time. The bottleneck in information processing occurs "upstairs" in the brain.

5. It is generally agreed that when the objective is persuasion, face-to-face contact (that is, the use of combined senses) is the most effective approach. Television would come closest to this preference model. Where single senses are used, the aural media are said to be superior to the visual media.

An important aspect of perceptual systems is the availability of some technical aids to perception. One of the communicator's major problems has been to make the invisible become visible to his audience. Advertising men have long done this through highly creative but sometimes doubtful procedures. Pharmaceutical companies, for example, provide visual interpretations of chemical reactions in the body—complete with flashing lightning, crashing hammers, and anything else that seems to get the point across. Similarly, some manufacturers of cleaning fluids and cleaning powders provide microscopic portrayals of what is happening on dirty walls, sinks, and floors.

Two principles are reflected in these illustrations. One is that the communicator must become increasingly aware of technical aids that expand the human senses. A microscope enlarges what the eye cannot ordinarily see; an infra-red camera sees in the dark; and a Geiger counter measures radiation that is otherwise imperceptible. To the extent that the images and readings of these devices can be visually presented and communicated to the audience, the process of perception is greatly aided.

A second principle implied in the above examples is that relatively unused senses may sometimes be more effective than the senses habitually employed. A convenient example can be found in the highly antiseptic cellophane world of the supermarket. Except for the background music intended to romance people into buying, the stimuli facing the customer are almost entirely of a visual character. The sense of smell has just about been eliminated. How many more hot rolls or cheese would be sold if people could smell them is a question that the marketing experts are just beginning to reexamine. By allowing the olfactory sense to reinforce the visual stimulation, communication and persuasion might be improved. Perhaps communicators must learn what restaurateurs have long known.

channel capacity

Everybody who travels knows that each port of entry can handle only a limited number of passengers or cargo at any given time. Communication engineers use this notion of port capacity in their technical consideration of the "channel of capacity" of the instruments for the transmission of messages. Psychologists also use this concept to describe the amount of information that the human being can process as determined by the physiological and psychological limits inherent in him or the situation.[17] This is largely the subject matter of information theory.

The mathematicians and engineers who deal in information theory are primarily concerned with the physical transmission of signals and their measurement in terms of the amount of information they contain.[18] Questions dealing with the truth, meaning, and usefulness of these signals are ignored; or, to put it another way, the emphasis on the technical aspect of communication is so dominant that the other two aspects—the semantic and the pragmatic—are virtually disregarded.

The communicator must, however, deal in all three aspects of communication. His emphasis is perhaps reversed, for the pragmatic or persuasive aspect takes precedence. But to do this, semantic success must have been achieved, and for this to happen, the message must be received by the audience. The technical aspect is, therefore, one of the necessary links in the chain of communication.

The communicator must also be concerned with the limited channel capacity of the perceptual system. A distinction between "sense intake" and "perceptual intake" is relevant because the capacity of the physical sense organs is thousands of times greater than the capacity of a person to perform discriminatory action. George Miller, in a classic paper entitled "The Magical Number 7, Plus or Minus Two: Some Limits on Our Capacity for Processing Information," argued that when a person has to make some absolute judgment about a stimulus, he is able to judge it in terms of a scale involving about seven categories.[19] He raises the intriguing question: "What about the seven wonders of the world, the seven seas, the seven deadly sins, the seven daughters of Atlas in the Pleiades, the seven ages of man, the seven levels of hell, the seven primary colors, the seven notes of the musical scale, and the seven days of the week?"[20] The suggestion, unproven, is that the number seven appears to have limited man's thinking.

There are three formidable obstacles that delimit the channel capacity of human beings. The first is man's limited span of attention—an individual can attend accurately to only a small number of items out of a larger number.[21] In reading a book, for example, only several words can be taken in at a quick glance. Similarly, a driver on a superhighway cannot be expected to read line after line of billboard copy. Although speed reading courses can help to increase a person's span of comprehension, limits are always present which the communicator must consider.

A second, although closely related limit to human perceptual capacity, is the principle of unity of attention.[22] In general, a person can pay attention to only one difficult task at a time. The popular way of saying this is that you can't do two things at once. Television can't be watched while you're reading a book.

The principle of unity of attention must not, however, be taken too rigidly. When one task is highly automatic and requires little or no conscious control, it is possible to engage in another activity. Everyone knows that listening to the radio while driving a car is possible. Moreover, if a person wants to pay attention to two conversations at once, he can rapidly shift his attention from one to the other. This shifting of attention is sometimes facetiously known as the cocktail-party technique. Another exception to the principle of unity of attention is that several activities may be so well integrated that they are really one. This is illustrated by the student who can listen to a lecture and take notes at the same time.

A third limitation to perceptual capacity is the need for man to avoid cognitive strain.[23] By operating at much lower than top capacity, he has reserve capacity to deal with emergencies. This notion is conveyed in a Cadillac ad which tries to convince the buyer of the need for additional cylinders to avoid falling rocks or to have that extra surge of power to pass someone in an emergency.

Perhaps it is true that one characteristic feature of leisure time is that people want to avoid strain. If so, the load a person carries during leisure hours must be lower than normal. Justification may, therefore, be found for the application of various readability formulas which keep words and sentences short, and ideas suitably spaced.

increasing channel capacity

What steps can the communicator take to overcome these limitations to channel capacity? Some hints may be obtained from information theory. The first suggestion is that attention be given to the efficient packaging of messages. Communicators must get at the essence of what they are trying to say and eliminate the nonessentials. The following illustration from a transportation problem may be helpful in understanding this concept.

People in New England who wanted orange juice used to import whole oranges from the South. After squeezing the juice from these oranges, New Englanders threw the rind and pulp away. Soon cost-minded distributors and customers raised the question of why it was necessary to transport all these parts that were headed straight for the garbage pail. The next step was to squeeze the juice in the South, can or bottle it, and ship the essential contents to New England. The transportation cost was reduced and the garbage disposal problem was alleviated. The illustration does not end here, however, for as we all know, technology provided a third step. Orange juice consists largely of water, an element New England has in great abundance. Why, then, ship water from the South to the North? So dehydration entered the picture. Concentrated orange juice is the result. The New England housewife now adds three parts of her own tap water to one part of southern orange and produces a quart of "Farm Fresh Juice" in about one minute.

Communication engineers are constantly working on the problem of eliminating all signals that are not essential in the transmission of information. The telephone industry decided, for example, to limit voice sound frequencies from five-hundred to five-thousand cycles per second instead of the fifty- to eighteen-thousand cycles per second that are perceptible by the human ear. It must be remembered, however, that although the essential part of a message is transmitted, something is sacrificed. This something, which is voice quality in the telephone example, may be an aesthetic experience in other illustrations. The question is whether such artistic elements are relevant to the objectives of the communicator. Information theorists say they are not.

A second suggestion derived from communication theory concerns the concept of redundancy, a measure of certainty or predictability. There are many forms of redundancy. The simplest one is the repetition of a signal. Other forms are built into our language through letters, words, and grammatical rules. Everybody knows, for example, that a *U* always follows a *Q*. Similarly, probabilities can be established for the letters which will follow the *U*. One of the purposes of information theory is to learn more about the statistical composition of language.

We know that the English language is about 50 percent redundant (or, expressed another way, its relative entropy is about 50 percent).[24] This feature enables us accurately to receive messages even under some conditions of noise, that is, under varying competing stimuli and forms of distraction. Following the same idea, if printed words are missing or blurred we can still make out the meaning. The Wilson Taylor "Cloze" procedure of testing the readability of messages is also based on the redundancy feature of language. Taylor deletes every *n*th word in a passage, and asks readers to supply the missing words.[25] The higher the ability to predict the word the higher is the readability.

Schramm says that one of the great strategy questions confronting mass communication is the amount of redundancy to employ.[26] As the readability formulas show, the most efficient writing is not always the most effective. Various rules of thumb also support a degree of redundancy: that two or more examples or illustrations should be given for each important rule or term in preparing technical training material; and that product names in broadcast commercials should be repeated three times. Thus, Schramm writes, "The art of being an editor or a program manager consists in no small degree of striking the right balance between predictability and uncertainty—right balance being defined as the best combination of satisfied anticipation and surprise." [27]

SELECTIVE PERCEPTION: THE ESTABLISHMENT OF PRIORITIES AND EXCLUSION LISTS

In the previous section, several perceptual obstacles to communications were considered. Emphasis was placed on technical factors, and to a lesser extent, semantic factors in communications. This section deals with factors that bear chiefly upon the persuasive aspect.

Two questions are involved. The first is: How will the attitudes of a person in the audience affect the reception of incoming messages? Because of the human perceptual limitations discussed in the previous section, it is generally necessary for an individual to select and accept only part of the total incoming sensory information. Selective perception is the name given to this process.[28]

It is not just a passive mechanism, however, for a person actively reaches out in order to find things in the environment that are important to him. Therefore, inside or so-called functional factors become the control center for a person's perceptual behavior.

A second question is: What does the person do with the information he receives? His own preferences in the form of needs, values, and linguistic habits will add to, subtract, and modify what is received from the outside.[29] The port of entry analogy again seems to fit. Immigrants who are compatible in terms of similarity or sameness in cultural patterns would more readily be admitted than strangers or anarchists who threaten the status quo. And those people who are admitted go through an "Americanization" program to further assimilate them into the population. The similarity of this process to that of perception is striking.

personal needs and values

What a person selects to see and how he will react to it is determined by three highly interdependent factors: personal needs, personal values and attitudes, and linguistic habits. The first of these factors—motives or needs—has already been discussed under the motivational design model of attitude change. The only point that should be added is that those needs of which a person is most deprived are given a higher place on his priority list. Psychologists refer to this process as lowering the threshold of perception.

The mirage phenomenon is also relevant in connection with personal needs. When the object needed for the satisfaction of a need cannot be found, the deprived individual begins to see things in his environment that aren't really there. The same phenomenon occurs in laboratory experiments. In an experiment by R. Levine, I. Chein, and G. Murphy, a number of subjects were asked to state what came to mind as they looked at a set of food pictures that appeared highly ambiguous because the pictures were glass screen.[30] The experimenters found that up to a point, the number of associations connected with food and eating increased hour after hour, as food deprivation became more severe. This experiment supports the adage that one sees what one needs to see.

Closely associated with needs are personal values. These work either in conjunction with or in opposition to needs. The mechanism is the same when personal values cause objects or information compatible with those values to be recognized and received more readily than stimuli which oppose these values. It is in contra-distinction to the needs mechanism when values cancel out or modify the operation of motives. Hedonism, in other words, is not given full play, but is held in check by the superego. A person may crave an alcoholic beverage prior to lunch, but he doesn't carry out this wish while on the premises of a Methodist institution.

Personal values are most closely related to the personality design to attitude change discussed in the previous chapter. A person must satisfy his needs in such a fashion that his image of himself is not damaged. Furthermore, ego defense is translated into a mechanism known as perceptual defense, and serves to shield a person from unpleasant stimuli.

There may be exceptions to this general rule, as Sherif points out. Sometimes people seem to seek out the things they dislike. Sherif refers to the Allport-Kramer experiments in which people with high prejudice scores judged more faces to be Jewish than did non-prejudiced subjects. Sherif concludes: "Such results are extremely difficult to explain in terms of contrasting mechanisms which defend the person from unpleasant stimuli and sensitize him to pleasant items." [31] Similarly, an article entitled "Do Rosy Headlines Sell Newspapers?" raises the question of whether scary headlines increase newspaper circulation.[32] Circulation figures, unfortunately, neither prove nor disprove this point. A conclusion to draw from these studies is that people don't always run away from stimuli that they find unpleasant. But when in doubt, it is better to go on the assumption that pleasant, ego-rewarding stimuli are preferred.

On a practical level, the factor of personal values is conveniently expressed in a principle of persuasion which Herbert I. Abelson expresses as follows: "A communicator's effectiveness is increased if he expresses some views that are also held by his audience." [33] The point seems to be that the communicator and the receiver are more likely to be joined together in a communication's link when they are "tuned" into each other in terms of values.

linguistic habits

In addition to personal needs and personal values, linguistic habits influence selective perception. It is well to remember the basic communication model at this point: the sender must "encode" his message into whatever conventional language symbols are employed; the receiver must in like form "decode" the symbols into a message that corresponds as closely as possible to the intended one. If, to take an extreme case, the receiver does not speak the same language as the sender, then communication does not take place for a "commonness" between the two is not established.

People's linguistic habits influence their behavior pertaining to selective perception on two levels: the cognitive and the expressive.[34] The cognitive level has received the most attention because it determines whether the communicator's message will be understood—whether the words and other signs used by him are familiar to his audience. Maximum understanding is expected with a close member of a family because a commonness of meaning is obtained over a lifetime of coexistence. Similar understanding is achieved among personal acquaintances and friends. Executives try to reach this level of understanding through orientation and training programs and by developing a breed of "organization men." Lower levels of understanding must be expected with mass audiences that have a variety of subcultural language codes. The use of "readable" English is a means of reaching a level of commonness.

The cognitive level, by itself, has many applications. For example, it permits the identification of persons and things and thereby makes it possible for a person to make discriminatory choices. The Eskimo who uses language that distinguishes three kinds of snow is more likely to see one of the three kinds when he steps out of his igloo than a New Yorker when he steps out of his apartment. And, conversely, a New Yorker can pick out the year, model, and make of a car when it is a block away, while the Eskimo would at best know that it was a vehicle. Such a consideration of people's repertoire of categories of thinking have broad significance. Many public relations efforts can prosper on thought clichés. But whenever a rational approach based on critical thinking is needed or desired, then attention must be given to an audience's familiarity with basic vocabulary on a given subject.

The stimulus-response design discussed earlier is a means of obtaining the necessary association between a name and its referent. Advertisers spend much money and time in getting brand names associated with products. Similar effort must sometimes be spent for public relations campaigns. One requirement of the Space Age is the need to acquaint the public with the new vocabulary of aerospace. The National Aeronautics and Space Administration (NASA) and its contractors have gone to great lengths to educate the public in the new vocabulary. For example, a Honeywell advertisement defined such terms as "launch," "yaw around," "brake," and "spin." The television broadcasts of space flights have been interspersed with technical descriptions of the launching equipment and the terms just mentioned. Without this educational background and learning of a new vocabulary, NASA and other organizations could not achieve their public relations objectives in a manner consistent with democratic values.

The second level of linguistics—the expressive—deals with how language shapes attitudes and feelings. Roger Brown refers to this as the "dispositional theory" of linguistics and says that "the meaning of a linguistic form appears to be the total disposition to make use of and react to the form." [35] Such a disposition, he argues, is essentially an attitude toward the person or thing named. The word "spider" might trigger off a negative attitude of avoidance, while the word "strawberry shortcake" would do the opposite. Such attitudes can be highly individualistic or they can be culturally shared by members of a group or a whole country.

Much progress has been made to explore the expressive level of language. A tool, the semantic differential, has been developed by Charles Osgood and others to measure the connotative aspects of the meaning of words and other symbols.[36] These connotative aspects are strictly psychological ones that reflect basic "emotive reactions." It is assumed that a human being is capable of only a finite number of ways of reacting to words and things. The crux of the semantic differential as a measurement device lies, therefore, in the determination of those finite dimensions of "semantical space" that provide the connotative meaning.

Three major dimensions have been studied: evaluative, potency, and activity. The evaluative factor, which is claimed to account for about half to three-quarters of the semantical space, refers to the attitudinal aspect already discussed; namely, how favorably or unfavorably a person responds to something. The potency factor is concerned with power and the things associated with it—size, weight, toughness, and the like. The activity factor is concerned with quickness, excitement, warmth, agitation, and the like. There are factors beyond these three—tautness, novelty, receptivity, and aggressiveness—but these account for a small proportion of semantical space.

The expressive level of language and the semantic differential have many applications in public relations and communication. Most fundamentally, they concern the attempt to gain favorable attitudes toward a person, product, or institution. The preoccupation with corporate image studies is ample evidence of the concern about engineering a preferred disposition to a corporation and its various manifestations. Other applications have similarly been attempted.[37] One study, for example, in the area of employee communication, sought to determine whether management and employee feelings associated with terms like "profit" were the same.[38]

The linguistic habits of people are an important variable in considering how people decide what to pay attention to in their environment. Combined with people's needs and values, the process of selected perception can be a potent factor in determining the effectiveness of communications. It serves as a screen through which a stimulus must pass. This screen can affect a stimulus in various ways: to filter it, impede or facilitate it, or distort it. The whole subject of perception should be viewed as a way of linking a communicator with his audience technically, semantically, and persuasively.

A person may alter his opinions and attitudes on the basis of current information and other stimuli. But his new tendencies are not always acted on immediately. Storage and transmission to the future are involved. Thus man's memory system is considered in the next chapter.

12 man's memory system

We broadly think of memory as representing what has been extracted and learned from the long, steady stream of incoming information. Experience tells us that only a pitifully small fraction of the total information to which man is exposed is even retained by him. Most of the impressions fade away in seconds. Only a few impressions remain to be coded into memory.

What every communicator wants to know is how his message can be given the preferred treatment of being remembered. For unless parts of it are retained in some form, the message cannot be said to influence behavior. Most persuasive situations in modern society do not call for an immediate reaction to a message as would be the case in a riot or other crowd behavior. The time of exposure to a message and action on it is typically separated by days, weeks, and months. Man's storage of information becomes an important consideration in a communication strategy.

Two aspects of man's memory system are of interest to us. First is knowing how it works so we can improve our chances of entering it and staying there. In this connection some standard knowledge about remembering and forgetting will be reviewed. Second, we want to examine some effects that previously stored information has on new information on the receiving platform of memory; this is called a question of timing. Both these elements are important in understanding the retention of information.

Usually we think about only one kind of memory, the permanent kind, and ignore the fleeting kinds of temporary memory. Yet we know that some information is retained just long enough to use it. D. E. Broadbent gives the example of a person who looks up a telephone number and remembers it just long enough to dial it.[1] If he wanted to remember the number for a few minutes longer he would have to repeat it to himself to keep the memory trace alive. There are certainly enough other illustrations, such as the casual chitchat that takes place over a cup of coffee, to suggest that a temporary memory system does indeed exist. Travers even subdivides this system into the memory trace which holds information only for a few seconds and the short-term system which holds information for perhaps as long as thirty minutes.[2]

Travers states that an effort is required to transfer information to the permanent memory—a process that probably takes a substantial period of time, in the order of twenty minutes.[3] This effort may take the form of placing information in temporary storage many times. This probably happens with the learning of advertisements. Another kind of effort is forthcoming when one knows that he will need certain information at some future time. This is another way of saying that motivation and an "intent to learn" must be present. These processes of storing information reinforce some of the principles discussed in Part II. Appeals that relate to a person's needs must be incorporated in a message and the message should be repeated, preferably in different contexts, a number of times.

Once information is stored in the so-called permanent memory system, how long does it last? The answer is not simple because some psychologists distinguish between failure of the memory system and failure of the retrieval system. We have all had the experience of not being able to recall something that at a later time is remembered. Evidence from cases in hypnosis and brain surgery suggest that what is learned is learned permanently and that any difficulty in recall is the fault of the retrieval system.[4] Most psychologists, however, concur that deterioration of the retention system itself can cause some memory failure. Commonplace tests of what people remember after listening to talk shows this. For example, as mentioned in Chapter 3, Nichols and Stevens report that people tend to forget from one-half to one-third of what they hear within eight hours and about 25 percent after two months.

The rate at which forgetting occurs depends on the nature of the materials used and the circumstances. The classical "forgetting curve" is based on the work of H. Ebbinghaus with nonsense syllables, meaningless words like HEX, GIX, and WUB. The curve, more correctly known as a retention curve, shows the percentage of the material retained after varying periods of time without practice. The curve typically falls rapidly at first and then gradually tapers off.[5]

With more meaningful materials more is learned in the first place and the amount forgotten is smaller. Prose is remembered better than nonsense syllables and poetry is remembered better than prose. Solutions to puzzles such as match tricks are easily remembered after a month when the principles involved are memorized.[6] A communicator should obviously try to make his message as meaningful as possible through a variety of techniques: relate facts and concepts to an audience's previous structure of knowledge and values; use imagery (photographic impressions); develop as many associations for the audience as possible; and use rhythm, as in poetry, to provide a flow and interconnection.

Before considering some of these and other aids to the communicator in greater detail, an important exception to the general pattern of forgetting—the sleeper effect—must be considered. The sleeper effect occurs when communication—for example, belief in the communicator's conclusion—rises for a period of time—three weeks is a typical interval—instead of falling as normally expected.[7] The same phenomenon also takes place in reminiscing: more details are remembered at a later period of time than at an early one.

There are several explanations for the sleeper effect. A major one is that the source of a message may have been questioned and doubted. This low credibility has a depressing effect on results when measured immediately after the communication effort. But over a longer period of time, the doubt over the source is forgotten sooner than the message content itself. Furthermore, the link between the source and the message is forgotten—disassociated—thereby removing the depressive effect on results. If, however, the audience is reminded of the source at this later time of measurement—that is, if the source is reinstated—the depressive effect is again apparent. The total effect then shows the typical pattern of forgetting, that is, the curve showing results drops over time.

A primary factor on which the rate of forgetting depends is the kind of learning material involved. Nonsense materials—words that don't mean anything—are most quickly forgotten. Meaningful materials, especially facts and concepts related to a person's previous structure of knowledge and values, are least forgotten.

What lessons does a communicator derive from these psychological findings? His first reaction may be that he doesn't want to expend money and effort on what will almost immediately be forgotten. This involves two considerations: (1) What is it that the communicator wants remembered? and (2) Can the message be kept short and still achieve its purpose?

deciding how much must be remembered

If a pharmaceutical company wants a customer to buy its sedative, two steps are required: the customer must know that if he can't sleep, a sedative is helpful, and he must remember the name of the brand.

The first step may be unnecessary if people are already aware of the connection between a sedative and sleep. This awareness may be part of the general culture as transmitted from person to person in the home, at school, or at work. If it is not, a public relations effort to include this fact in school health programs might be attempted. Sometimes a competitor's efforts along these lines might be used as a foundation. If, however, nothing has been done, the campaign must include this step.

It might be accomplished by a simple statement, diagram, or picture which associates a sedative with sleep. If the credibility of the communicator or the medium is high, additional information may be unnecessary. High credibility is thereby rewarded, whereas low credibility must be compensated for by further communication efforts.

The second step—remembering the brand—involves at least one complication. Will the customer have to *recall* the brand name or merely *recognize* it? Everybody who has taken examinations knows that a multiple-choice question is easier to answer than a fill-in or an essay question. Recall places a greater burden on a person than recognition. The amount of learning can be lower where recognition is required.

In order to decide which form of remembering is required, reference must be made to the action situation—that is, the place where a purchase takes place. Fortunately for most producers and sellers, modern shopping in supermarkets places a light burden on the customer. He need only recognize his favorite brand. But unfortunately for the pharmaceutical company whose product cannot be placed on counters, the customer must usually recall the name of the product and the brand. He might ask the druggist to show him several brands or list the ones he has in stock. But customers don't usually do this. And besides, the pharmaceutical company knows that every druggest may have his own preferences.

One way to reduce the costs of forgetting, then, is deliberately and precisely to determine what a person needs to remember in order to engage in the desired actions.

Another way to save money and effort in a campaign is to eliminate those parts of a message that are likely to be forgotten almost immediately and express what is said in ways that facilitate remembering. Caution must be exercised in deciding what and how much to eliminate from a message. Although some things may rapidly be forgotten, they may nonetheless make a contribution to the communication process. The audience may have been reminded of former experiences, motives may have been aroused, an argument made more convincing by the richness of data, and in general, a context provided for the core of the communication. Most of the material may not be remembered, but it helped to build up an acceptance of the communicator's message.

Psychology can make a contribution to the communicator by showing how the memory process works. It is similar to that of selective perception, in which stimuli are selected and often distorted in the process. Similarly, the memory assimilates new information on the basis of several principles: what seems compatible with the principal theme of a message, what provides good continuation, what least burdens memory, and what fits into stereotyped expectancy and preexisting clichés.

These principles are derived from an article by Gordon W. Allport and Leo J. Postman called "The Basic Psychology of Rumor." [8] Everybody knows that as a rumor spreads from person to person, the original message is distorted and exaggerated in parts, yet some resemblance of the original remains. This effect is more prominent in laboratory studies than in field studies. In the latter, distortion may be completely eliminated for a variety of reasons: a rumor is usually heard more than once, subjects communicate only on their own initiative, the less reliable rumor transmitters are excluded, and the planted rumors have usually been relatively simple, uncomplicated, and with a minimum of irrelevant detail.[9] Hence the following descriptions of and explanations for the kinds of distortions that occur are drawn from the laboratory studies of Allport and Postman.

One kind of distortion is called *leveling*: "As rumor travels, it tends to grow shorter, more concise, more easily grasped and told." The authors conclude that in terms of the number of details remembered, "social memory accomplishes as much leveling within a few minutes as individual memory accomplishes in weeks of time." [10] This finding suggests that when communication effects are dependent upon the transmission and reinforcement of messages from person to person, the problem of memory is compounded. The authors point out, however, that a short concise statement is likely to be faithfully reproduced, that the possibilities of distortion are reduced as there is less detail to select from, and that rote memory serves to hold simple material in mind.

The mass communicator's tendency to keep messages simple thus receives support. The power of slogans that require no effort to retain is also recognized. In effect, the communicator has done the leveling for the audience. Even when fuller information is provided, the message is reduced to a small package that the audience member can easily carry away.

A second distortion discussed by Allport and Postman is called *sharpening*. This is the reciprocal of leveling: the selective "reporting of a limited number of details from a larger context." [11] Sharpening is determined by several factors. One of these is language. Odd, attention-getting words are remembered and familiar symbols such as church and cross tend to be mentioned readily. Second, time and space references are sharpened in various ways. Time references tend to be changed to the "here and now" because this is of greatest interest to people. Quantities are exaggerated and transposed with prominence in physical space. Movement is stressed and there is a tendency to ascribe movement to stationary objects. Finally, a story or message is sharpened on the basis of the labels used by the communicator to orient the audience. Since these labels tend to be used to introduce what follows, the primary effect—remembering first things best—tends to reinforce the effect of labels.

assisting the memory

A communicator can increase the chances that his message will be remembered if he facilitates the operation of the memory system—if he works along with it rather than against it. By examining some further properties of the memory system, particularly the indexing process, some ways of assisting the memory have been discovered.

As stated earlier, man has only limited capacity to store uncoded incoming information. He is well designed for the purpose of monitoring what is going on in the environment but is poor at retaining much of what he observes. If he looks at a picture or movie he cannot recall all the details in it or the sensations he experienced. He simplifies his task by placing much of the material in the background and concentrating on a portion of it, the "figure." He further simplifies it by taking advantage of his extraordinary capacity to learn and retain verbal information. By internally expressing "in his own words" what he sees, he codes incoming information in a form that he can remember.

Travers speculates that in the case of at least some material, the visual information received is recoded into an auditory form and is retained in this form. The use of some kind of label for a visual display also likely facilitates the retention of nonverbal visual information. For example, a person who visits a cathedral may be helped in retaining information about the structure by saying to himself that the style is "perpendicular Gothic." [12] Travers strongly suspects that the human permanent memory system is mainly a verbal one. Man does have some kind of crude primitive visual memory but it is generally quite imprecise.[13] From these speculations, Travers concludes that any encouragement given to a learner to verbalize and talk about the experience he wishes to remember would facilitate its storage.

Human information storage is not like computer storage. A computer stores information in only one place, while man stores the same information in several parts of the brain; a computer's storage is a *collection* of information, while man's is a "consolidation"; and man uses a kind of organization called "cognitive structure" not found in a computer.[14] Some other recognized structuring of the human memory is that information is catalogued in some temporal sequence and that there is an arrangement of objects in space. The practical value of this knowledge about man's memory system has not been fully explored. Travers does make one recommendation—namely, that "one of the tasks of the efficient teacher is to help the student fit the knowledge he acquires into a number of different cognitive structures, so that the knowledge can be used in a number of different contexts." [15] The same lesson would apply to communicators other than teachers.

Another aspect of the memory system that has received much attention is the role of labeling and indexing. As stated earlier, a retrieval system independent of the memory system may exist. Indexing is central to this retrieval system as well as to the prior intake of information. Man needs some sort of inventory of what is stored in his permanent memory; and some sort of retrieval process must operate that tells him where to look in his files of experience. The problem is similar to that faced by librarians and designers of information retrieval systems. One of their great challenges is to design "descriptor languages" that code everything that is stored.[16]

Karl Deutsch in his book, *The Nerves of Government,* refers to indexing in another sense. He says that every person and organization needs information about his or its "state of consciousness." This is provided by "secondary messages" that deal with the changes in the parts of the system. Consciousness thus consists of the collection of internal feedbacks of these secondary messages. It is on the basis of this consciousness that many decisions are made. If the system overrepresents certain secondary messages or if the secondary messages misrepresent primary ones (incoming information) then the decisions are distorted. The system's scanning of the environment for new information would also be disruptive by this false consciousness.[17]

The obvious way in which this knowledge about the indexing process in man's retrieval system can be of help to the communicator is to remind himself to use the same vocabulary as that of the user, especially in the parts of the message that serve as the index. Percy H. Tannenbaum demonstrates this lesson in his article, "The Indexing Process in Communication." He advises the communicator to include key "message parts" in his message that will serve to attract attention and mobilize preferred reactions. The cue word or phrase in the message should correspond with one of the "index cards" of the receiver so that it connects with the memory system. The result is that the part of the message we call an index will exercise an inordinate effect on the meaning of the message. And we can also conclude that the message stands a better chance of being stored for future use.[18]

SOME QUESTIONS OF TIMING

The practical questions of time are not couched in terms of the psychology of remembering. They are expressed in terms of how many exposures of a message are required in order to have impact, how to relate a communication to other things that are happening at the same time, and how to prepare an audience for something that will or may happen at some future time. Psychologists, however, have also made some contributions to these questions. They can be viewed as ways of combating the forces of forgetting and aiding the forces of remembering.

how many exposures should be planned?

The most obvious way of overcoming the effects of forgetting is to repeat the message as often as necessary until learning takes place. This practice can be even further enhanced when audience participation is feasible. The messages that are repeated should vary from time to time in order to get the maximum value from practice. As pointed out by Edwin R. Guthrie, one of the values of practice is that the same learning takes place in different contexts.

To the extent that the communicator wants the learned behavior to take place in varying contexts, he should include the most likely action situations in his repetition of messages. Advertisers are most adept at this when they show how a beverage, for example, might be served in different ways for different occasions. Hopefully, when these occasions arise, the customer will remember the appropriateness of the beverage.

When a message is repeated often enough so that learning and perhaps overlearning has taken place, the concept of *booster shots* is useful. A booster shot gets to the core of a message—the part or parts that would be sharpened in rumor transmission. Since this is the essence of the message and since the supporting evidence for the conclusion has been given previously, such abbreviated repetition is often adequate.

A final consideration in planning the number of exposures is supplementing the action-provoked message. The supplement is appropriate when, as in political campaigns, the moment of decision and action is concentrated. An extra push may be helpful to translate favorable attitudes into action, to overcome minor resistances, and to introduce additional motives to induce the action. Supplementation also occurs in fundraising when, after the foundation of the campaign has been laid, someone calls on the potential donor.

relating a message to surrounding events

An important, money-saving factor in timing is the attempt to coordinate one's communication efforts with surrounding events. The primary advantage of riding on the coattails of a major event is that a good deal of what would otherwise have to be communicated has already been disseminated and accepted. Second, such events represent "ultimate reality" to people. They may distinguish between what Walter Lippmann calls the pseudo-environment—the words and pictures used by others to describe what is "out there"—and the real environment, in which people feel they are witnesses to events on the part of self-interested parties and the uncontrived or public events.

To take advantage of surrounding events, a communicator must be informed on what is likely to or will take place in the near future. Being an avid reader of the mass media is the usual technique. Each mass communicator, however, has his own schedule of events and his own "pet ways" of keeping informed about happenings in that segment of the environment in which he is interested.

A way to hedge against the future is to prepare for events that are likely to take place. An inoculation is provided against what others may do or a foundation is laid for your own communications. The name given to these efforts is "preparatory communications."

preparatory communications

One theory of forgetting is that memory traces are competitive: one destroys the other. If something is learned and nothing else takes place in a person's life, the thing is remembered. Two groups of cockroaches learn the shortest route through a T-maze to food. One group is then restrained so that no interfering activity can take place. The other group is allowed to go about its normal routine. The findings indicate that the frozen cockroaches forget nothing while the unfrozen ones who had interfering experiences have to do some relearning.[19]

Interference of one learning activity with another is more likely to occur when the similarity of the materials being learned is high. The businessman's analogy would be that one identical or highly similar product is competing with the other—that is, they are substitute products. However, it is also possible that the learning of one thing can be transferred to another. In the businessman's language this happens if the products are complementary—for example, an increase in the sale of bacon may increase the sale of eggs. Fortunately for the communicator, he is readily able to identify which messages interfere with or reinforce his learning.

Interference can work in both directions of time. When prior learning interferes with subsequent learning, it is called *proactive inhibition.* When new learning interferes with prior learning, it is called *retroactive inhibition.*[20] The latter is involved in counter-propaganda efforts; the former is involved in building up resistance to future propaganda.

One of the most illuminating experiments on resistance to future propaganda was conducted by Irving Janis, Arthur Lumsdaine, and Arthur Gladstone in an article called "Effects of Preparatory Communications on Reactions to a Subsequent News Event." In early June of 1949, a group of students was given an "optimistic" radio report on Russian A-bomb developments. The program took the position that Russia would not be able to produce a stockpile of atomic bombs for a long time to come. Follow-up measures from the experimental group and a control group were obtained three months later—a few days after President Truman announced that the Russians had indeed exploded an atomic bomb. The results indicated that those who had previously been exposed to the "optimistic" communication showed resistance to the news. They showed significantly less change in the pessimistic direction than did those who had not previously been exposed to the optimistic report. The pessimistic view was that the Russians would soon be able to produce large numbers of bombs and that the possibility of an outbreak of another world war was more imminent.[21]

This study is, therefore, an example of how a communication on the subject of Russia's ability to produce atomic bombs partially immunized people to future information that was incompatible with what was originally learned. The illustration also has a second feature—what was originally learned served to reward the audience because of its favorable content, whereas subsequent news was pessimistic and unrewarding. This feature loaded the dice in favor of the proactive inhibition concept.

The general principle of inoculating people to help them resist future propaganda has been further studied. McGuire and Papageorgis point out the analogy to the medical situation in which the resistance to disease of a person raised in a germ-free environment is developed by pre-exposing him to a weakened form of virus so as to stimulate his defenses.[22] In a communication situation, resistance to persuasion of a person raised in an "ideologically clean" environment is developed by pre-exposing him to weakened forms of counterarguments or to some other belief-threatening material strong enough to stimulate his defenses against belief, but not so strong as to overcome it. The purpose of some of the experiments along these lines is to discover what kinds of forewarning are most effective in raising resistance to later attacks.

The subject of memory completes our review of the psychological processes important in persuasive communication. The five basic designs of persuasion discussed in Part II were based on the psychology of learning. The two chapters of Part III dealing with man's intake and storage of information showed the link between man and the stimuli persuasive communicators prepare. We now move beyond the focus on the individual and consider the social system in which he functions.

FOUR

designs for
interpersonal
and
mass
communication

13

the sociology
of
communication

Repeated reference has been made to the receiver or audience of communication. It was assumed that this target of the persuasive communicator's efforts could directly be reached without any mediation by the social system in which each target audience is embedded. Furthermore, since our interest in Part II was in psychological designs to influence beliefs, attitudes, and behavior, the references were usually in terms of the individual. Only in the discussion of the social design was explicit reference made to the persons and groups that influence how an individual thinks and acts. We learned from this design that a communicator cannot think of his audience as a collection of isolated individuals.

The sociological perspective of communication is essentially built on the premise that the human relationships and social structures surrounding an individual are not passive but exert an influence, often powerful and dominating, upon him. Recognition of the two-step flow in mass communication acknowledges that personal influence must be considered in predicting and determining the effects of mass communication. Other people not only serve as modifiers of a person's attitudes but as links in a network of communication. They transmit messages originated elsewhere. These are often distorted and editorialized upon; hence the initial sender of a message loses control over its content and impact. He also loses his monopoly position in the persuasive situation because these links in the transmission belt of communication initiate their own messages, which might conflict with those of the sender. These possibilities strongly underscore the need to consider the social matrix that surrounds an audience and through which messages flow.

Another reason to consider a sociological framework is that when the persuasive communicator serves as a change agent for a social action program, the social system becomes his major concern. In these programs, the social system serves in a threefold capacity: as the context or social medium through which an action program is carried out, the target of an action program, and the source of the resources necessary to complete it.[1] Although the mass media are still important channels of communication with members of the community, conversations with key individuals, informal discussions at meetings and conferences, and speeches to important groups are likely to command more attention and time. Interpersonal communication and speech communication therefore become critical. Even with these forms of communication, however, a structure exists and the patterns of a social system are followed.

AN OVERVIEW OF THE SOCIAL SYSTEM

An extension of the social design in Part II to a full consideration of the social system required for a sociological treatment of communication is represented in the figure below.[2]

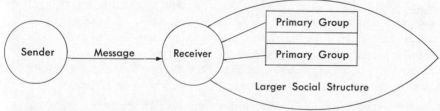

The receiver is seen as influenced by the primary groups to which he belongs and both directly and indirectly by the larger social structure. This larger structure, consisting of social organizations and institutions, serves as the source of the groups' and individual's values and goals. Earlier references made to the Western Electric studies and studies of the American soldier in World War II reflect this orientation of starting with the larger social structure and working back to the individual through his primary group.

Sociologists use many concepts and models to define the larger social structure. The term "social system" is used to describe social organization in dynamic terms. It refers to the interaction of a plurality of individuals in a common situation. A family is a social system, as are morning coffee groups, work groups, a woman's club, the PTA, the school board, the community, city, county, state, and nation. Thus the concept varies in inclusiveness and complexity.

Talcott Parsons provides a more complete definition of a social system: it "consists in a plurality of individual actors interacting with each other in a situation which has at least a physical or environmental aspect, actors who are motivated in terms of a tendency to the 'optimization of gratification' and whose relation to their situations, including each other, is defined and mediated in terms of a system of culturally structured and shared symbols." [3] Two other systems are referred to in this definition. One is the personality system: "the orientation of action of *any one* given actor and its attendant motivational processes. . . ." [4] In retrospect we can say that much of Part II explored this system. The other system is the cultural, which, although reflected in both the personality system and the social system, has an independent existence. It consists of inherited systems of ideas or beliefs, expressive symbols, and value-orientations.[5] People's general views regarding the nature of the universe, the relations of man to the universe, and the relations of man to man are contained in cultural values. Language is also a part of culture and reflects the basic categories into which prior generations have fitted and interpreted and coded their experiences, dreams, and wisdom.

The social system is of particular importance to us because it provides useful categories for the major settings in which communication takes place. It helps us to elaborate upon the simple model presented earlier in this chapter. A setting is not to be confused with the channel or medium of communication; it refers to the characteristics of the social system in which the sender and audience are located. Four such settings are discussed in this and the next two chapters: [6]

1. The social relationship of two persons in social contact, for example, in spontaneous conversations, interviews, and other encounters such as between doctor and patient, husband and wife, parent and child, teacher and pupil, and other dyads.

2. The small social group of three or more people in face-to-face contact, for example, the primary group of the family, an informal clique of workers, a problem-solving group in business, or a therapy group.

3. The social sub-system: organizations and associations, for example, employee communications in a bureaucracy, community council meetings, public speaking situations.

4. The total system: the mass audience and its social groupings, for example, the electorate, the general consuming public and various sub-groupings based on demographic variables, political preferences, ethnic characteristics, and interests in sports, music, and so forth.

This fourfold classification of social system settings relates to the usual division of communications into interpersonal communication and mass communication. Interpersonal communication deals mainly with the social relationship and with small groups, and mass communication with the total system. Falling in between is the social sub-system. The remainder of this chapter deals with the first of these social system settings.

INTERPERSONAL COMMUNICATION
IN A SOCIAL RELATIONSHIP

The prototype of interpersonal communication is that of two persons in face-to-face contact who are reciprocally relating to each other. Each sees the other as a unique personality. Fritz Heider, a pioneer in the field of interpersonal relations, describes it as the "relations between a few, usually between two, people. How one person thinks and feels about another person, how he perceives him and what he does to him, what he expects him to do or think, how he reacts to the actions of the other— these are some of the phenomena that will be treated." [7] While it is possible to draw on such stereotypes as social class, religion, and education to figure out the likely attributes and attitudes of the other person, the social encounter itself allows a great deal of information to be collected about him. The ideal of more fully understanding the "field of experience" of the receiver can better be realized. Even many aspects of the personality design previously discussed can be applied to a social relationship between two people.

Most human communication occurs in conversations which are spontaneous, often unexpected, and rarely planned. These conversations provide inherent satisfaction of personal needs. As indicated in the frontier-breaking book, *Interpersonal Dynamics,* one kind of personal need satisfied by interpersonal relations is simply the purpose of fulfilling itself, such as in friendship or marriage. [8] These are basically emotional transactions between people that exist for no visible instrumental end. But it must not be forgotten that interpersonal feelings are the basic, raw data of all interpersonal relationships. A second kind of personal need that is satisfied is that of confirmation: either to aid in personal development, such as in attaining personal identity, or to help comprehend external reality. For example, a young boy might associate with an older one because he gives him a sense of being grown up. Moreover, as illustrated in the social design, other persons define social reality and, especially in ambiguous situations, even physical reality.

As persuasive communicators we must be aware of the influence that these casual, informal conversations have on the attitudes of people. We are not, however, likely to intervene in these interpersonal encounters. But there are two other functions of an instrumental nature fulfilled by interpersonal relations which are highly relevant to our purposes. One of these is a relationship formed to effect change or influence, as exemplified in such diverse activities as psychotherapy and "brainwashing," seduction and persuasion, indoctrination and socialization. These efforts often involve small groups as well as a relationship between two people. The second instrumental function exists to further a goal or task, as viewed in the reciprocal behavior of doctor and nurse or pilot and copilot. The substance of much verbal communication in formal organizations serves this purpose.

Despite the informality of most interpersonal conversations, a structure can be discerned, for they resemble a minature social system. Moreover, strategies are applied even on this level, not only in the instrumental relationships which are more likely to be somewhat planned, but in the personally satisfying relationships. Finally, interpersonal communications involve not only speech communication but nonverbal, tactile, and visual cues. We shall now discuss each of these three characteristics of interpersonal communications.

structural aspects

Most of us pay attention to only one aspect of communication: content and its information value. But human communication is a multilevel phenomenon and thus involves meta-communication. As suggested by the Greek prefix "meta" which implies "about," communication also "defines both what the message is *about* and how its sender conceives of his *relationship* with the receiver." Although meta-communication has special application to psychiatric situations, it also applies to everyday situations: "Thus, it is not necessary for a sales girl to precede her question 'May I help you?' with the definition of her relationship to the prospective buyer by saying, 'I am a salesgirl and my function here is such and such. . . .' Normally, the buyer can be expected to know this from the situational context. . . ." [9]

Of particular interest from a structural viewpoint is whether a relationship between two people in symmetrical or complementary. In a symmetrical relationship the partners establish and maintain equality. Its positive aspect is that it allows for mutual respect, trust, and spontaneity. In an optimal case, each partner feels free to be himself. In a complementary relationship, such as with a mother and her baby, the partners accept and enjoy differences. Often there are two positions: the primary, superior or "one-up" partner who defines the nature of the relationship and the other secondary, inferior or "one-down" partner who accepts and goes along with this definition.[10]

A stable, healthy relationship must have both patterns and these must interchange both in time and in areas of competence. It is demonstrated "that in a symmetrical relationship a runaway results in an escalating pattern of increasingly frustrating competitiveness, while in a complementary one a runaway leads into growing rigidity and exasperation." [11] Conflicts also arise when one partner defines a relationship as symmetrical and the other as complementary, as happened in an interchange between a mother and her twenty-one-year-old daughter. The mother saw the relationship as a complementary one, with herself in the superior position, while the daughter sought to define the relationship as symmetrical, one between equals.[12] Relationships can get even more complicated when, for example, a wife demands of her passive husband, "I want you to dominate me." This request is a trap, for the message creates the paradox of defining the relationship as symmetrical and complementary at the same time.[13] Further interpretations will have to be left to psychiatrists, for the purpose here is to demonstrate that messages may contain cues about the kind of relationship that exists between two people.[14]

Also using the perspective of meta-communication, Eric Berne in his best-seller *Games People Play,* studies structural aspects of communication by examining each partner's "ego state." He asserts that each person has three ego states: that of parent, child, and adult. In a parent ego state a person responds as his father or mother would or would want him to; in the adult state a person acts autonomously toward an objective appraisal of reality; and in the child state he is fixated on relics from earlier years and acts as if he were carrying a little boy (or girl) around inside of him.[15]

Berne maintains that when we communicate with others we speak from one of these states. Satisfactory relations can continue only as long as the response is complementary. The meaning of complementary differs here from the way it was used earlier. Berne says that a response is complementary when it is "appropriate and expected and follows the natural order of healthy human relationships." [16] That would happen if you speak as an adult and the reply is given as an adult. Communication breaks off, however, when a cross-transaction occurs. For example, suppose a husband's message is adult to adult as in the question "Do you know where my cufflinks are?" The appropriate adult response might be "On the desk." But the response is cross-transactional when it is given as a child: "You're always blaming me, just as my father did," or, "You always blame me for everything." Or it might be as a parent: "Why don't you keep track of your own things? You're not a child any more." [17]

Although these transactions—as Berne calls them—are most dramatic in interpersonal communications, they can also be seen in larger social settings. James Pilditch applies these ideas to the corporation by asking: "How many strikes occur because bosses behave as parents to children when they should be speaking adult to adult?" And in another area he asks: "How much advertising fails because it is wrongly positioned: (parental when it requires an adult response, or adult when it needs a parental response)?" [18] Such structural aspects of communications which are usually hidden in a message must not be overlooked.

strategies and manners

Social interaction is not only structural but is often guided by a deliberate strategy of creating certain impressions in others. This is the thesis of Erving Goffman's insightful book, *The Presentation of Self in Everyday Life*. A person acts as if he were an actor on a stage—when he steps into the "front region" of life from the privacy of his "back region," he must act according to a plan and follow certain rules.

A person's strategy is to guide and control the impressions that others form of him. He does this because he knows he will be treated in accordance with how highly he is regarded. Hence he tries to deceive others into believing he is worth more than is actually warranted or more than people would ordinarily ascribe to him. In a sense he is a counterfeiter. Why does he seek self-enhancement? We can readily understand that certain jobs require an act.[19] A waiter, for example, must make his customer feel relaxed and important; creating the right atmosphere and establishing an air of status are a part of restaurant service. Along similar lines, a person in a professional role may consider impression management as a way to build up his client's confidence in him. But there may be more personal motivations for self-enhancement. Some people have a strong need for self-esteem which requires the receiving of approving responses from others. The possibility also exists that self-enhancement is based more on self-deception than on the deception of others.

The strategy of impression management is executed in a kind of information game that people play with one another. It is assumed that people need information about one another, not only out of curiosity but to determine the proper behavior. A Japanese, for example, is described as needing to know his own relative status in an interaction situation, "since it is in status that one finds the cues for reciprocal behavior." [20] In many social interactions this information is not directly available but must be inferred from gestures and minor cues. Besides "the expression that he gives," Goffman says that a person also has an "expression that he gives off." [21] Most people are not conscious of the latter or have only partial control of it.

As everyone who reads or watches spy thrillers knows, these games are intensified when the stakes are large and the other person is seen as a competitor or enemy. Goffman refers to these enlightened dealings as "strategic interactions": "the calculative, gamelike aspects of mutual dealings."[22] Many examples and techniques from the spy literature are cited; for example, smoking a pipe serves as a screen to conceal or dampen any unintentional reaction of a spy that would give him away.[23]

Besides serving personal motives, impression management is part of a "working consensus" that interactors establish. They agree on certain perceptions of each other and arrive at a common definition of a situation. A typical conversational encounter is thus a little social system in which each person has involvement obligations.[24] Various rules of etiquette must be observed: a person must appear spontaneously involved in the conversation and not allow his attention to be distracted by other thoughts or people; he must not be self-conscious and focus too much attention upon himself; nor must he become "consciously concerned to an improper degree with the way in which the interaction, *qua* interaction, is proceeding"; and finally, he must not be distracted by another participant as an object of attention, for example, by a person who acts with affectation and insincerity.[25]

As stated earlier, nonverbal communication plays a large role in social encounters. We shall now examine some of the major dimensions of this aspect of communication.

nonverbal communication

The usual models of communication such as the Shannon-Weaver model presented in Chapter 2 refer to the sender, message, channel, and receiver. The message element is usually assumed to consist of words. Silences do not figure into the meaning and other nonverbal materials are usually subsumed under "noise"—distortions of the message. While these assumptions may be permissible in mass communication, they are indefensible in interpersonal communication, especially on the social relationship level between two persons. Ray L. Birdwhistell, a major contributor to the field of kinesics—the study of communication through body motion—says that most of the time words express only the smallest part of our social meaning—just 30 to 35 percent of it.[26] He feels that communication must be defined in broader terms than the production of words and their proper usage and must certainly include kinesics.[27]

Body language, the colloquial term for kinesics, deals with a wide variety of signals, messages, and channels: bodily contact, proximity, posture, physical appearance, facial and gestural movements, and direction of gaze.[28] In everyday life we are aware of the preening behavior of the man when he adjusts his tie and smoothes his hair, or of a woman who engages in flirtatious behavior by resting one hand on her hip or leaning forward and talking with great animation. We also recognize cultural differences in such behavior; for example, at the sight of a pretty girl the Italian pulls on one of his ear lobes, an Arab strokes his beard, and the Englishman assumes an overly casual stance and elaborately looks away.[29]

What all these examples show us is that we get an entirely different picture of communication if we make use of the channels of all sensory modalities, not just the auditory one used in speech. For example, we can refer to a kinesthetic-visual channel and an odor-producing olfactory channel.[30] As commented upon by Birdwhistell:

> The student of body motion behavior, as he becomes a more practiced observer, becomes increasingly aware of the apparently endless movement, the shifting, wriggling, squirming, adjusting, and resituating which characterize the living human body in space. If the entire human body becomes the organ for communicative movement as an analog to the vocal apparatus as the organ of speech, how can he hope to deal with the flood of information which he observes? [31]

Fortunately, the literature in this neglected area of communication is growing. A few illustrations and interpretations from it will be helpful in further sensitizing us to the richness of this new language.

Lawrence K. Frank says that "the skin is the outer boundary, the envelope which contains the human organism and provides its earliest and most elemental mode of communication." [32] In a sense, then, bodily contact is the most basic type of social behavior. It symbolizes an increased intensity of involvement with the other person, sometimes of a sexual nature. Or it may indicate hostility, anger, aggression, or coercion. The experience is immediate and transitory, ordinarily limited to two persons, and ends when contact is removed. Frank believes that:

> Without tactile communication, interpersonal relations would be bare and largely meaningless, with a minimum of affective coloring or emotional provocation, since linguistic and much of kinetic communication are signs and symbols which become operative only by evoking some of the responses which were initially stimulated by the tactile stimuli for which these signs and symbols are surrogates.[33]

That part of our language which is expression—deals with feelings—certainly reflects tactile terms. Jessie Bernard cleverly and dramatically uses the terms "stroking" and "striking." [34] Echoing Frank, she says that "as infants need physical caressing or stroking in order to live and grow, even to survive, so also do adults need emotional or psychological stroking or caressing to remain normal." [35] The "stroking" function is performed by positive expressive talk that raises the status of the other, gives him help, and rewards him. Reassuring smiles, silent applause, asking for clarification, an opinion, or for suggestions in conversation represent this kind of stroking behavior. Bernard says that our traditional cultural norms command women to be generous in strokes and sparing in strikes. Expression language becomes "striking" in nature when it reflects disagreement, rejection, antagonism and deflation of the other's status. When one person says "Lovely party" and the other answers "Sure is. It's like the party I once attended at the White House . . .", the first person has been struck while the second one strokes himself. [36]

Proximity is another dimension of body language. The possible range that two people in a social encounter can establish is determined, at the lower limit, by the factor of visibility and audibility. Based on the range, Edward T. Hall suggests a four-point classification of degrees of proximity: intimate, casual-personal, social-consultative, and public. [37] These differ from each other not only in distance but in that different sets of senses predominate. For example, at a casual-personal distance (about five feet) vision and hearing are used, but in the intimate range smell, touch, and even taste play a part. It is also observed that closer degrees of proximity are usually combined with a shift of orientation away from the head-on to the side-by-side.

A person's posture reflects his attitude, status, and emotional state. An akimbo position toward someone indicates dislike; an open-arms posture by a female shows a liking toward the other person. With regard to status, Goffman observed that at staff meetings of a psychiatric hospital, the high-status people, such as psychiatrists, sit in a relaxed posture— lying slumped in their seats with feet on the table—while the junior people would sit more formally and further back. [38] A look at sculpture reflects the many ways in which emotions are depicted by posture; for example, a bowed head shows sorrow, dejection, or reverence.

The expression of emotion is amplified in facial and gestural movements. It is mainly the face that reflects the main emotions of happiness, surprise, sadness, fear, anger, disgust/contempt, and interest. [39] Speakers must watch facial signals, for they provide continuous feedback on whether the audience understands, is surprised, agrees, and so on. Eye movements also indicate audience reactions. That is why, after ending a long utterance, a speaker is likely to look up. Facial expressions can, in addition, reflect audience attitudes. Approval-seeking subjects, for example, tend to smile more and use more head nods and gesticulations. Speakers themselves may find that their own facial expressions act as meta-communications that modify or comment upon what is being said or done at the time. The dictionary of gestures is even more symbolic and varies enormously with different cultures. In our culture we see that a hand to the nose expresses fear, fist gestures indicate aggression, a finger at the lips shows shame, and an open hand dangling between the legs suggests frustration.

The three aspects of interpersonal communication in a social relationship that we have discussed—the structural, strategic, and nonverbal—are most evident on this level. We have seen, however, that they also apply to groups larger than two persons. This shall be apparent in the next chapter, which deals with interpersonal communication in small groups.

14 interpersonal communication in small groups

Society abounds with informal and formal small groups. Our daily lives can be plotted by movements from and to family groups, work groups, and play groups. In each we do a great deal of talking and listening, mostly spontaneous, but on some occasions and in some places we deliberate about what we're going to say, and plan minor strategies as to how we can fulfill our needs and accomplish our goals. Especially in the more formal settings of work, some small group meetings require planned presentations that resemble public speaking.

Our focus in this chapter is mainly on the task-oriented group which is engaged in problem solving and decision making. Our perspective and concern is twofold. First, as members and leaders of groups we want to be able to participate effectively and, at least sometimes, to exercise influence. Especially as leaders we want to know why some small groups are successful and others are not. We want to understand the dynamics of group action sufficiently so that we can predict with some degree of probability the likely reactions of others to our communication acts. Second, our perspective may be that of an outsider whose communication strategy calls for working with groups. This is the typical case of social action programs. Although knowledge of group interaction is still important, greater yet is our need to understand group structure, communication networks, and leadership.

We already have a background from the discussion of the social design (Chapter 8) about the motivations for group membership and the enormous social influence exercised by groups on individual attitudes. We shall now build on this foundation by first discussing social interaction in small groups and then small group networks and opinion leadership.

SOCIAL INTERACTION IN SMALL GROUPS

Social interaction in small groups is a compromise between two forces: the individual member's biological nature and personality, and the role, culture, and environment that impinge upon him. A. Paul Hare shows the relationship of these elements in the following conceptual scheme: [1]

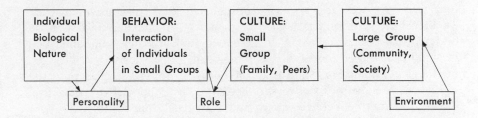

The scheme shows that one of the dimensions that must be observed in social interaction is how much an individual is concerned with the satisfaction of his own needs and the expression of his personality as compared with a social orientation to group goals and norms. Through his "role"—the expectations of group members toward the position he occupies—the member is linked to the group and the larger social system. In informal groups this role is not assigned, but achieved through the process of interaction. Role differentiation and a hierarchical structure among members results. The culture is defined by group norms and the more general guidelines and expectations established by society. Since a member belongs to many groups whose goals and values do not necessarily coincide, there is likely some inconsistency in attitudes and behavior. Hence there are forces for both compliance and deviation from group norms. A group leader in particular must be aware of all these elements that affect social interaction.

The key feature of social groups is the possibility of face-to-face interaction among all its members. The following most commonly used definition of a small group by Robert Bales reflects this and allied features:

A small group is defined as any number of persons engaged in interaction with each other in a single face-to-face meeting or a series of meetings, in which each member receives some impression or perception of each other

member distinct enough so that he can, either at the time or in later ques-
tioning, give some reaction to each of the others as an individual person,
even though it be only to recall that the other person was present.[2]

A size of between two and twenty members most commonly fulfills the
above requirements. Moreover, a mere collection of persons such as
found at an airport gate would not count as a group. Just how much
interaction would have to take place to qualify as a group is an uncertain
matter, since the definition must of necessity be somewhat indeterminate.

Speech books make many additional distinctions among different
kinds of small groups (and those blending into the larger audiences of a
public speaker). James N. Holm, for example, distinguishes between a
conference and a meeting.[3] The former is defined as a gathering of from
four to twenty persons who have convened to think together as a team.
Theoretically, no member should try to defend a predetermined opinion
or stand or to persuade others to accept it. Full and free communication
in an atmosphere of cooperation is the essential characteristic. A meeting,
on the other hand, is defined as an occasion for presenting prepared
messages.[4] Members expect to see themselves as either active or passive.
The active ones deliberately try to attain a predetermined objective. Our
analysis of small group interaction pertains chiefly to the conference,
although many observations will apply to a meeting as well.

interaction analysis

The most obvious feature that can be observed in a group is who
talks how much to whom. These facts tell us what the group's communication network is and how much traffic each channel carries (the interaction rate).[5] More difficult to analyze is the content of interaction. The
aim is not to deal with any specific subject matter, but with the kinds of
statements made and acts performed. Many systems have been developed.
For example, Chapple simply divided all interaction into two types, action
and silence.[6] The most widely referred-to system, however, was developed
by Bales, who uses twelve categories for the direct observation of the
interaction process as shown and classified in the chart on p. 157.[7]

The observer categorizes each "unit act" into one of the twelve categories. A unit act is a bit of behavior—mainly verbal but also nonverbal—
that can provide enough of a stimulus to elicit a meaningful response from
another person.

Several characteristics of these categories should be noticed. The
first is that half of them deal with task activity (4–9) and half with social-
emotional activity (1–3 and 10–12). Both are necessary for group performance and survival. Besides working on solutions to a problem, a group

PROBLEM-SOLVING GROUP OBSERVATION CATEGORIES

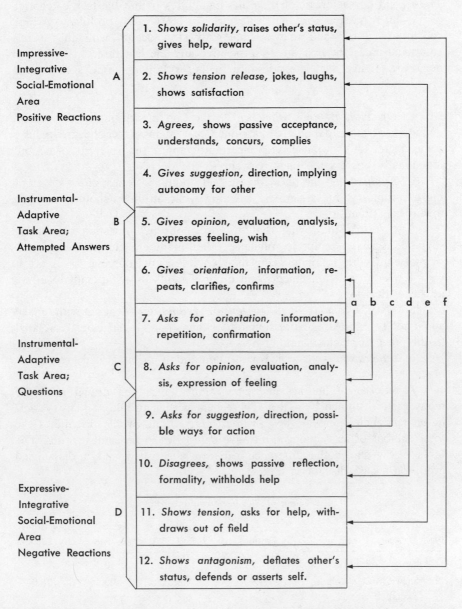

Impressive-
Integrative
Social-Emotional   A
Area
Positive Reactions

1. *Shows solidarity,* raises other's status, gives help, reward

2. *Shows tension release,* jokes, laughs, shows satisfaction

3. *Agrees,* shows passive acceptance, understands, concurs, complies

Instrumental-
Adaptive
Task Area;   B
Attempted Answers

4. *Gives suggestion,* direction, implying autonomy for other

5. *Gives opinion,* evaluation, analysis, expresses feeling, wish

6. *Gives orientation,* information, repeats, clarifies, confirms

Instrumental-
Adaptive
Task Area;   C
Questions

7. *Asks for orientation,* information, repetition, confirmation

8. *Asks for opinion,* evaluation, analysis, expression of feeling

9. *Asks for suggestion,* direction, possible ways for action

Expressive-
Integrative
Social-Emotional   D
Area
Negative Reactions

10. *Disagrees,* shows passive reflection, formality, withholds help

11. *Shows tension,* asks for help, withdraws out of field

12. *Shows antagonism,* deflates other's status, defends or asserts self.

a b c d e f

A subclassification of system problems to which each pair of categories is most relevant:
    a. Problems of orientation   d. Problems of education
    b. Problems of evaluation   e. Problems of tension-management
    c. Problems of control   f. Problems of integration

must make decisions and release the tension that task performance creates. The second characteristic of the Bales categories is that the task categories divide into passive "asking" categories (7–9) and positive "giving" categories (4–6), and that a similar division occurs with the social-emotional area: the first three are positive and the last three (10–12) are negative. Finally, the categories are further subdivided into six problem areas:

1. *Orientation*—the "what is it?" question of arriving at a common definition of the situation. It is assumed that members of the group have some degree of ignorance and uncertainty about the relevant facts, but individually possess the facts relevant to the decision.

2. *Evaluation*—the "how do we feel about it?" question of developing a common value system by deciding what attitudes should be taken toward the situation.

3. *Control*—the "what shall we do about it?" question of making suggestions that attempt to influence other members and to arrive at a way of controlling or influencing their common environment.

4. *Decisions*—agreements and disagreements in an attempt to arrive at a final decision.

5. *Tension management* or *tension reduction*—dealing with naked and directly explosive expression of feelings that are specifically related to the preceding act of another person.

6. *Integration*—concerned with maintaining an integrated group.

A number of findings and conclusions have been drawn from the many groups studied by Bales. These deal with a profile of activity, act-to-act tendencies, and a who-to-whom matrix. The profile distributes the total number of acts among the twelve categories in percentage rates. The table below shows the difference between a satisfied and a dissatisfied group on a case discussion task: [8]

Meeting profiles in percentage rates

Type of Act	Satisfied	Dissatis-fied	Av. of the two	Av. rates by Sections
1. Shows Solidarity	.7	.8	.7	
2. Shows Tension Release	7.9	6.8	7.3	25.0
3. Agrees	24.9	9.6	17.0	
4. Gives Suggestion	8.2	3.6	5.9	
5. Gives Opinion	26.7	30.5	28.7	56.7
6. Gives Orientation	22.4	21.9	22.1	

Type of Act:	Satisfied	Dissatis-fied	Av. of the two	Av. rates by Sections
7. Asks for Orientation	1.7	5.7	3.8	
8. Asks for Opinion	1.7	2.2	2.0	6.9
9. Asks for Suggestion	.5	1.6	1.1	
10. Disagrees	4.0	12.4	8.3	
11. Shows Tension	1.0	2.6	1.8	11.4
12. Shows Antagonism	.3	2.2	1.3	
Percentage Total	100.0	100.0	100.0	100.0

Most noticeable in the satisfied group is the higher rate of suggestion followed by positive reactions (agreement) than the dissatisfied group. Otherwise the profiles do not substantially differ. Notice, however, that attempted answers—giving orientation, opinion, and suggestion—are more numerous than the asking for these reactions. One of Bales' recommendations for running a conference relates to this profile. He suggests that the group start with the facts if possible, then move on to their feelings about them, and then ask what should be done about the problem. Make sure, he says, to lay the groundwork before getting to specific suggestions. He also notes, incidentally, that this recommended order is the exact opposite of that which is characteristic of formal parliamentary procedure. A second recommendation is that if the leader scents trouble, he should try to break off the argument and backtrack to further work on the facts and direct experience.[9]

His analysis of act-to-act tendencies is related to the problem of group equilibrium that deals essentially with the reduction of disturbances. Bales says that there is a "tendency of the group to swing back and forth between attempts to complete the task and attempts to maintain the group and to satisfy the needs of its members." [10] A review of some of the typical reactions to certain acts amplifies on this problem. When a person attempts an answer, he is likely to get a positive or a negative reaction. This likelihood increases as the person moves from a prior act of giving orientation to one of giving opinion, to one of giving a suggestion.[11] Furthermore, as statements become more "directive" and "constrictive," the reactions are more likely to be negative.

A person who wants to play it safe is advised to ask questions. Questions receive reactions in the task activity categories and tend to avoid the sanctioning ones of the social-emotional area. Thus if a member finds that he has created strain resulting from disagreement and argument, he can always backtrack to questions which then serve as a "neutral way out." For those members who are in the thick of competition for status, there is a price to pay. Asking questions is a low status act that only those who have a fixed high status or have accepted a low status can afford to pay.[12]

The who-to-whom matrix provides further insights into status effects. By examining the total number of different possible combinations of who is speaking and to whom for a given time period, it is discovered that groups with designated leaders of higher status allow less equal participation for members than groups with no designated leader.[13] High ranking men also include more attempted answers in their profiles and address more acts to the group as a whole than lower ranking men. These have more reactions, both positive and negative, and address more of their acts to specific individuals, often to those of higher status.[14]

With continuing social interaction, role differentiation and leadership appears. Some people communicate more than others, a tendency that increases with the size of the group. But more importantly, different kinds of leaders emerge. The two types that have received the most attention are the "idea man" and the "best-liked man."[15] Group members apparently distinguish between those whose company they enjoy and those whom they think can help them to realize the group goals. The idea men have a higher concentration than the best-liked men in the task area, hold the floor for longer periods of time than others, are often the highest interactors, and, incidentally, have a low F-scale score—meaning that they are permissive rather than authoritarian. The best-liked men have a higher concentration in the social-emotional area, as indicated by their tension-release acts of joking and laughing. The perfect kind of leader is one who combines both qualities. In fact, Argyle says that it is essential that a formally appointed leader should carry both task and social roles.[16]

In this section on group interaction our perspective has been primarily internal—that is, as a member or leader of a small group. We shift now to the external perspective of a communicator who seeks to influence group action or members' attitudes as part of a larger strategy of communication.

SMALL GROUP NETWORKS AND OPINION LEADERSHIP

Passengers on the New York City subway system who want to check on how to get from one place to another consult the rapid transit map. This stylized map shows the transportation network, a geometrical figure consisting of lines connected together by their ends. Their shapes and lengths only broadly outline the geography of the space represented, for number and connections are important, not magnitude.

A communication network is much the same; only the nodes—the ends of the lines where they are united—represent persons and the connecting lines represent channels of communication. To diagram the flow of communication among members of a small group, dots, lines, and arrows show who sends messages to whom. If successive patterns were examined over a period of time, we would have a picture of the social structure of the group and the relationships among members of the group.

In this chapter we examine the small group network and its opinion leaders. These patterns which are easily discernible in the small social system of a group also serve as a prototype of community networks and opinion leadership.

contrived groups

The properties of communication networks and how they affect certain aspects of the group process are most clearly seen in the classical experimentally created groups created by Alex Bavelas and Harold Leavitt.[17] The basic ways in which five people can be linked to one another was varied. Idealized patterns could be obtained through the controlled conditions established. The typical experimental arrangement is for a number of people to sit alone in small adjacent cubicles and to be allowed to communicate with one another by passing written messages through slots in the wall between cubicles.

Four main communication patterns were established by Bavelas and Leavitt: the circle, chain, Y and wheel. Visually it is easy to recognize that the main difference in the patterns is the degree of access each individual (represented by a dot) has to others. The person in the center of the wheel has access to all others; the individuals at the ends of the chain have access to only one other. The arrow going in both directions indicates that each individual may send and receive messages.

One of the contributions of Bavelas is that he developed a measure of centrality that indicated how close each position was to all the others. In its simplest form, centrality is measured by the minimum number of communication links that must be used to get from one position to another. Based on this measure, the most central position is C in the wheel; next most central, position C in the Y; next, position C in the chain. All positions have equal centrality in the circle.

Behavioral differences produced by different communication patterns were most clearly correlated to the measure of centrality. It is the wheel, which contains the most central position, that excelled in accuracy of results, location of recognized leadership, and speed of performance. These results feed down progressively with the Y in second place, the chain in third, and the circle last. The circle, however, excelled in two respects: the general satisfaction of its members was greatest and they were best in correcting errors in performance (although they committed the most errors).

Although caution must always be exercised when transferring laboratory findings to real-life situations, the similarity of the Y pattern to the formal organization and the wheel to the informal group is suggestive. The Y pattern (and the wheel in particular sub-units of an organization) is used to get a task performed efficiently. In contrast, the circle pattern (representing an informal group) is used to maintain morale and keep the organization integrated.

Social structure as reflected in communication networks affects performance and job satisfaction. Furthermore, an alteration in a communication network changes the social structure and the kind of behavior that such a structure will make possible or probable. This is why many managements are abandoning the concept that real-life organizations are single "networks" in favor of a more realistic view of them as a number of networks superimposed.[18] Each network handles a certain class of messages under given circumstances. The platoon leader of a combat infantry group rigidly enforces the chain of command; the platoon leader of a group of engineers, however, forms a circle type of interaction to discuss an unusual construction problem facing him. Similarly, as Harold Leavitt suggests in *Managerial Psychology,* organizations may provide for special group meetings in which the usual rank considerations are dropped (to the extent that such absolute disregard of consequences outside of this temporary closed group can be ignored).[19]

sociograms as reflecting real groups

Groups are not only formed by leaders or management; they emerge spontaneously. There are free-forming groups such as a circle of close friends. Practically every person belongs to some such group. In a study conducted in Lansing, Michigan, for example, only 4.5 percent of the respondents interviewed reported that they had no friends.[20] There are also forced-choice small groups such as the family and fellow workers. Even if values and norms are not shared at the beginning there is a tendency to do so as interaction continues.

It is obvious that informal groups abound. There are so many that, as reflected in one study of a small section of a metropolitan area, there were more than two hundred informal groups unknown to institutional authorities who studied the area. And we can only speculate how many more were unknown to the investigation.

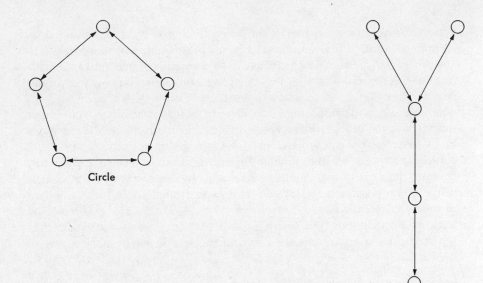

Circle

Y

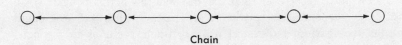

Chain

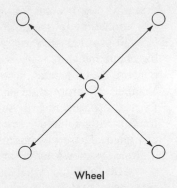

Wheel

FOUR COMMUNICATION PATTERNS

An instrument, the sociogram, was developed by J. L. Moreno to identify informal social groups and to measure informal social relationships between individuals on the basis of attraction, rejection, and indifference.[21] The result of showing the connecting lines among individuals is a network similar to those we have been discussing. Those individuals who received a disproportionately large number of choices from other members of the group are like the individuals in the most central positions in the Bavelas-Leavitt groups. In the language of sociometry, they are called stars: they are the popular figures or, if they receive certain key choices, they are power figures. These are obviously strategic individuals in the group because a message to them would more likely be transmitted to others than if the message reached an isolate; someone who receives no choices. Furthermore, the message may be editorialized upon and thus the stars may serve to influence how the message is acted upon.

gatekeepers and opinion leaders

A more general terminology for these central positions has gained currency in the communications field with the use of the terms "gatekeeper" and "opinion leader." The term gatekeeper is used to describe those individuals who control a strategic portion of a decision-making channel so as to have the power to make the decision between what goes *in* or *out*.[22] Gatekeepers also serve as transmitters within networks and can decide on the shortest and fastest links to other positions in the network. A gatekeeper may or may not fulfill an additional role: to serve as a *model* for opinion—to influence as well as to pass on information. The term opinion leader is used to emphasize the influential aspect of the transmission of information even though the opinion leader may not also be a gatekeeper. He performs the function of sanctioning messages for the group by: (1) checking the accuracy or truthfulness of information, (2) assessing the benefits of recommended actions for group members, and (3) evaluating messages in terms of conformity to group goals and norms.

Both roles—the transmissive and the influential—must be considered by communicators who want to introduce new ideas to a group. Their concern is to locate those group officers or members who control the channels of information and influence. With reference to the Bavelas and Leavitt experiments, those in positions of highest "centrality" must be found; with reference to sociometry, those who are "stars" must be identified. These persons may or may not be the same as the officers of a group as shown by organizational charts.

How likely is it that the formal leaders of a group will be receptive to new ideas, that is, to serve as innovators? It can be argued that it is part of a leader's job to keep the members informed of outside events and ideas that are relevant to the group's activities. This function must, however, be weighed against the known characteristic of a leader as the champion of existing group norms. If the preservation of the status quo is important to the group, the leader is especially likely to be hostile to change and to perceive part of his job as protecting members from alien ideas. He may even find new ideas menacing to the maintenance of his leadership position if their application requires an educational background and skills that he lacks.

Homans, in a section of a book dealing with status and the risks of action, suggests other possibilities.[23] If a leader is highly accepted and attributed with high status he can disagree with group judgment without taking a large risk. If the group turns out to be correct, he will have sacrificed a certain amount of esteem, but not a critical amount because he has a large reservoir of it to fall back on. If the group's judgment turns out to be incorrect he will have increased the esteem in which others held him "as a possessor of rare abilities." Thus a leader with acknowledged high status may cooperate in introducing a new idea while a person of middle status will not. His disagreement with group judgment involves a higher risk. As stated by Homans:

> . . . if the man of middle status conforms to the group's judgment and the group turns out to be right, his position as an accepted member is confirmed, and it needs confirming more than does that of an upper-status member. If he conforms and the group is wrong, he does not lose anything: he has only been a boob with the rest, who are in no condition to turn on him. If, on the other hand, he refuses to conform, and the group's judgment turns out to be right, he may really hurt himself in status; he is not so far from the bottom that a single misstep will not bring him appreciably closer to it.[24]

In a large group that has divided its work into specialized areas, committee heads or experts may serve as gatekeepers and opinion leaders of new ideas. What has been said about leaders may, however, apply to the subleaders. The search for an effective access point to a group may center on informal leaders who serve as opinion leaders. They may be more willing to serve as innovators if they feel that the group's interests are being served. If the new idea impresses them sufficiently, they may be willing to challenge the existing leadership and even to form a new group.

varieties of opinion leadership

In deciding which persons in a group to approach to gain access to it, a communicator should consider variations in opinion leadership. As

Banfield points out in his book, *Political Influence,* the amount of influence possessed by someone is meaningless to assess unless it is specified: "Who has influence with whom and with regard to what?" [25] The person whose advice is sought on a political question is not the same as the one whose advice is sought on a stock market question. Because of distinctions among the types of persons who are consulted, communicators who wish to work through opinion leaders should choose the kind suitable to their requirements. Three pairs of opinion leaders have been distinguished: vertical and horizontal, monomorphic and polymorphic, and local and cosmopolitan.

The traditional concept that opinion leadership always flows from the high social class or status levels to low ones is no longer realistic. In its place is the recognition that opinion leaders appear on every level and work horizontally within each level—as well, perhaps, as extending to other levels. More broadly stated, social status no longer exclusively explains the basis of opinion leadership, for social status is only one of several factors.

Two additional social characteristics—life cycle (phases of family life and child-rearing), and gregariousness (extent of contact with other people)—are considered by Elihu Katz and Paul Lazarsfeld.[26] In their study of four influence areas—movie-going, fashion, marketing, and public affairs—social status was clearly the least important characteristic.[27] It was only in public affairs that more opinion leaders were found in the higher than lower status levels and more people from low levels directed their inquiries to people of higher status than their own.[28] In contrast, in marketing and fashion, the influencer and influencee were usually of the same social status.

The life cycle was the most important factor in opinion leadership among women, especially for movie-going and to some extent in fashions and marketing. Gregariousness was in between the life cycle and social status in importance, and played a particularly large role in public affairs.

In summary, social status is clearly not the sole or most vital factor in opinion leadership and the flow is not typically downward from high to low status levels.

The distinction between monomorphic and polymorphic opinion leadership is in respect to the "sphere of activity in which they exert interpersonal influence." [29] The monomorphic ones exert influence in one narrowly defined area while the polymorphic ones exert influence in a variety of areas, perhaps unrelated. The references already made to Katz and Lazarsfeld indicate that the principle of specialization used in the division of labor in large organizations also applies to opinion leadership.

The third distinction—between locals and cosmopolitans—is based on the opinion leader's scope of interest in subject matter.[30] The locals are "preoccupied with local problems, to the virtual exclusion of the national and international scene"; the cosmopolitan is concerned with the world outside. In the language of communication networks, the local is oriented to his single network of interpersonal relations while the cosmopolitan is oriented to several networks, particularly outside ones. The local was typically born in the community where he lives and his entire career progression has been there; the cosmopolitan was typically born elsewhere and his career progression has been in an organization or profession.

The base of influence of each is of interest. The local, as might be expected, derives his influence from his numerous contacts. He not only knows as many people as possible but he knows them in personal terms. He is thus able to provide sympathetic understanding. His basis of credibility is trustworthiness. In reference to the functions of opinion leadership, he excels in serving as a transmitter and sanctioner—not, however, of information in terms of scientific accuracy but in terms of his group's benefits and standards.

The cosmopolitan derives his influence through his occupational status—from the prestige of previous achievements and previously acquired skills. He has "been around" and this is why he is sought out for advice. His credibility is based not on sympathetic understanding but on expertise. Because he is an avid consumer of the mass media, he "provides a transmission-belt for the diffusion of 'culture' from the outside world to the 'cultural leaders'" of a community.[31] In terms of the opinion leader functions, he likely excels as a gatekeeper: he can serve as a sanctioner of information by checking the accuracy of a viewpoint, and he can serve as an originator of new ideas.

From a communication viewpoint, one of the two types of opinion leaders may seem more useful than the other. The cosmopolitan might, for example, be seen as more receptive and understanding of outside ideas. But the local is needed to gain acceptance of an idea by the local group. Hence a communicator should plan to work with both types of opinion leaders.

As stated earlier, this review of group networks and opinion leadership is applicable not only to the small groups that have been the focus of this chapter, but to larger social systems as well. We turn now to a discussion of communication in larger social systems.

15 communication in larger social systems

Individuals and groups do not live in isolation but are embedded in larger, widespread social networks. We leave the primary group of the family to work in an office or shop that is typically part of a larger bureaucratic organization. During the week we may attend a meeting at a union hall, a professional society, a trade association, or a local PTA, and we may in addition go to a movie, the theater, a church, and listen to a public speaker at a political rally. In all of these activities and social settings communication takes place.

Although we are participants in these social networks, our chief concern as persuasive communicators is the planning of communications to reach groups, organizations, and voluntary associations. Sometimes we want to reach everyone in a community or larger social system or everyone who falls into a certain social grouping. Our approach to these social units is determined by our role and purpose. As internal communicators —editors of employee publications, members of an employee relations or public relations department, or staff person with many speaking obligations—our purpose is to keep members informed and motivated to accomplish the common goal of the organization.[1] As public communicators working for a particular organization or cause, we view these social units either as convenient channels through which we reach people or as total units whose cooperation is needed. For example, a trade association interested in a pro-business vote in a state election may seek the cooperation of business firms and through their employee publications, public

speaking opportunities, films, and other means try to reach the large segment of the population that is employed by them. But a community action group would be more interested in winning the support of significant community leaders and groups than in reaching large numbers of individuals.

Larger social systems contain two major communication settings. The first is in the extended groups to which people belong in various organizations and associations. While face-to-face communications also exist in these social units, they are supplemented by more formal oral communications, often resembling the characteristics of public speaking, and by a wide variety of written communications. The whole range of organizational communications starts with the style of interpersonal relations and ends with the mass media. The second major setting for communication in large social systems is the system as a whole. Our focus here is on the mass audience of heterogeneous people and on the social groupings which comprise it. The techniques and technology of mass communication are here applied.

COMMUNICATION WITH ORGANIZATIONS AND VOLUNTARY ASSOCIATIONS

Unlike a communal society that is structured largely by non-specialized kinship organizations, modern industrialized ones like ours have an abundant number and variety of social units beyond the primary groups. Sociologists use a variety of terms to describe these units. Francis E. Merrill calls them secondary groups because they reach out from the primary group into many types of institutional and bureaucratic structures.[2] Secondary groups are less intimate, personal, and inclusive than primary ones and regard each other mainly as means to ends, rather than as ends in themselves. Thus people interact with a segment of their personalities rather than with the entire personality. Relationships are usually entered voluntarily and with purpose. Sometimes an actual or implied contract augments the primary group mechanism of status by stating and defining the mutual duties and obligations of each party.

Another term, "association," is used by Maciver and Page in their classic, *Society,* to describe the social units of a community or larger society. They define an association as "a group organized for the pursuit of an interest or group of interests in common."[3] Their definition is so broad that it includes virtually all purposeful organizations, including the family. We are interested, however, in what they call the "great association"—the large-scale organization with its impersonal or secondary relationship and its specialization of functions.[4] General Motors, the

government of the City of New York, and the American Cancer Society are examples of such organizations. These large structures still contain informal primary groups and other face-to-face relationships, but most relationships are based on highly differentiated roles and hierarchical structures. In many of these roles, a member develops the typical passive attitude of an audience member rather than an active participant.

The term "social institution" is also used to refer to social units. But as Joseph S. Himes points out, a social institution involves more than a complex, bureaucratic organization like the United Nations; it refers to the intangible sanctioned rules of social action.[5] When people refer to the institution of marriage, money, or slavery, they stress the rules of the relationships involved rather than the organizations in which they occur.

For our purposes we can lump together the most essential economic, political, and cultural social units and call them organizations. But we need another term, called voluntary associations, to refer to the myriad secondary groups to which so many Americans belong.[6] People join these groups to give themselves a greater understanding and control of a segment of the environment in which they operate. These associations are, accordingly, typically categorized in terms of such selective interests as:

—Veterans, military, patriotic,

—Civic, service, or both,

—Lodges, fraternal, or professional,

—Cultural, educational, college, or alumni,

—Social, sports, hobby, or recreational,

—Church or religious,

—Political or pressure.

These voluntary associations serve as intermediaries between their members and either the general public or community decision makers. Their support is also often solicited by organizations that want to expand their political base or give the appearance of community support. Banfield gives the following example:

> The civic association may serve as a "front" for the organization and as its ally. As a "front," it says things which the organization cannot well say for itself either because it would not be believed or because saying them would provide a response from employees, competitors, customers, or others which the organization does not want. The organization's interest in the issue may be (or be thought) narrowly selfish, and its arguments, however well-founded, may be discounted on this account; the civic association, because it speaks for a broader interest, can appeal more plausibly to the public interest.[7]

Although voluntary associations often speak in terms of the public interest, their perspective is actually more selfish in that they try to reflect the views, values, and goals of their members.[8] Because many of these associations involve a high degree of participation by their members, they are, however, vehicles for the expression of democracy. No one engaged in a social action program can afford to ignore them.

With the addition of voluntary associations to the organizations that comprise a society, our review of the basic subsystems of society is completed. We turn next to the nature of communications among these subsystems and then to ways of selecting the most influential audiences in a community setting.

identifying influentials and active participants

A change agent for a social action program is advised to obtain the support of "legitimizers" and "active participants" who will do the work.[9] Legitimizers are persons who possess social power and can therefore provide support, guidance, authority, justification, or "license to act" in a specific social action program. This social power is based on authority, influence, or both. To identify individuals who possess formal authority is simple and direct, for those persons who occupy important organizational positions are selected. Thus leaders might include elected political officials, higher civil servants, business executives, officials of voluntary associations, heads of religious groups, leaders of labor unions, military officers, and others.[10]

Identifying individuals who possess informal social power or influence is more difficult. A reputational approach is often used whereby leaders are identified through the opinions or judgments of other members of the social system, who tell the researcher who they think the leaders are.[11] Various criteria and procedures of concensus, such as employing a panel of experts, can then be used to decide which persons appear to be operating as leaders in the community.

The reputational approach—also sometimes called the sociometric approach—was used by Floyd Hunter in his study of the *Community Power Structure* in a large southern city of about 500,000.[12] He identified forty persons who as a group constituted the top leadership of Regional City. They decided on all the big issues facing the community—issues like labor policy, expansion of educational facilities, public health and welfare services, the sales tax, traffic control, and plans for a proposed regional development. These men worked behind the scenes and were represented and supported by sub-leaders, the persons who executed the policies and decisions of the top men.

Not all communities have a single group of leaders. In place of a single power network, New Haven has a multiple network.[13] With each of three issue-areas, the composition of the leaders involved was different. Of the total of fifty different individuals who initiated or vetoed policies, only three leaders did so in more than one issue-area. The very few influential persons in a community who have influence over decision making in a broad range of issue areas are sometimes called "top influentials." [14] Where they exist, these people are the prime targets of change agents who seek legitimization of their causes.

Another group of people, the active participants, must be reached by change agents. These are not persons who are involved in making key decisions in the early stages of a social action program, but the ones who do the work. They have characteristics similar to the subleaders in Robert Dahl's study of New Haven.[15] They come from all the layers of social classes but their financial position, educational attainment, and social status is somewhat above that of their fellow citizens. Specifically, more of them were age forty or over, males, lived in the top three residential areas, had white-collar occupations, were educated beyond high school, had annual incomes over $10,000, and owned their own homes. They were also heavily represented in voluntary associations. Studies show that membership in these associations is unevenly distributed.[16] In all instances the distribution takes the form of a J-curve with the majority of the population concentrated at the low participation end of the scale. The persons who are members of voluntary associations not only serve as a source of subleaders and active participants in social action programs but are known to constitute a high proportion of those who are classified as opinion leaders.

Let us now examine the communication patterns used by the leaders of organizations and associations.

communication in organizations and communities

The boundaries of all human organizations are defined and limited by the reach and efficiency of their communication networks. One way in which large-scale organizations and larger social structures can grow in size is by merely forming a chain of coupled systems.[17] This is essentially the nature of "line communications" in a bureaucracy which follows the "chain of command" as diagrammed on the organizational chart. The leaders of rank-and-file worker groups report to a department head; the various department heads form another group who report to a division head; and so on throughout the organization. The person or group on the top has the formal authority to coordinate the efforts of all the members of the organization to achieve a common goal.

Communication along these channels compounds the barriers of communication faced in ordinary conversation. The men on the top cannot possibly be kept informed of every detail; downward messages are misunderstood in an effort to please the boss and to anticipate his wishes; upward communication is distorted with the great concern for "giving the boss what he wants" or to "cover up" mistakes. Thus an organization has a system of multiple filters with each person at a strategic point serving as a gatekeeper of what information to pass, modify, or suppress.[18] Language poses a further difficulty for where a high degree of division of labor exists, people use the specialized vocabularies of their trade, profession, and social class. As semanticists have pointed out, even the same words have different meanings because of people's different associations with them.[19]

In community communication networks some of the features of large-scale organizations are even further magnified and new ones are introduced. The total range of specialization of purpose is even broader among a community's social units and thus the backgrounds of community leaders and active participants differ more widely. The perception of a common purpose which theoretically prevails in private organizations and associations usually does not exist in a community at large. Representatives from various groups meet to arrive at a consensus on various specific issues and projects. But unless the force of government or of events compels them to agree and act, there is no hierarchical structure that has the legitimate authority to impose a solution and command performance. Hence the reliance on persuasive communication is greater in the social system of a community.

Another difference between organizational and community communication patterns is in the methods of communication used. In organizations, those members who have the greatest need to work together and communicate with one another are placed in close physical proximity. Hence interpersonal communication is facilitated. On a community level, get-togethers and meetings must be specially arranged and some travel is necessary. Meetings tend, therefore, to be less frequent and more planned and controlled so agendas can be completed.

Public speaking is a prominent form of communications in the community and among the various trade and professional associations in society. One of the major attributes and strengths of public speaking is that like the mass media, large audiences can be reached. But unlike the mass media some of the persuasive characteristics of interpersonal communication are retained. The latter feature is implicitly incorporated in such definitions of public speaking as James N. Holm's: "public speaking is planned conversation with a group of listeners." [20] A speaker is advised to analyze his audience in order to discover what kinds of people it contains and what common interests exist. Furthermore, the possibility should not be overlooked that the audience is indeed a true group, possessing a set of habits or ways of behaving to which they all conform.[21] To overcome the tendency for audience members to be passive and react as isolated individuals, some writers recommend various techniques to increase active participation. Among these are the buzz group, which breaks down a large group into small units to facilitate discussion; the use of question cards; the assignment of listening teams, audience reaction teams, or observing teams; and various role-playing scenes.[22]

Many organizations consider public speaking so effective that they establish speaker's bureaus. As Lawrence S. Jeppson points out, this is sometimes done strictly for the public relations purpose of creating good will.[23] Other times a careful program of speaking engagements for organizational representatives is planned to win support for a cause. The cumulative effect of individual public speeches often approaches the result achieved through mass communication, a form of communication to which we now turn.

COMMUNICATION WITH MASS AUDIENCES AND THEIR SOCIAL GROUPINGS

A feature of modern, literate, urbanized, and industrialized societies in democratic countries is the presence of the mass media of communication and a corps of professional communicators. Countries in transition from traditional to modern society find that the exchange of information becomes more complex and formalized and that some things that were once done by individuals now require social institutions.[24] As stated by Daniel Lerner, a country goes through three phases:

> Urbanization comes first, for cities alone have developed the complex of skills and resources which characterize the modern industrial economy. Within this urban matrix develop both of the attributes which distinguish the next two phases—literacy and media growth. There is a close reciprocal relationship between these, for the literates develop the media which in turn spread literacy. But, historically, literacy performs the key function in the second phase. The capacity to read, at first acquired by relatively few people, equips them to perform the varied tasks required in the modernizing society. Not until the third phase, when the elaborate technology of industrial development is fairly well advanced, does a society begin to produce newspapers, radio networks, and motion pictures on a massive scale. This, in turn, accelerates the spread of literacy. Out of this interaction develop those institutions of participation . . . which we find in all advanced modern societies.[25]

All developing and modern nations need an extensive and rapid system of public communication that enable ideas and information to be disseminated throughout society.

Charles R. Wright, following the ideas of Harold Lasswell, outlines four functions performed by mass communication: surveillance, correlation, transmission of culture, and entertainment.[26] Surveillance, or the handling of news, is the collecting and distributing of information about events in the environment. Not only are individuals helped because they have a "tool for daily living," but society as a whole benefits because it has a system for providing news that is essential to the economy and other institutions and, in case of emergency, speedy warnings. With the help of the media, impending danger from hurricanes, floods, or military attack can be reacted to more successfully. In the case of civil disturbances, this surveillance activity can work both positively and negatively. On the positive side, disrupting rumors can quickly be stopped and corrected. For example, according to the Kerner report, "rumors significantly aggravated tension and disorder in more than 65 percent of the disorders [of 1967] studied by the Commission." [27] But on the negative side, there is controversy over whether television actually stimulates riots—perhaps by building expectations that "our city will be next" or by helping to enlarge a disturbance in progress.[28]

The second function of mass communication, correlation, is of an editorial or propagandistic nature; interpretations of information about the environment are provided and prescriptions offered for conduct in reactions to these events. This function is of significance to the organizations and associations who purchase or otherwise obtain the use of the mass media to propagandize their viewpoints and thereby preserve their political power. The transmission of culture, the third function, is an educational activity that communicates a group's store of social norms, information, values, and the like. This function comes closest to providing the "cement" that holds society together. The young are socialized to society's values and when the mass media bring the deviant behavior of older people to public attention, the social norms of society are enforced. The last function, entertainment, serves to amuse people irrespective of any instrumental effects it might have. One can draw an analogy between this function and that of the social leader in small groups who, by joking and laughing, provides tension release for others.

Numerous definitions of the mass media and mass communication have been advanced. Their usual common denominator is that large, anonymous, and heterogeneous audiences are reached simultaneously.[29] However, some authorities disagree. Joseph Klapper feels that the size of the audience is secondary to the feature of impersonal transmission. The mass media therefore include radio, movies, books, newspapers, and magazines but exclude personal address, the drama, and other face-to-face communications.[30] Gerhart D. Wiebe restricts the mass media to those which are readily available to most of the public, "including a sizable number of people in all major subgroups," and whose "cost is so small to the individual that they are generally available to these same people in a financial sense." [31] Wiebe's reference to subgroups and to "intermediate and special-interest communications" anticipates the current trend toward giving greater consideration to the specialized social groupings that comprise a mass audience.[32] Before discussing this trend, the mass audience approach shall be examined in greater detail.

the mass audience

In the mass audience approach the individual is treated as "mass man." Individual differences are ignored and the common qualities of man are addressed. The stimulus-response and cognitive designs discussed in Part II are most relevant because they treat man in the most generalized terms as responding to the most universal human drives and the values of mass culture. The aim of mass circulation publications and broadcast networks is to attract the largest possible audience. Audit Bureau of Circulations figures and Nielsen ratings call the tune.

Content analysis studies of the mass media are, therefore, a useful form of audience analysis. An analysis of magazine fiction by Berelson and Salter, for example, shows that the characters used in the stories usually possess the following features: they are usually "American," enjoy high economic status, possess desirable occupations, marry only within their group, and seldom violate any American traditions.[33] An interpretation offered by the authors is that "the heterogeneity of the audience to whom such stories are directed may necessitate the use of the broadest symbols of identification." [34] Such descriptions do not necessarily reflect reality, but to the extent that media people try to mirror society as it exists and succeed in so doing, a content analysis is a valuable form of audience analysis.

To humanize "mass man" the content of the impersonal mass media is designed to draw on many social influences. The journalist's search for a "human angle" to a story, and the use of "warm" personalities on radio, television, and in film are in a sense surrogates for interpersonal influence. The knowledge that the mass media are read, listened to, or watched by other people adds the additional social element that the experience is being shared with others.

Ralph H. Turner and Lewis M. Killian have taken this last element as the basis of a fourfold classification of possible reactions to the mass media. They are:

1. No uniform response by a general anonymous, amorphous, dispersed population.
2. Uniform response by many disparate individuals to some content, but without interaction or sense of being a large body of coreactors.
3. Uniform response and sense of other people who are like-minded.
4. Collective behavior: extensive interaction and various types of concerted behavior.[35]

The first type of response is randomly individualistic and inappropriate for forms of entertainment where the response is a matter of individual taste. From a public communication viewpoint, however, this kind of response represents a dispersion of effort without the predictability of results that is desired.

The second and third types of responses are the ones typically expected from mass communication. The second type makes the two minimum assumptions that there will be a common "focus of attention"—namely, on the stimulus presented—and that there will be a common response on the part of a number of separate, dispersed individuals. The efforts of radio and television commercials to induce the purchase of the advertisers' products is the most prevalent example. Another example, a classic, is the Kate Smith War Bond Drive during World War II. Her radio marathon is given credit for the sale of $39 million worth of bonds in the first drive and $110 million in the second drive.[36]

These examples of the second type of response may spill over into the third when people react out of a sense that others are like-minded. When purchases are motivated by social emulation or a fad, the third type of response is exemplified. Similarly, when people vote for a candidate because they think others will vote for him, the bandwagon effect is illustrated and characterizes the third type of response. Finally, we might consider the kinds of consensus that represents acquiescence for the sake of conformity. Pluralistic ignorance—not knowing that "everyone else" in a group privately has beliefs different from those expressed publicly for the sake of conformity—is an example.

When people begin to talk to one another about what they saw or heard and decide on common action, then the fourth type of response occurs. One of the best examples is the effect of Orson Welles' radio drama, "War of the Worlds." This radio broadcast in 1938 created a panic situation. Cantril gives this description of it:

Long before the broadcast had ended, people all over the United States were praying, crying, fleeing frantically to escape death from the Martians. Some ran to rescue loved ones. Others telephoned farewells or warnings, hurried to inform neighbors, sought information from newspapers or radio stations, summoned ambulances and police cars. At least six million people heard the broadcast. At least a million of them were frightened or disturbed.[37]

Illustrations of collective behavior such as the one just described are sometimes taken as proof that the mass media are enormously effective in influencing behavior. Caution must be exercised, however, in normally expecting such potent results. Not only are such instances rare, but their power grows out of the stimulation that the mass media give to supplementary interpersonal communication. It is more realistic to expect all of the four types of responses to mass communication just discussed.

social groupings

The concept that the general population consists of a diffused mass audience has gradually been supplemented or replaced by the view that the public is a collection of everchanging specialized social groupings. A social grouping—also called a social category or statistical group—consists of people who share a common characteristic but do not interact with one another on a face-to-face basis. Included might be "those who follow sports events, those who own radios, those who read the 'slick' magazines (or some other type, say the 'pulp'), those who are potential buyers of bonds or stocks, those who are reform-minded, those who are status conscious (a sizable element in this country), those who are seeking romance, those who fear radicalism, those who are interested in peace, *ad infinitum.*" [38]

Companies who in the past have concentrated almost exclusively on the mass audience are now exploring the concept of "market segmentation." [39] This is an attempt systematically to describe customers and potential customers by differentiating them from the public as a whole by reference to social groupings. Use of demographic dimension by such characteristics as sex, age, income, education, occupation, and so on is most prevalent. Hence if market research demonstrates that high-income professional families are the best potential customers of sailboats and motor cruisers, then the "class" media would be used. Specialized appeals can be incorporated into the advertisements and, to the extent that the grouping serves as a reference group, an attempt can be made to make it salient.

In the current era of social change, the demographic basis of identifying social groupings is being augmented by finer and more discriminating criteria. A person who has spent a year or two in an academically fifth-rate college should not be lumped into the same single bracket of "college educated" as a Ph.D. from Harvard. Important differences would be overlooked, for their income, outlook, habitat, and life style vary considerably and affect their purchase decisions.[40] Hence in the search for meaningful dimensions of market segmentation geographical, cultural, socioeconomic, and personal differences among customers are examined.[41]

The media have responded to the demands of market segmentation and the desire to reach social groupings within the general population. Theodore Peterson pointed out some years ago that the big successes in the years ahead for magazine publishers would be among magazines that "pinpoint their appeal to some clearly defined audience with special taste, needs or interests." [42] The *New Yorker,* he says, is an illustration, for it never pretended to be a magazine for everyone; its pitch is to the sophisticated, urban reader with money.[43] With the increasing numbers of people who are CATV (community antenna television) subscribers, even greater promise can be held out for the social grouping approach. By June 1969, 2,321 systems were operating in the United States and serving twelve million people.[44] The potential of CATV is that it can send selected messages to a few small neighborhoods which, in turn, often contain residents within a given range of income, life styles, political attitudes and other attributes of social groupings.

In the next chapter we shall examine a type of social grouping that has received the greatest attention by sociologists. This is the concept of social class that continues to serve as a way of looking at subcultures within society. It has been found useful in thinking about market segmentation, political campaigning, economic education programs, and, in general, about ways in which large groupings of people look at the world.

16 the influence of social class on attitudes and communication

Social class is one of the most important variables in the sociology of communication. It affects a person's chances with regard to education, occupation, income, and marriage. As described by Leonard Reissman, it "creates a social mold that is so inclusive that the individual is seldom free of it." [1] Not unexpectedly, therefore, social class influences attitudes, behavior, and communication style and content.

The first section of this chapter describes the concept of social class, its measurement, its relationship to political and economic attitudes, and application to sociopolitical information programs. The second section of the chapter relates social class and the related concept of status to how persons communicate with each other and the kind of language they use.

DEFINING SOCIAL CLASS

Every society ranks its members according to prestige or power based on such valued attributes as wealth, skill, or power. These ranks or social layers describe an aspect of society known as social stratification. [2] Our language represents the rough way in which such rank order exists. Various groups of people are referred to as "the higher-ups," "the in-betweens," and "the low-downs." Societies vary in the number of social layers they contain and the ability of members in one layer to move upward into another. A caste system is the extreme version of social stratification.

We typically describe American class structure along the lines presented by W. Lloyd Warner and his associates in their classic study of "Yankee City"—a New England coastal town near Boston.[3] Based on this study, Warner declared that there were six groupings sharp enough to be called classes. As summarized by Joseph A. Kahl, these are: [4]

1. *Upper-upper,* 1.4 percent of the total population. This group was the old-family elite, based on sufficient wealth to maintain a large house in the best neighborhood, but the wealth had to have been in the family for more than one generation. This generational continuity permitted proper training in basic value orientations, and established people as belonging to a lineage.

2. *Lower-upper,* 1.6 percent. This group was, on the average, slightly richer than the upper-uppers, but their money was newer, their manners thus not quite so polished, their sense of lineage and security less pronounced.

3. *Upper-middle,* 10.2 percent. The moderately successful business and professional men and their families, but less affluent than the lower-uppers. Some education and polish were necessary for membership, but lineage was unimportant.

4. *Lower-middle,* 28.1 percent. The petty businessmen, the school teachers, the foremen in industry. This group tended to have morals that were close to puritan fundamentalism; they were churchgoers, lodge joiners, and flag wavers.

5. *Upper-lower,* 32.6 percent. The solid, respectable laboring people, who kept their houses clean and stayed out of trouble.

6. *Lower-lower,* 25.2 percent. The "lulus" or disrespectable and often slovenly people who dug for clams and waited for public relief.

Both subjective and objective methods are used to measure social class. Subjectively it can be determined either by asking a person to which he believes he belongs or asking others to rank him. In a specialized equalitarian and fluid society such as ours, the difficulty of this measurement is apparent. When the great majority of Americans are asked to identify themselves as belonging to the upper, middle, or lower classes, they say that they belong to the middle class. However, if the wording of the question is changed so that they must choose between upper, middle, working, and lower classes, more than half in many communities identify themselves with the working class.

Objective methods are based on the possession of some valued attribute such as family background, wealth, skill, education, place of residence, income, and power. The criteria chosen and the weight given to each vary with communities, regions, and countries.

By examining *The Social Register* we get some idea of the qualifying criteria for the large majority of the upper class in the country as a whole.[5] These criteria include a person's college and class, probably one of the older Eastern colleges like Harvard, Yale, and Princeton; the clubs to which he belongs; his address, which is likely to be in a fashionable and expensive residential area; and the fact that he is so-and-so the II or III, showing the importance of family lineage. It is obvious that the qualities of a person independent of his achievements are important.

Warner, in his study of "Yankee City," put more emphasis on occupation and income. His Index of Status Characteristics lists occupation, with a weight of 4; source of income, with a weight of 3; house type, with a weight of 3; and dwelling area, with a weight of 2.[6]

Because a high value is placed on occupation and income in the United States, the term socioeconomic status (SES) is often preferred to social class. As Reissman points out, "the idea of status has been much more warmly accepted as somehow sounding less harsh, less final, and less materialistic than *class*." Furthermore, he says, the term *status* does not violate "professed values of equality and the equal accessibility of opportunities." [7] This emphasis on achievement is reflected in *Who's Who in America*, which is primarily a list of people whose occupational achievement has been outstanding.

The variety of subjective and objective methods used to measure social class is evidenced in Delbert C. Miller's *Handbook of Research Design and Social Measurement*. One of these is a widely used socioeconomic status scale attributed to Alba M. Edwards. He uses six major occupational groupings, each of which is purported to have a somewhat distinct economic standard of life and to exhibit intellectual and social similarities: [8]

Professional, technical, and kindred workers

Business managers, officials, and proprietors

Clerical and sales workers

Craftsmen, foremen, and kindred workers

Operatives and kindred workers

Unskilled, service, and domestic workers

Since it is based on United States Census classifications, it is useful for all kinds of comparative purposes.

Another method of measuring stratifications is through occupational prestige and esteem. Miller's *Handbook* reports on one of these, Paul K. Hatt and C. C. North's Occupational Prestige Ratings.[9] In these ratings, for example, a U.S. Supreme Court Justice is ranked the highest with a score of 93, a college professor is scored 90, a lawyer 86, an airline pilot 83, a public school teacher 78, a reporter on a daily newspaper 71, a policeman 67, a barber 59, a truck driver 54, a bartender 44, and a shoeshiner 33.

Whatever measuring device is used, the essential point is that social class is significant to an understanding of attitudes and behavior. The measure chosen must reflect the idea that people in a given social stratum have many common experiences as a result of their place in the economic and social order. These common experiences explain how their attitudes are molded.

SOCIAL CLASS AS A GUIDE TO POLITICAL AND ECONOMIC ATTITUDES AND BEHAVIOR

One of the most widespread and acceptable political notions is that rich people are conservative and poor people liberal or radical.[10] This idea stems principally from Karl Marx's emphasis upon the "material basis" of society and the class conflict he expected to result from it. It would appear to follow that an individual's social class as defined by his occupation would affect his political and economic attitudes.

studies in political sociology

The view that attitudes and social class are related was supported by two early studies, one by Arthur W. Kornhauser [11] and the other by Richard T. Centers.[12] Both authors based their conclusions on the findings of public opinion polls: Kornhauser upon evidence drawn from several independent public opinion sources and Centers upon a battery of questions which he formulated. Some of the questions used by Centers are shown below because they illustrate the kinds of politico-economic attitude issues where class interests and values are manifested: [13]

> 5. As you know, during this war many private businesses and industries have been taken over by the government. Do you think wages and salaries would be fairer, jobs more steady, and that we would have fewer people out of work if the government took over and ran our mines, factories and industries in the future, or do you think things would be better under private ownership?
>
> 6. Which one of these statements do you most agree with? (1) The most important job for the government is to make it certain that there are good opportunities for each person to get ahead on his own. (2) The most im-

portant job for the government is to guarantee every person a decent and steady job and standard of living.

7. In strikes and disputes between working people and employers do you usually side with the workers or with the employers?

Both Kornhauser and Centers found marked differences in the political attitudes expressed by people in different income and occupational groups. People in the higher groups generally believed in "adherence to the status quo," while those in the lower groups believed in social change in the "liberal" or "radical" direction. More specifically, Centers reported that "a substantial degree of relationship is also found between political behavior and occupational status. The higher groups are characterized by much greater support of the traditionally conservative Republican Party than is the case with the lower occupational strata." [14]

These findings are consistent with what is known as the "interest group theory of class." As defined by Centers: [15]

This theory implies that a person's status and role with respect to the economic processes of society imposes upon him certain attitudes, values and interests relating to his role and status in the political and economic sphere. It holds, further, that the status and role of the individual in relation to the means of production and exchange of goods and services gives rise in him to a consciousness of membership in some social class which shares those attitudes, values, and interests.

Kornhauser offers some explanations that account for the varying political outlooks of different social classes. One explanation is that people with certain success-bringing attributes and attitudes rise from lower to higher positions in the socioeconomic scale. Another reason lies in the "differential influences" that surround each socioeconomic group and affect its development.[16] Probably the most important explanation is that on the basis of "people's major motivations and opportunities for their gratification at the several income levels ... personal maladjustment, frustration, and unrest are likely to be greater, on the whole, as one descends the socioeconomic scale." [17] It is this dissatisfaction that produces a more prevalent desire for a changed world.

The simple relationship between social class and politico-economic ideology reported by Kornhauser and Centers was modified and elaborated upon by later studies. In *The People's Choice*, the authors point out that "the crucial factor is not so much a person's objective occupation as his own opinion of his social status." [18] This consideration was especially important in determining how such marginal groups as white-collar workers and foremen would vote.

A study by Mark Abrams of "Social Class and British Politics" further shows the danger of gross oversimplification. The working class in England is often assumed to loyally vote for the Labour Party while the middle and upper classes vote for the Conservatives. Abrams states, however, that only slightly over 60 percent of the working class has voted Labour in recent elections.[19]

One explanation for the lack of unitary political attitudes among members of the working class is that they do not all identify with it. This was illustrated by the following question that was put to a sample of 500 working-class men and women: "The people of this country are sometimes put into these five classes. Which one would you say you belong to? Upper middle class, middle class, lower middle class, skilled working class, labouring working class?" Only 56 percent replied that they were working class, 40 percent described themselves as middle class, and the remaining 4 percent were unable or unwilling to consider themselves part of any class group.[20]

Further findings did not, however, show that those who identified themselves with the middle class voted for the Conservatives. Many who rated themselves middle class still voted for Labour—24 percent, to be exact. And among those who described themselves as working class, 22 percent supported the Conservatives. Abrams conjectures that with rising affluence the future electoral success of the Labour Party will depend on the number of workers who will remain loyal to Labour despite their identification with the middle class.[21]

A study by Richard F. Hamilton of American workers shows a similar pattern. Wealthier workers who were at higher skill levels were not more politically conservative than poorer workers at lower skill levels. Based on surveys conducted in 1955 and 1956, he found only a very small difference in the direction of greater Republicanism among the skilled.[22] But when he asked questions related to issues of concern to workers, the traditional relationship of attitudes to occupational level prevailed. Majorities at all skill levels favored government guarantees of jobs and of medical care. The percentages in favor increased with skill category; for example, 59 percent of the skilled were in favor of job guarantees in contrast to 58 percent of the semiskilled and 72 percent of the unskilled.[23]

This distribution of attitudes does support the explanation (earlier discussed in connection with Kornhauser) that deprivation influences positions on domestic economic issues. But worker position on party choice cannot be accounted for only on the basis of occupational level or social class. Hamilton says that "it would appear that genuinely sociological factors such as group membership, pressure, and influences should be considered as likely explanatory factors." [24]

The field of political sociology now recognizes that the social status of individuals or groups does not by itself determine political behavior.[25]

The kinds of factors mentioned by Hamilton must also be considered, for they serve as intervening variables. For example, semiskilled workers who are organized by a powerful industrial union are consequently more likely to act in terms of the "interest theory" of political behavior than workers who are not so organized. Hence studies are needed, according to Bendix and Lipset, that deal with those factors "which increase or decrease the likelihood that a man will support the political movement linked with his class." They list three types of studies that are relevant: [26]

1. *Voting studies.* These specify the elements which are associated with party support. They deal with the effects of factors such as varying status, type of work, property ownership, unemployment or insecurity, community social structure, social mobility, exposure to cross-class experiences, on the propensity of people to identify themselves with or against their class politically.

2. *Studies of political participation.* These have thrown a great deal of light on the linkage between participation and class position, and have made manifest the ways in which the normal operation of the social structure serves to weaken the political effectiveness of movements based on the lower class by reducing the involvement in politics of their potential followers.

3. *Public opinion and attitudes.* Analyses in this field have outlined a number of consistent variations in the values and attitudes of different classes, making understandable some of the political behavior of these groups which is not directly tied to interest. For example, the lower classes while liberal (leftist) in their attitudes on economic issues, tend to be less liberal on noneconomic issues, for example, civil liberties, race relations, immigration policy, and so forth.

The third kind of study dealing with public opinion and attitudes is of particular concern to persuasive communicators. Being able to predict a group's attitudes on the basis of social class and its related occupations would surely be helpful. Such attempts have been made with reference to specific issue areas:

1. *International affairs issues.* As summarized by Alfred Hero of the World Peace Foundation, certain international affairs issues are favored by business, professional and even white-collar groups more than by manual, particularly unskilled workers.[27] These issues include economic aid to neutralists, freer trade, liberalized relations with Communist coun-

tries, and an emphasis on conciliation, negotiations, and other nonmilitary means in U.S. foreign policy. On the other hand, socioeconomic status has had little bearing on views of the United Nations, technical assistance, world relief, military aid, collective security, and the size of our own defense establishment.

2. *Civil rights and treatment of deviants.* Seymour M. Lipset reports that on such issues as civil liberties for unpopular minorities, civil rights for Negroes, and corporal punishment for criminals, the lower strata are less liberal than the more well-to-do.[28] In a measurement of prejudice toward Negroes, F. R. Westie found that the higher the socioeconomic status, the less the prejudice.[29]

3. *Federal intervention in the economy.* Alfred Hero reports that majorities of Americans have approved of federal intervention in the national economy and federal action for social welfare. Specifically, "such programs as regulation and prohibition of child labor, old age pensions, social security, public works, slum clearance, urban renewal, low-cost housing, federal responsibility for full employment and unemployment compensation, aid to education, veterans' benefits, assistance to depressed areas, anti-poverty legislation have been favored by clear majorities of those venturing opinions." [30]

In connection with these domestic economic issues, the authors of *The American Voter* offer self-interest rather than ideology as an explanation for attitudes held.[31] Their conclusion is based on a Domestic Social Welfare Scale which ranks persons along a continuum of attitudes on the desirability of governmental action in areas of domestic social welfare. This finding reinforces the general notion that although many sociological factors must be considered in determining the exact impact of social class on attitudes, it remains as a major source of influence.

application to sociopolitical information programs

Soon after the end of World War II many American businessmen were worried about the spread of the collectivist ideology in Europe and feared that the same would happen in the United States. As a result American business launched what William H. Whyte, Jr., an editor of *Fortune,* called the "Great Free Enterprise Campaign." [32] The general objective of this campaign was to get others "to think *right* about economic matters." [33]

At first the campaign was waged largely by means of institutional advertising. The Advertising Council played a leading part in awakening American business to the need to "sell business to America." Gradually, however, businessmen felt that the best way to reinforce belief in the American business creed was by reaching their own employees through "economic education" programs.[34]

These programs varied in purpose, scope, and technique. The most publicized aim of economic education was to make employees aware of the danger of "collectivist" government legislation and to .enlist their support in the defense of free enterprise. An example is Alcoa's *Voting Is Your Business*. This program encouraged employees to register and to vote.[35] Open partisanship was avoided, but employees were urged to "vote intelligently," to take the "long-range view," and to recognize the kind of change that was desirable. The medium of small group discussions was mainly used to reach employees.

Other purposes of economic education were to improve collective bargaining and employee cooperation and productivity. Businessmen believe that there is a close connection between an employee's satisfaction with his economic share and his understanding of the economic system. Such satisfaction would temper unreasonable union demands. Furthermore, improved employee understanding and appreciation of management problems and decisions would elicit a higher level of cooperation in the attainment of company goals. Plays such as "The Dynamic Economy," films such as "Productivity: Key to Plenty," and group discussions were the major media used to accomplish these additional purposes.

The question that confronts the persuasive communicator is whether information campaigns of this sort can truly accomplish the intended purposes. In Chapter 7 we concluded that a cognitive approach is inadequate in changing attitudes toward our economic and political system. Some of the programs use the social design in that group discussions are held. The chances of producing better results are thereby enhanced. But in the light of our discussion about social class and its effect on economic and political attitudes, can we provide better answers to how these attitudes can be influenced?

If, as Centers, Kornhauser, Lazarfeld, and others believe, occupational status is of crucial importance in determining an individual's political attitudes, then only as the proportion of people engaged in different occupational groups is shifted upward can a change in attitudes be expected. This upward shift has been and will continue to be brought about as more economic activity is shifted from agriculture, mining, and manufacturing to the service industries. The shift will be further accelerated as technological improvements and the calculus of factor costs brings about that age of automation when most of the workers will be highly skilled technicians working alongside professionals.

The distinction between objective and subjective methods of identifying a person's social class may also be pertinent as workers become more affluent. A person who objectively would be classified as a member of the working class might subjectively classify himself as belonging to the middle class. Which social class, then, reflects his political and economic attitudes? We know that a person's reference group can exert a greater influence than his membership group. Take the fact that white-collar workers are politically more conservative than manual workers.[36] This conservatism is explained by Centers as the greater tendency of white-collar workers compared with manual workers to identify with the middle class. The result is that:

> Among the white-collar workers, this self-labeling makes a greater difference in attitudes—65 percent of the 'middle-class' white-collar workers have conservative socio-economic attitudes, compared with 38 percent of the 'working-class' white-collar workers. Among manual workers, subjective class identification makes much less difference in attitudes—37 percent of 'middle-class' manual workers have conservative attitudes, compared with 25 percent of the 'working-class' workers.[37]

Those who use opinion surveys to evaluate employee communication programs should consider the effect on attitudes of the self-labeling of social class by employees.

SOCIAL CLASS AND COMMUNICATION

A person's status and social class affect his communication behavior. Among the dimensions of behavior that are affected are the persons with whom he communicates; the content of what he says; the frame of reference he uses for this content; the linguistic categories and stylistic devices he uses; and the function that he intends communication to serve.

gaining status through communication

How some basic patterns of communication are affected by status is seen in the results of a study of small groups by Harold H. Kelley. He experimentally created high-status and low-status subgroups for the purpose of studying the effect on communications within and between the two status levels. He also introduced the factor of mobility between the two status levels.[38]

The finding of greatest interest in Kelley's experiment is that communication serves as a substitute for belonging or being able to move into a high-status position by low-status persons who have little or no possibility of promotion. This tendency was particularly evident in the amount of task-irrelevant content that low-status persons communicated to high-status persons (as well as low-status ones). Irrelevant messages consisted of suggestions for getting better acquainted, wondering about the real purpose of the experiment, and expressing dissatisfaction with the job.

The last type of message—communicating negative attitudes about their own job—was significantly more frequent than with high-status persons. The high-status persons apparently restrained themselves in addressing criticisms of their own job to the lower status group. This restraint was greatest among those who were told that demotion to a low-status position was possible. The factor of mobility may well alter a person's subjective identification with a particular status, and as his reference group does, so does his communication behavior.

Another finding by Kelley is that high-status persons restrain themselves against expressing confusion with their task—a fact that might show incompetence in their handling of responsibility. Barriers to such communications help to preserve the authority relationships that exist in an organization. Recognition of a status leads to efforts to preserve such status. The field of consumer behavior offers other examples of how communication relates to status. Product advertising is replete with art work and copy that hint of status enhancement through product ownership. Persons depicted in ads serve as the Joneses with whom Americans proverbially try to keep up. And the Joneses do not have to live next door, for as George Katona points out, "Our standard of behavior, and of consumption as well, may be determined by reference groups to which we do not belong rather than by face-to-face groups." [39]

Chapin's 1927 analysis of social class was based on the material life styles of people. He observed the presence of various household items and rated them.[40] As expressed by Kahl, the assumption is "that people symbolize their own class values by the way they furnish their living rooms, and that their friends in turn judge them by the symbols they observe." Plus points were given for such items as hardwood in contrast to softwood floors, and the presence of bookcases filled with books, newspapers, periodicals; negative points were given for alarm clocks and sewing machines. While criticisms can easily be made of Chapin's system, the purpose is simply to indicate how status can be ascribed on the basis of different possessions.[41]

Since the affluent 60s when more Americans have been able to afford standard packages of consumption goods, many kinds of possessions such as television sets and refrigerators can no longer be used as a basis of class differentiation. Furniture, wearing apparel, and other items that put one's taste and one's knowledge of correct status symbols on trial still, however, relate to social class.

Shopping in certain stores is itself a status symbol. An "inferior-class" person may, for example, visit a high-status store and thereby at least temporarily assimilate some of the store's taste. But there are penalties in shopping where a person does not "fit" in a social-class sense. An example cited by Pierre Martineau tells the story:

> In a study of department stores and shopping behavior, it was found that the Lower-Status woman is completely aware that, if she goes into High-Status department stores, the clerks and other customers in the store will punish her in various ways. "The clerks treat you like a crumb," one woman expressed it. After trying vainly to be waited on, another woman bitterly complained that she was loftily told, "We thought you were a clerk." [42]

The style of advertising helps the individual to make a class identification. The super-sophisticated, clever ads appearing in the *New Yorker* and *Esquire* may be obscure to inferior-class people. The same may be true of different styles of radio and television commercials. That there is a relation between class and communication becomes apparent.

status differences reflected in communication

Another study sheds light on the relationship between social class and communication. An analysis of differences in how people in the lower class and middle class expressed themselves in describing a disaster situation was made by Leonard Schatzman and Anselm Strauss. They found differences between these classes striking, and concluded: "Communication across group boundaries runs the danger—aside from sheer language difficulties—of being blocked by differential rules for the ordering of speech and thought." [43] The differences that went beyond the factors of intelligibility, grammar, and vocabulary were in the number and kind of perspectives used by a person, his ability to take the listener's role, his use of classifying or generalizing terms, and his use of devices of style to order and implement communication.

A lower class person tends to describe an event as seen through his own eyes in a straight, direct, narrative manner. He uses *they* and *we* without clear referents, and uses few qualifying, illustrative, or summary statements. His reference is to acts and persons of particular people, not of categories of people. His frames of reference are limited and he uses crude temporal connectives like *then, and,* and *so.*

A middle-class person may describe an event from the perspective of another person or organization; he uses many devices to supply context and to clarify meaning; his use of concrete imagery is overshadowed by the abundance of conceptual terminology; and he tends to impose overall frames of his own to structure his comments.

Both general and specific recommendations flow from studies like the above. Generally speaking, the need is reinforced for every communicator to consider the field of experience of his audience and to remember that cross-class communication has its own built-in barriers. Specifically, a persuasive communicator must not delude himself in thinking that the mere application of a readability formula will adjust a message to the field of experience of the reader. Dissimilarities between the writer's and reader's ethnic origin, family upbringing, education, place of residence, work experience, and social life will obstruct communication. Besides a readability formula to measure the difficulty of meaning, a writer must consider cultural aspects of words. In part, these aspects deal with the connotation of words as measured by a semantic differential test. But for the fullest removal of cultural barriers, a writer must be like a good novelist who has lived in the same social contexts as the characters he depicts. There may be some arguments in favor of choosing writers from the ranks of marginal men—men who stand between two social classes that attempt to communicate with each other.

17

blending interpersonal and mass communications

A communicator does not have to choose between interpersonal and mass communication but can blend them. The whole range of these forms of communication should be seen as available in the preparation of a media mix. The blending should be based on such considerations as the size and composition of the audience reached by a medium and the power of each to inform, persuade, and evoke action.

Thus the fact that several media reach the same audience should not be judged as redundancy in the media schedule but as a way of blending the performance capability of each medium into a mix that will achieve desired results. For example, one medium may inform and create favorable predispositions; another medium, usually some form of personal influence, may win acceptance of an idea and produce action.

SUPPLEMENTING THE MASS MEDIA

That the mass media by themselves have limited effect in conveying information, changing attitudes, and influencing behavior is a generally accepted conclusion. Joseph T. Klapper summarized some of the arguments for this position when he said: "mass communication ordinarily does not serve as a necessary and sufficient cause of audience effects, but rather functions among and through a nexus of mediating factors and influences. These mediating factors are such that they typically render mass communication a contributory agent, but not the sole cause, in a process of reinforcing the existing conditions." [1]

In an article dealing with "propaganda for social objectives," Lazarsfeld and Merton made a similar observation. Success of propaganda efforts, they said, depends on the presence of three conditions: (1) monopolization, (2) canalization, and (3) supplementary face-to-face contact. Monopolization helps a campaign because counterpropaganda is eliminated or minimized. This happens when the media are controlled by one group or no motive for opposition exists, as, for example, in many fundraising efforts. Canalization implies that basic attitudes and values are not changed; a campaign accepts and uses existing behavioral predispositions by simply applying them to the propagandist's limited and presumably compatible objectives. The need for supplementation by face-to-face contact not only demonstrates the limited effectiveness of the mass media but the desirability of the blending principle. [2]

the two-step flow

The need for supplementary face-to-face contact and influence is the crux of the theory of the two-step flow of mass communications. It was first formulated in *The People's Choice*, a study by Lazarsfeld, Berelson, and Gaudet of the 1940 presidential campaign. Candidate preference and vote decisions, it was discovered, were based more on face-to-face communication and influence than on the mass media. Information disseminated by the mass media to what was presumably the general public was first picked up by opinion leaders and only then transmitted to the general public. These leaders exceeded nonleaders in exposure to the mass media and were more highly interested in the campaign than followers. [3]

This two-step flow theory was later elaborated upon in Katz and Lazarsfeld's book, *Personal Influence—The Part Played by People in the Flow of Mass Communication*. [4] It was a rediscovery of people, of the role and relevance of interpersonal relations, not only in public affairs but marketing, fashion, and movies. As summarized by the authors, "The whole moral of these chapters is that knowledge of an individual's interpersonal environment is basic to an understanding of his exposure and reactions to the mass media." [5]

The description of who served as opinion leaders and what functions they performed was earlier discussed in Chapter 14. At this point, however, the distinction betwen the influence function and the relay function of opinion leaders must be restated. Katz and Lazarsfeld focused on the transmission of influence, not only of information. Other studies that demonstrate the need to combine mass media with interpersonal communication deal only with the transmission of information or "news."

One group of such studies concerns public knowledge of events of great public significance. As summarized by Walter Weiss, "Roosevelt's death and Kennedy's assassination were known by more than two out of three people within the first fifteen to thirty minutes after they were made public by the media; and 95 percent or more were knowledgeable within the first hour and a half." [6] With regard to Kennedy's death, approximately half the general public were first made aware of Kennedy's death through radio and television, and the other half—more likely late receivers of information—through personal sources. Many of the latter, however, turned to the broadcast media for further news and confirmation.

Another group of studies which shows the supplementary role of interpersonal communication is that of S. C. Dodd and his associates. These are studies of the diffusion of messages on civil defense contained in leaflets dropped on American communities from airplanes. The findings deal with such variables as these: how rapidly a leaflet message is disseminated to various percentages of community households, who serves as the carriers of information, and to what extent the stimulus (frequency and density of air drops of leaflets) must be increased to achieve greater communicative effect. [7]

One of the significant findings is the clear dependence on interpersonal networks. This dependence is higher when few leaflets are dropped (low redundancy condition) than when many are dropped (high redundancy condition). Under the low redundancy conditions, "nearly two-thirds of the knowers come in contact with the information through social channels," while under conditions of high redundancy, one-half of the knowers learned the message via social diffusion channels. An incidental finding was that young people under sixteen were more likely to transfer the information by word-of-mouth than were older people.

It is findings like this one that led DeFleur and Larsen, associates of Dodd, to write:

> In more recent times it has been realized that mass media information is received, passed on, distorted, assimilated, rejected, or acted upon in ways which are in part determined by the operation of various social and social-psychological systems at various points of transmission and reception as the flow of information takes place. Therefore, for the student of mass communication the operation of primary groups, role structures, voluntary associations, personality variables, and vast complexes of other variables related to the operation of 'diffusion networks' have become a new research domain. The developing model of the operation of the mass media couples the mass communication process to the social networks of family, work, play, school, and community. [8]

the diffusion process

The combination of the mass media with interpersonal communication is most prominently demonstrated in the diffusion process. This is a type of decision making over time which involves the acceptance and utilization of an idea by an individual. Rogers defined the diffusion process as the communication of an innovation (a new idea) from one individual to another in a social system over time.[9] The theory was developed by rural sociologists who were concerned with the adoption of new agricultural practices such as the use of hybrid corn seed.[10]

We can view the diffusion process as an extension of the two-step flow. What is different is that the diffusion process emphasizes the final stage of adoption and not just the relay function by which an individual receives new ideas from any relevant source and passes them along to others.[11] With regard to the multi-step flow of information and influence, the two-step flow model often ends up being a multistep one in which mass media messages may travel through several layers of personal relationships before reaching intended audiences or wider publics. Furthermore, our designation of media must be more flexible and comprehensive. When speaking of mass media we should sometimes think of other formal, impersonal communications such as professional meetings and publications; and when speaking of interpersonal communications we should sometimes distinguish between local and outside sources or between friends and professional peers.

The diffusion process considers five stages along with the sources of information as expanded and distinguished above. These are summarized below.[12]

Stage in the Diffusion Process	Sources of Information (Media)
1. *Awareness:* exposure to an innovation but lacking complete information about it and lacking motivation to seek further information.	Impersonal or nonlocal communications—usually involving mass media or such sources as specialized and technical media, technical personnel, salesmen, and governmental personnel.
2. *Interest:* motivation to seek additional information; cognition stressed.	Personal communication increases in importance as compared to first stage.
3. *Evaluation:* weighing of advantages and disadvantages of an innovation in order to decide whether or not to try.	Personal communication most important—primarily from local peers but also from change agents.
4. *Trial:* probationary use of an innovation on a small scale by an individual in order to determine its utility in his own situation.	Commercial change agents are most important at this stage, principally for early adopters.
5. *Adoption:* individual decides to continue full use of the innovation.	Individual experience with trial.

The stages represent a logical sequence of rational decision making. They may, however, be rearranged or omitted in such special situations as the presence of coercion, unusual trust in a change agent, or despair with current practice.[13]

The categories of the five stages have to some extent been discussed in another context, for they can be compared to phases in attitude change. In *Communication and Persuasion,* for example, the analysis of experiments in attitude change is often made in terms of whether the audience: (1) attended to the message; (2) understood it; and (3) accepted it.[14] The attention phase is roughly equivalent to the first awareness stage of adoption; the understanding or comprehension phase to interest; the acceptance phase to evaluation; and the action phase to trial and adoption.

The information sources associated with each stage of the diffusion process are differentiated by Rogers chiefly by whether they are impersonal or personal, and, second, by the kind of personal source employed, that is, whether it is a cosmopolitan or local source. The impersonal media, chiefly mass media, contribute mostly to making people aware of an innovation; in a sense, they provide preliminary information. Although impersonal media are also useful in the interest or knowledge stage, personal communications begin to enter. There is presumably a motivational element as well as an informational one in such personal communications. These reach a peak in the evaluation stage where, as Rogers points out, people would rather believe people than facts. In the final two stages—trial and adoption—social influence continues to play an important role, but an individual's own experience with the innovation predominates if such experience can be satisfactorily interpreted by him.

Of special significance to advertising and public relations is the role that change agents play in the evaluation and trial stages. A change agent is defined as "a professional person who attempts to influence adoption decisions in a direction that he feels is desirable."[15] Technical assistance workers in industrially underdeveloped countries, county extension agents, detail men of pharmaceutical companies who promote medical drugs with physicians, and salesmen and dealers of new products are cited as examples by Rogers. A change agent has much in common with a gatekeeper in that both serve to link separate social systems or networks together.

But when a gatekeeper is a commercial change agent, his integrity is questioned by the people he seeks to change. His vulnerability is best understood by seeing him in a conflict situation: he is responsible to the bureaucracy that pays him, but he must simultaneously satisfy the need of the so-called local client system—the people he seeks to influence. His credibility is impaired if he appears to execute the demands of the bureaucracy while disregarding the expectations of the client system.[16] This happens to a commercial change agent when people feel that he promotes the "over-adoption of new ideas to secure higher sales."[17] These findings suggest that a public communicator's credibility will be low when he is seen as ignoring the interests of a public in favor of his employer's interests.

Two applications of the diffusion process illustrate the concept. The first example is in the medical field, where drug companies play an aggressive role in disseminating information about new drugs, and the second example is an agricultural marketing program in the Philippines.

The adoption of the drug *gammanym* excellently demonstrates the role of interpersonal communication in the diffusion process. Sixty-seven percent of the 141 doctors who were interviewed said that their first source of information about gammanym came from personal contact rather than literature.[18] The drug companies obviously played a large role, for the detail man was given credit by 57 percent of all the doctors; and with regard to literature sources, 18 percent of them referred to drug house mail and another 4 percent to drug house periodicals. As suggested by our review of the role played by different media in the first stage of awareness, colleagues played a small role—only 7 percent of the doctors first heard about the drug from other doctors.

But this and other diffusion studies dramatically show that "mere possession of information concerning the availability of an innovation is almost never a sufficient cause to explain its adoption." [19] In the adoption of hybrid seed corn among Iowa farmers, a study shows that while over 90 percent had heard of the new seed by 1934, less than 20 percent had tried it by then.[20] With gammanym, doctors acted quickly after learning of the new drug, but only 10 percent acted on the basis of one source of information; the other 90 percent reported that two or more media contributed to their decision.[21]

The role of different media at different stages in the diffusion process is further shown in the "interest" stage and the "evaluation" stage. In the interest stage the informal channels (such as neighbors and friends), agricultural extension agencies, commercial channels, and so on played a role equal to the mass media.[22] And in the evaluation stage the informal and more professional sources of information predominate.[23] Thus a sharp distinction must be drawn between media that "inform" and those that "legitimate" action.

The importance of a doctor's colleagues is shown in the identification of which doctors were early adopters of the drug. Those who were most closely integrated in the medical community—that is, who were the more frequently named by colleagues as a friend or a discussion partner—were more likely than others to be innovators with respect to the new drug. The authors of this study conclude that the importance of integration is explained by two central factors: "(1) interpersonal communication—doctors who are integrated are more in touch and more up-to-date; and (2) social support—doctors who are integrated feel more secure when facing the risks of innovation in medicine." [24] As an example of social support, it was discovered that doctors were more likely to prescribe the same drugs as their sociometric colleagues when called upon to treat more puzzling diseases.

The second example of the application of the diffusion process is a case study of an agricultural marketing program in the Philippines. A subsidiary of Esso Standard Eastern, Inc. sought to win support of Filipino farmers, distributors, and civic organizations for expanded use of chemical fertilizers. Along with constructing adequate production facilities and a widespread distribution system, plans were made to win farmer acceptance of fertilizers. These plans included the following:

1. *Dealer relations.* Dealers and independent businessmen were selected and trained to help in the marketing of fertilizers. These persons were chosen from local community leaders who were either agriculturists or very knowledgeable in agriculture. This feature of the plan acknowledges the role of personal communications in the adoption process and the criteria considered important in selecting these commercial change agents. Emphasis is given to the local characteristics of these opinion leaders but an effort is made to add agricultural expertise. These dealers are particularly important in stages two, three, and four of the adoption process.

2. *Field demonstrations by "farmer cooperators."* Throughout the Philippines, leading farmers were invited by company agronomists to participate as farmer cooperators in a series of field demonstrations. These selected farmers were asked to grow their crop in their usual way in one plot and raise the same crop, fertilized according to company specifications, on an adjoining plot. Field days were conducted as soon as the effects of the company's recommendations had shown visible proofs. Neighboring farmers were then invited to see actual field results. This feature of the plan emphasizes the trial stage, although it is a vicarious experience for observing farmers. At least they can "see for themselves" and to the extent that the local farmer has credibility based on local community membership the experiment would be believed. Government agricultural representatives are also invited to act as resource persons in field days and farmer meetings.

3. *Publicity.* A combination of mass media and interpersonal communications were used to disseminate the results of the company's farm demonstration program. Radio, print, brochures, and other point-of-sales materials were used. Movies were made of the processes involved and the results of farm demonstrations. These were shown during farm meetings.[25]

summary

The blending of the two major media approaches—interpersonal and mass communication—is not only a possibility but a requirement. In theory, as pointed out by Lazarsfeld and Merton, and in practice, as shown by the University of Washington studies and a lobbying situation, a prudent combination of both approaches is desirable.

The resultant process calls attention to the local contexts of attitude change that starts with information and ends with adoption or rejection of an idea. The goal, then, is to fulfill some purpose; the means are the media that are selected.

SUBSTITUTING FOR THE MASS MEDIA

The review of theories of how the mass media are supplemented by interpersonal communications helps to free the communicator from rigid, stereotyped approaches to audiences and media. The modern communicator must be flexible and imaginative in his approaches if he is to be effective in solving new, complex communications problems.

The new challenges facing communicators are numerous. Two are discussed below. The first is in pressure group communications. As the role of government grows in our economic system, business reacts by countervailing methods such as inaugurating or intensifying pressure group activities. The second is in finding substitutes for the mass media when they are unavailable or prohibited by government or social sanctions.

pressure group communications

The right of a citizen "to petition the Government for a redress of grievances" is a highly organized activity known as lobbying. The major technique involved is communication of some kind. Lester W. Milbrath defines lobbying as "the stimulation and transmission of a communication, by someone other than a citizen acting on his own behalf, directed to a governmental decision-maker with the hope of influencing his decision."[26] Such activities are here called pressure group communications.

Two strategies of communication are often treated as opposing alternatives: to create a favorable climate of public opinion for a given issue through appeals to the general public, *or* to influence legislators and other decision makers through intermediaries. Restated in media terms the alternative is between the mass media or interpersonal communication.

Milbrath compares these and other approaches to lobbying. Attempts to set the stage or create the climate within which government decisions are made are called public relations campaigns. These he finds less efficient and more costly than other methods, but very effective when they are big and clever campaigns.[27] Attempts to approach decision makers through constituents and friends are discussed as another technique. A part of this technique, approaches by constituents, is rated higher than other techniques by the most knowledgeable lobbyists, those who have had experience on the Hill or who are on a legislative relations staff.[28] Both the public opinion strategy and the opinion leader strategy have their merits.

When a really important lobbying matter arises these should not be seen as mutually exclusive approaches. On the contrary they should be combined. This strategy was demonstrated in the classic case of Du Pont's divestiture of 63 million shares of General Motors stock. To avoid penalization of stockholders who would have to treat receipt of shares as dividends received and for other economic reasons, Du Pont sought legislation from Congress to amend the tax laws so that distribution of stocks would be appropriately based on a return of capital.

The Du Pont public relations staff and management, as described by Harold Brayman, decided upon a dual approach. The first approach was not to work through intermediaries but for the then president of Du Pont, Crawford H. Greenewalt, directly to talk to leaders of Congress in both parties and practically all of the members of the House Ways and Means Committee and the Senate Finance Committee.[29]

Speaker John W. McCormack of Massachusetts was so impressed with this approach that he said substantially the following to a friend of his:

> You know, Clarence, I've just had a most refreshing experience with a businessman. He was the president of the Du Pont Company, Crawford H. Greenewalt, and it was the first time in the 30-odd years that I've been a member of Congress that the head of one of the six or eight largest corporations in the United States came to my office to talk directly with me on a problem that gave him concern. It was about the recent decision of the Supreme Court in the General Motors case.
>
> He came straight to the point without beating around the bush, without talking about his maiden aunt who had gone to the same school with my mother, or anything of that sort. He was forthright, he knew the facts, and he explained them clearly.
>
> I listened attentively, and he persuaded me of the justice of his case. And after he left the office, I trotted down the hall to the office of Wilbur Mills [Chairman of the Ways and Means Committee] and said, "Wilbur, the president of the Du Pont Company has just been in to see me about the problem he has as a result of the recent Supreme Court decision, and he has persuaded me his case is a good one. I think, Wilbur, you should get this bill out before your committee and consider it carefully; and if you and your committee agree with me, get it out on the floor so we can vote on it." [30]

Harold Brayman, in commenting on the advantages of this approach, says that "not only are principals more effective in dealing with principals in governmental matters than anyone else can be, but it is only by this method that there can be created in government circles the confidence in business integrity and the faith in sources of information which make it possible to secure favorable action." [31]

Aware that legislators could not act if their constituents were hostile to what was sometimes called the "Du Pont tax relief bill," normal, national media outlets were used to create a favorable climate of opinion. Many years of public relations investment in creating a good public image of Du Pont was considered a help in this effort. Stockholders too were given attention and kept informed of developments. Many of these stockholders wrote to Congressmen and kept Du Pont informed of replies received.

This case study in Du Pont's pressure group communications demonstrates the value of combined personal and mass communication approaches.

substitutes for the mass media

National mass media, particularly network television, constitute an ideal form of communication whenever the American general public is the target audience. Political campaigns by presidential candidates and advertising campaigns by national brands are the classical examples. What would a candidate or national advertiser do if national television coverage were unavailable? This is not just a rhetorical question, for the treasuries of some political candidates have been limited. In the case of national advertisers, some have deliberately avoided national television—the liquor industry, for example—and others such as the tobacco companies are contemplating doing the same. What, then, are the alternatives?

Conglomerate Mass Media. As an alternative to a single national mass medium—namely, network television—a conglomerate of other media can be scheduled that will reach the same size audience. Leaving out the development of cable television, which collectively may in the future reach all the homes that television networks now do, conglomerate mass media would mainly use the print media, chiefly newspapers and magazines. The combination of local audiences and of specialized audiences receiving professional or various special-interest publications would reach almost as many households and individuals as do television or radio. Although Marshall McLuhan's glorification of electronic media can be accepted and the printed media seen as comparatively "flat," new creative possibilities are being explored by visual communicators.

Crowds and Concentrated Flows of People. The next best alternative to conglomerate mass media is the sum of large crowds. Every theatre, sports stadium, cinema, convention or concert hall, church, school, factory office, or open space where large numbers of people assemble qualifies. These confined environments can be categorized and ranked in terms of size of audience, frequency of attendance, composition of audience, the possibility of disseminating messages, and the appropriateness of the event and place for particular types of messages. Among the media that might be used are playbills and other programs, posters, sky-writing, blimps, lapel buttons, and pickets.

In some cases, companies selling consumer products have sponsored special shows as a vehicle for advertising and supplementary good will. Schlitz, for example, reached a total of half a million people in New York City in twelve concerts at six parks in 1965. Jazz festivals have drawn as many as 200,000 young people.

Another way of conceptualizing a crowd is to think of rapid, concentrated flows of people. In a given hour or day large numbers of people travel on certain highways and cross busy intersections; use air, train and bus terminals; ride on planes, trains, busses or trolley cars; park in shopping centers and garages; and visit tourist attractions.

The conventional media of billboards and posters are most appropriate for flows of people. They can be reinforced by multimedia approaches through light and sound techniques.

Finally, the automobile should not be ignored because it is the most widely used means of transportation and is used many hours weekly. It should be seen as a highly confined physical space in which family members and friends sit for many minutes or hours at a time. The concept of media should include such devices as messages on tape cassettes, road maps, touring guides, and various accessories such as coin or cigarette dispensers.

Social Groups. What we earlier considered as a supplement to the mass media under the heading of the two-step flow can also be considered as an alternative for the mass media. The many kinds of social groups include most persons, for virtually everyone belongs to a primary family and work group. In the United States we also have numerous secondary groups such as voluntary organizations to which about 55 percent of Americans belong. While this approach is undoubtedly complicated and time-consuming, it is theoretically a plausible substitute for reaching national audiences.

To cover a wide audience, an enormous range and number of activities with regard to these social groups must be undertaken. Family groups might be penetrated by placing messages on food containers and packages, printing messages on games played at home, or on household accessories such as telephone book covers and ash trays. Church groups might be reached through bingo games and church fairs.

This burden can be substantially reduced by identifying social groups that have a high multiplier—that is, whose members are opinion leaders who transmit to others and whose recommendations are accepted by them.

The interplay of interpersonal and mass communication has been particularly evident in this last of five chapters on the sociology of communication. All the chapters, however, serve to expand on these two concepts of interpersonal and mass communication. Besides establishing the framework for Part III, Chapter 13 examined the dimensions of social interaction in a social relationship between two persons; Chapter 14 did so in the small group setting. In Chapter 15 we viewed the total society in terms of communication within and among organizations and associations and in terms of reaching mass audiences and its subgroupings. Chapter 16 placed a magnifying glass on one of the ways of classifying social groupings—namely, on a social class basis. Finally, in this chapter we saw how all the approaches could be blended.

18

the media of communication

The media of communication are the avenues over which messages reach an audience. They may be viewed in technical, transportation terms: What routes can best carry what load and types of cargo to desired destinations at what costs? The goal is to get the cargo to the receiver without spoilage, damage, or loss. In this sense, the media should ideally function as passive conduits for messages.

But "the medium is the message," Marshall McLuhan has declared.[1] He would have us believe that it is not what is said that counts but the medium through which it is said. The medium becomes master over the content.

McLuhan overstates his case to gain recognition for the active role played by the media. A reasonable interpretation of his assertion is that the media interact with messages to shape the experience of the audience. Each medium has a preference for certain content and affects the attitude of the viewer. For example, television is seen as a "cool" medium because its low definition requires audience participation; radio is a "hot" medium for the opposite reason.

The publicity that McLuhan has given to the media makes it clear that more than technical characteristics of media must be considered. Since we are mainly interested in the persuasive impact of communications, media characteristics will be viewed in psychological terms.

This approach was favored by Carl Hovland in his chapter, "Effects of the Mass Media of Communication," which appears in the *Handbook of Social Psychology*. After discussing the effects of individual media on general behavior and the comparison of one medium with another in terms of achieving some desired effect, he stated his preference for a different approach: one that emphasizes the particular facts which differentiate the media from one another.

These factors, based on psychological processes that explain human behavior, are: "(a) attracting and holding an audience, (b) providing information, (c) changing attitudes and opinion, and (d) inducing action along particular lines." [2] This basic outline will be followed in the discussion below.

ATTRACTING AN AUDIENCE

Attention is the factor that serves as the connecting rod between a medium and the intended audience. This is why the power of a medium to attract an audience is a primary consideration.

The communicator is chiefly interested in two questions: (1) What proportion of the population do different media reach? (2) What kind of people are attracted to which media? Most of the information available on these questions concerns the mass media.

size and composition of audience reached by different media

When the communicator uses the mass audience approach he assumes that these media reach most if not all the people in a given geographical community. Fortunately, this assumption is true. According to a study by the University of Michigan's Survey Research Center, all but 1 percent of private dwelling units are covered by at least one of four mass media: newspapers, magazines, radio, and television.[3] Furthermore, half of the dwellings in this nation-wide survey are reached by all four of these media.

Looking at the media individually, the availability and "reach" of the various media in 1969 was as follows:[4]

—Daily newspapers: 1,752 newspapers with circulation of 62.5 million.
—Weekly newspapers: 9,326 with 18 million circulation.
—AM radio stations: 4,321 stations.
—FM radio stations: 2,181 stations.
—TV stations: 666 stations; 84.6 million sets in 95% of American homes.
—Cable TV: 2,000 systems reaching 3 million homes.
—Movies: 19,000 theaters.

These statistics are, of course, relevant only to show the potential audience that can be reached by different media. The problem of selecting specific newspapers, magazines, television programs, and so on still exists.

These decisions involve various methods of media selection which will be discussed in the next chapter.

In most communication situations it is important to know what *kind* of person is reached by a medium, as well as how many are reached. Audience composition is typically described in terms of demographic variables such as age, sex, marital status, education, occupation, religion, place of residence, and ethnic and racial background.[5] Most advertising and opinion survey studies refer to these variables.

Media usage varies among persons of different demographic descriptions. Among some of the main findings are these: [6]

(1) *Age.* In general, the world pattern is that media use tends to increase from childhood to middle age and then drops off slightly. Newspaper reading, for example, reaches a peak somewhere between the ages of thirty and fifty. Movies are somewhat an exception to the general pattern because usage is at a maximum in the teens and then drops off. A survey by the Opinion Research Corporation, for example, states that "almost three-fourths (72%) of the admissions during the survey week (June and July, 1957) were people under 30 years of age and 52% were under 20." [7]

(2) *Sex.* The high status of women in America is reflected in their being slightly heavier users of the mass media than men. The Survey Research Center study shows that the percentage of women users is from 2 to 8 percent higher than male users. In other Western countries men show their superiority by at least being heavier users of newspapers than women (although women maintain their lead in the use of radio). In Arab countries and southeast Asia, extremely low status of women is shown in the fact that they read and listen considerably less than men.

(3) *Education.* Usage of mass media tends to increase with education. This is easily explainable for newspaper and magazine consumption because literacy is an audience qualification. Most nonreaders are in the "grade school and lower" category. It may surprise some people that the pattern of increased usage with education also applies to television, that is, the television audience is not overloaded with viewers of less education than the national average. Radio listening, however, is different; it readily reaches people in lower educational levels.

(4) *Income.* The pattern here is about the same as with education. Radio again appears as the best way to reach the low-income groups. Magazines, on the other hand, are consumed by higher income groups. Price is an important factor. This reason also helps to explain why the higher income groups make the best showing as "multiple media users."

(5) *Religion.* One of the most interesting findings is that people of the Jewish faith are the highest media consumers.

(6) *Region.* With the exception of movies, the percentage of non-users of the mass media is highest in the South.

(7) *Urban-rural.* People in rural areas tend not to use the media as much as city people. When further breakdowns are made, it is found that usage is highest in communities of intermediate size, for example, in the suburbs, rather than in the largest cities.

the degree of attention aroused

The media consumption habits of people tell only part of the story. A person may be "linked up" with a medium, yet the link may be thread thin. Whether a thin, casual connection as contrasted to a thick, solid one exists determines the kind of message that can effectively be communicated through a given medium. If the object is to remind people of some company name, the thread-thin connection is adequate, but if the object is to get new facts or associations across, "thicker ply" will be required. These connecting links refer to the degree of attention aroused by a medium. The following factors help to explain the attention-arousal power of a medium:

(1) *Flooding the Senses.* A medium that surrounds us with stimuli obviously leaves us with little choice but to attend. Movie screens that encircle us and stereophonic sound systems that bombard us are bound to capture our attention. To what extent this advantage of multimedia presentations can be extended to individual media is difficult to say. Film floods our senses more than television, and television more than radio. Whether several rather than one of our senses is used is one way to measure the attention-arousal capacity of a medium. The fullness and intensity of each kind of stimulus must, of course, also be considered. The real test is the extent to which a medium leaves us free to perform a competing activity, such as driving while listening to the radio.

(2) *Conditions of Viewing.* Although the situation surrounding a viewer may not seem to be a medium characteristic, it must be considered if certain situations are more associated with a given medium than others. A billboard at a train station, for example, commands a lot of attenton if there is nothing else to look at or do. The subway traveler who hangs on a strap and is pinned between two other passengers probably has memorized every word of the poster at which he is forced to stare. This is the true

definition of a captive audience situation: no alternative is left open except to attend to a designed message.

(3) *Immediacy of an Event.* When a medium seems to have the power to transport the viewer to the source of the event, the communications situation becomes more compelling. A news event seen live on television makes a situation seem real, immediate, and alive. Not a pseudo-environment, but an actual one involves the attention of the listener and viewer.

POWER TO CONVEY INFORMATION

Once contact with an audience is made, and its attention held, the objective is to convey the desired information. The scope and complexity of the information must be examined to determine the media characteristics that are necessary. Five are particularly important.

(1) *Sense Modality Involved.* A chief difference among media is that they present different sensory stimuli. Print involves the eye, radio the ear, television and sound film both. The question is whether the burden of conveying certain kinds of information is better handled through one medium than another. Chapter 11 reviewed some of the major findings about the comparative advantages of the visual and auditory channels as reviewed by Joseph T. Klapper and others.[8]

Perhaps, as Erwin P. Bettinghaus points out, it seems reasonable to suggest the hypothesis that the communicator ought to make use of as many senses as possible in communications since people gain all the information they have through the senses.[9] Unfortunately, the studies made by physiologists and psychologists on the subject of multiple communication channels are either too technical to be of much practical value, or simply reinforce well-known techniques. For example, a voice is helpful in describing and directing an audience's attention to unfamiliar objects in a visual display.

The communicator will probably find that the material with which he works in most situations dictate which sense modalties must be used. Occasionally, however, he faces special problems. A picture of raw rubber, for example, will never convey what the product really looks like in a research laboratory. There is a smell, texture, and vibration to butyl rubber that requires direct experience. When this is the case, the communicator must extend his thinking about media. He must consider the open house, the plant visit, and the traveling display. Whether he realizes it or not, he is thinking about which sense or combination most effectively achieves his objectives.

(2) *Presentation of Motion.* Some information is most efficiently conveyed by the use of motion. If the object is to show how something is assembled, for example, a training film is a preferred medium. In one film design, the technique of "implosion" was profitably used. Each part of an assembly was shown separately and then "jumped" into place from the display by animation.[10] This is truly making use of the motion picture.

(3) *Audience Control of Exposure.* One reason complex material is often taught better by print is that the reader is able to follow his own pace. He can look back whenever he wants; he can read some parts rapidly, other parts slowly. The viewer, in other words, has control over the presentation of material. This feature is an aid to learning.

Such individual control is primarily a characteristic of printed material, but it can also be applied to other media. For example, the Air Force has developed a "Handy Dandy" projector which enables the assembly man or student to look at a film or a single frame as long as he wants and therefore pace his own learning.[11] Teaching machines also possess this feature. In contrast, classroom lectures provide only a slight opportunity to control the pace. Members of the audience can frown or raise their hands and thus signal the speaker to slow down or repeat.

Control is at a minimum with the broadcasting media. Immediate feedback from the whole audience is not feasible. An effort to duplicate the results is made, however, by the use of live studio audiences and by the incorporation of criticism of past performances into future performances.

(4) *Accuracy of transmission.* Especially when legal or accounting information is involved, accuracy of transmission is essential. Accuracy can mean two things. The first is that the same symbol the sender transmits is reproduced at the receiving end—$1,000 appears as $1,000 at both ends. This might be called technical accuracy. Another form of accuracy is semantical. What counts is whether the intended meaning is transmitted.

The printed media are unquestionably superior in the technical sense of accuracy. Word for word, figure for figure, and picture for picture a message is reproduced as intended. Similarly with the broadcasting media, the words and images that appear in one home are the same as those in another—assuming that the receiving sets are in good condition.

But the reason school classes are held despite the existence of books and other mass media is that books do not always succeed in getting their meaning across accurately. Active two-way communication is often necessary. The teacher must test the knowledge of the pupil; the pupil must ask for clarification when needed. Face-to-face situations are superior for semantical accuracy.

(5) *Active Versus Passive Conditions of Learning.* The more involved a person is and the more he participates in the communication process, the greater the likelihood of learning. To a large extent, the media with wider sense modalities, such as movies, seem to involve a person more.

Also important is the extent to which a response is required of the viewer or listener. One of the advantages of the teaching machines is that the student knows he must respond with an answer. In addition, he is given the opportunity to repeat a response.[12]

WINNING ACCEPTANCE: CHANGING OPINIONS AND ATTITUDES

Understanding is one thing, acceptance another. If a medium possesses attributes that not only create understanding but lead to audience acceptance of a suggestion as well, then this medium has an advantage over others. One of the attributes that may be operative is the prestige of the medium. No general conclusion can be drawn, however, except that the prestige attributed to a medium varies with particular audiences, the degree of politcal control associated with the medium, and the novelty of it.

Closely associated with the prestige of the medium is the extent to which the credibility factor is given scope to operate. A radio speech by a recognizably trustworthy person is probably more credible than the same speech read by an unidentified person. This is because the radio is an aural medium that has the capacity to convey some qualities of the speaker's personality and intent as well as his content. This factor can easily be manipulated. For instance, it has been suggested that some national leaders might appear much more trustworthy and powerful if only the voice were heard than if they were also seen on a television screen.

Acceptance is also dependent on many social factors. In what social context is a newspaper read, or television watched, compared to movie-going? To what extent is instantaneous feedback present so that the speaker can alter his appeals to suit the audience and the mood?

Although these considerations go far beyond the media, the way in which media can involve different social situations should be recognized. Sometimes a social influence is introduced into an impersonal medium by reminding people that they are part of a larger listening audience. A desired social context can also be arranged by selecting an appropriate distribution channel for printed media. An employee publication sent to the home will be read in a family context, while distribution in the plant will involve working relationships, besides possibly wasting company time.

Finally, the temporal factor must be considered. People are in different moods during different times of the day or week or year; they have different energy levels in the morning, the afternoon, or evening, and they also have different motivations operating. A sleeping pill ad, for instance, should obviously appear around midnight and not in the late morning.

Most of these considerations involve proper placement and scheduling of a communication within a given medium. But different media provide greater discretion and certainty of timing than others. A message on radio or television will reach people at a precise time of the day and week; the same message in a daily newspaper will probably reach most people within the day but not necessarily; messages in magazines will likely be read over a longer time span.

INDUCING ACTION

The real test of the effectiveness of a communication must be found in how people's behavior is influenced by it. Media must be examined for the opportunities that they provide to induce action. The communicator's control over the time and place of exposure is sometimes relevant. Suppose, for example, that the management of an outdoor museum located outside of Boston wants to increase attendance. It might succeed by using a medium that will trigger a spontaneous decision by people to make the museum their destination for a Sunday drive. A Sunday morning announcement on the radio following the news and weather report may serve as this trigger. Radio here permits the proper timing. Similarly, a road sign reaches people in a situation that might be conducive to a desired action. The generalization is that a medium that can reach people at a time and place close to the "moment of decision" has the power to induce action.

In the above example, an existing motivational structure was assumed. There are other situations in which the power of a medium to add motivational elements is crucial. The power of the face-to-face medium comes largely from the fact that pleasing the other person becomes an end —a motive—in itself. A person may vote only because he knows that some friend with whom he had a political discussion will ask whether he voted.

The same mechanism of rewards and punishments that other people provide helps to explain the effectiveness of getting people to make a public commitment in a group situation. Kurt Lewin's classical experiment showing the superiority of a group decison over the lecture method for producing a change in food habits is partly explained by this factor.

In internal communications, the power of using line management as a primary or supplementary channel of communication is similarly explained by the authority relationship which is involved. When a foreman speaks on safety, the rules are more likely carried out than if a safety director who only occasionally appears does so.

Another factor that must be considered is the existence of an appropriate "social mechanism" through which an individual can express himself, that is, translate his attitudes into action. Wiebe points out that one factor in successful commodity advertising is the existence of a retail store—the social mechanism. But, he asks, what should a citizen do when he is urged to form neighborhood councils to combat juvenile delinquency? Listeners are unrealistically expected to form their own social mechanisms without the help of "blueprints" suggested by the media.[13]

19

media selection and placement

A knowledge of media characteristics serves as a background for the specific decisions and activities of media selection and placement. The aim of media selection is to choose a specific medium or combination of media that will reach the desired audience with the kind of message needed to achieve objectives. A media schedule is the usual way to summarize the decisions made.

Media placement is the presentation of materials to a medium for publication, broadcast, or other form of dissemination. When the medium is controlled by someone other than the communicator, the rules governing acceptance must be known and followed. These rules must particularly be observed with publicity materials for which no advertising fee is paid. In such cases, a communicator must really keep two audiences in mind: the ultimate target audience and the gatekeepers who control access to this audience.

MEDIA SELECTION: CONCEPTS AND METHODS

The typical approach to media selection is to list all of the media alternatives available. For some purposes the entire range would include interpersonal as well as mass media. But in the fields of advertising and public relations, media selection is usually restricted to the mass media and specialized periodicals read by segments of the public.

These media are typically classified in terms of the human senses or technical characteristics of the media. We speak of visual, aural, and audio-visual media; or of the printed word, the spoken word, and the image. Every communicator must prepare his own list and keep it updated. Robert C. O'Hara in *Media for the Millions* classifies newspapers and mass periodical literature as printed media, feature films and documentaries as filmed media, and radio, television and recordings as electronic media.[1]

Such a listing is usually accompanied by suitable descriptions which are applications of the media characteristics discussed in the previous chapter. For example, radio is granted the advantage of speed of transmission over print but the latter allows a reader to set his own pace.

Beyond such a general introduction to the media, two more specific steps must be taken. One is the preparation of a media strategy; the other is the media schedule itself.

media strategy

The media strategy relates media selection to other elements of the communications process, primarily the objectives and the target audiences, showing what role the media are expected to play.

For example, an investment promotion office in the United States of a small foreign country sought to interest American businessmen in constructing factories in its country. It decided that advertisements were a way of attracting such direct investments. The target audiences selected were chief executives of manufacturing companies and the heads of their international and marketing divisions. Special attention was to be given to executives in those selected industries which the country most wanted to attract. Another audience was to be specialists in banking who advise clients on investments and foreign situations.

The media strategy stated that two functions could be performed by the mass media and business publications: to direct attention to the current investment opportunities in the country, and to confer status upon the investment promotion activities. The advertisement part of the total promotion program could subsequently fall into two phases: the attention-getting and status-conferral phase, and the tactical support phase for field activities. The first phase concentrated on general business publications that were prestigeful and reached an internationally minded group of executives and on other specialized business publications that reached influential persons in connection with foreign investment decisions. The second phase concentrated on business publications in specific industrial fields and on regional newspapers.

After this kind of thinking and strategy statement, the stage was set for the preparation of a media schedule.

media schedule

The media schedule lists the names of newspapers, magazines, broadcast stations and programs, and other media; it also specifies facts about dates and times when an advertisement or commercial is to appear, size of the ad or length of the commercial, audience reached, total media cost, and cost per reader or viewer. Many variations in the details included appear.

For the investment promotion example given above, the media proposed were as follows:

A. Generalized Business Audience
   1. *Wall Street Journal*
   2. *Business Week*
   3. *New York Times*
B. Specialized International and Banking Audience
   1. *Business Abroad*
   2. *Bankers Monthly*
   3. *Banking*
C. Specialized Industry Audiences (some examples)
   1. *Chemical Week*
   2. *Iron Age*
   3. *Textile World*
D. Regional Audiences (some examples)
   1. *Chicago Tribune*
   2. *Pittsburgh Post-Gazette*
   3. *Dayton News Journal Herald*

Specific media information is obtained from basic reference manuals and from information directly provided by a publisher or broadcaster. Among the most widely used information sources are: [2]

—Ayer's Directory of Newspapers and Periodicals—Covers the U.S. and its possessions, Canada, Bermuda, Cuba, and the republics of Panama and the Philippines. Other information: population of states, cities, towns in which publications appear, frequency and type of publication, lists trade, technical, farm, and foreign language publications. Maps, statistics.

—Bacon's Publicity Checker—Enables user to reach by mail or telephone more than 4,300 press contacts, magazine editors, daily newspaper business/financial editors, and news services and syndicated columnists. List only those publications known to use publicity material. Each maga-

zine listed has been coded by its own editor to show types of publicity material used.

–Standard Rates and Data Service—Has separate sections: business paper section, general magazine section, newspaper section and radio-TV section. Gives advertising rates and includes circulation figures and other information related to these media. List of all publications participating in Audit Bureau of Circulation or Controlled Circulation Audit.

–Editor and Publisher International Year Book—Directory of newspapers—daily newspapers of the U.S., Canada, Great Britain, Latin and Central America, and other foreign countries, foreign language papers in the U.S., Negro newspapers, newspaper and advertising associations, clubs, stations affiliated with newspapers. Gives personnel, advertising rates, circulation of daily papers in the U.S. Schools and departments of journalism.

–Gebbie's House Magazine Directory—Covers 4,000 house magazines in the U.S. Listed alphabetically under name of issuing company or organization which is briefly described. Facts include name, address, editor, printer, type of print, frequency, length, and circulation figures, along with an analysis of subscribers and a description of content.

–The Working Press of the Nation—Lists personnel of newspapers, radio and television stations, news magazines, newsreels, syndicates, columnists, feature writers, and so forth.

media selection systems

Tremendous progress has been made in recent years in electronic data processing as well as in use of mathematical models in studying various forms of decision making.[3] Some of these techniques have now been applied to the process of media selection. Several systems will briefly be reviewed to illustrate the possibilties of electronic data processing in the field of public communication.

One system of media selection is a logical extension of an individual's attempt to list the periodicals, newspapers, and other media of special merit with regard to a client's communication problem. Such lists are simply combined into one huge "master list" with appropriate indexing and cross-indexing. This is what Public Relations Aids, Inc. has essentially done. They describe their media system as follows.

> Public Relations Aids has the only comprehensive public relations media system in the world. It covers more than 50,000 trade journals, consumer magazines, Sunday supplements, specialized editors of dailies, weeklies, syndicated association newsletters and house organs. It is the result of two years' intensive study by experienced public relations men, and is kept up-

to-date by a staff of full-time research assistants. Mechanized in accordance with modern data-processing principles, the system breaks down the media into some 2000 categories, sub-categories and cross-categories for speedy, highly efficient selection. The Public Relations Aids media system can be used for release mailings, for press conference invitations, and as placement contact file.[4]

This then, is basically a giant filing system, constantly kept up-to-date, that uses categories which are practical for public communication purposes. The principles but not necessarily the equipment of electronic data processing are used.

A second system of media selection is made possible by the existence of such giant filing systems in combination with computer storage of information. By using equations in conjunction with mathematical models, various kinds of media selection problems can be described, analyzed, and solved. The problem might, for example, be to allocate a limited budget to a media schedule that theoretically would reach the widest audience. Such a problem can easily be rephrased as one of "optimization" and can be solved through the use of linear programming. *Printers' Ink* describes this process as follows:

The linear model merely examines the equations that describe a particular situation in the computer for every possible combination of media; it then selects, from the many millions of possible combinations, the one that provides the maximum number of exposures for a given budget size. The computer then prints out a list showing the media selected and the number of insertions in each medium.[5]

The actual process involved, however, is not quite as simple or objective as it sounds. The computer must store such relevant information as the size and type of audience attending to a medium and weights must be assigned to such factors as the difference in effectiveness between a four-color and a black-and-white ad. Not all variables and values can economically be stored, so human judgment is not entirely eliminated. But by quantifying most variables, the media schedules can quickly be displayed and judgment applied.

Besides linear programming, another mathematical model called "Simulmatics" can be employed. It is a computer method of simulating different decisions and strategies. It makes pretesting an idea possible before it is actually put into operation. Here is how a media-mix simulation works. A computer would store information on about 3,000 individuals who have various demographic characteristics. The distribution of these characteristics is representative of the actual population—as reflected, for example, by U.S. Census sources. Besides this information, each individual represented in the computer has his unique media habits assigned in a manner to match previous survey findings. Each of thirty-five magazines, each of two hundred television programs, each of 160 newspapers, for example, is used or not used by individuals with their own unique frequency. Further information such as the exposure probabilities for different times of the day, by day of week, by page or size of ad or story, and so forth, can be added.

Once this information is stored, a given communications campaign can be simulated and an estate made of how much comes through to each individual. As summarized by Ithiel de Sola Pool in a speech given at the 15th National Public Relations Conference:

> The simulation consists essentially of holding up the media output to the audience and recording what part gets through to whom. Its use is to answer what-if questions about what would be changed if you used a different set of media in your campaign. One can run each of several alternative propaganda campaigns to see what reach is achieved by each.[6]

There is considerable disagreement among communication experts as to the value of electronic data processing and mathematical models for such purposes. Among the objections raised are that the formulas that must be used may eliminate some judgmental factors, perhaps the crucial ones, and that the weights given to factors in the formula tend to be fixed even though each situation requires a separate weighting schedule. Progress in the computer field is so rapid, though, that many of these problems will be overcome. As long as the benefits of eliminating hunches and guesses exceed costs, electronic media selection systems will gain in use and acceptance. There will still be lots left for humans to do both as feeders and programmers of computers and as judges of computer results. The psychological aspects of media choice are sufficiently complex to require human intervention.

MEDIA PLACEMENT

The most severe test of media placement is faced by the public relations man who wishes to have his publicity materials accepted by media editors. For this reason most of the comments will deal with his problems and experience. He often uses the term media relations for this step in the process of communication.[7]

A newly appointed public relations man is for this reason advised to become acquainted with the newspaper editors, local broadcasters, wire service editors, and others upon whom he is dependent. What the public relations man should seek to discover is what Warren Breed calls the medium's policy: "the more or less consistent orientation shown by a paper, not only in its editorial but in its news columns and headlines as well, concerning selected issues and events." [8] Such a policy reflects not only a medium's concept of how it should serve its readers but also its built-in biases. These preconceptions, prejudices, stereotypes, and ideologies may be those of a particular editor or publisher or they may be embedded in the traditions and practices associated with the institutional framework of a medium.

The literature of communication usually includes material dealing with the history and operation of the press, radio, television, and film. This knowledge is valuable to the extent that a communicator can better adapt his messages to the needs and practices of these media. The generalities learned must, however, be supplemented with specific knowledge about the personal preferences and biases of specific editors. This is why media experience is so often required as a qualification for public communication work.

Even with this experience, the communicator should review the more common tensions that arise between him and media people. William M. Pinkerton's article, "Businessmen and the Press," [9] is helpful in this respect. Pinkerton covers many subjects: newsworthy business events or occasions in which newsmen have expressed special interest; personal factors which affect the relations between businesses and newspapers; attitudes of editors toward "free space" requests; attempts by businessmen to suppress unfavorable news and to influence editorial opinion; and a list of guides in dealing with reporters.

Many of Pinkerton's themes are explored further in an Opinion Research Corporation survey, "The Press and Business." [10] The importance of media relations is emphasized because some of the most critical comments by the press are made about public relations agencies where one might expect the best media relations. Unfortunately, one of the complaints that newspaper editors have about public relations agencies is that some lack knowledge of newspaper practices and problems. They do not have what newsmen call "good news sense." More serious problems listed in a survey made by Opinion Research Corporation are that they "have insufficient knowledge of company and its personnel; they are "an unnecessary step in the information flow"; they "cause delays in getting information"; and they "provide inaccurate, distorted information." No wonder that 40 percent of the 228 editors interviewed felt that there was no advantage in dealing with public relations agencies.

On the other hand, when advantages of dealing with public relations agencies were listed, the following comments were included: better understanding of newsman's views, cooperation, broader outlook, better preparation of material, accessibility. The value of an agency obviously lies in how good it is. And its value is measured in terms of how helpful it is to the media while remaining dedicated to the best interests of the client and having particular knowledge about his organization and activities.

The essence of media relations is to establish and maintain contact with the working press and to develop a mutual understanding of each party's objectives, needs, and problems. The news and magazine editors know that companies want to project their images, and business editors recognize their possible influence on the reputations of the companies they write about. What editors ask for is greater cooperation; a free flow of honest, accurate information; a more liberal definition of legitimate requests for information; more personal contact with responsible executives; greater promptness in dealing with the press; and competent public relations people. Newspapermen are highly critical of the refusal by companies to talk on some topics, especially those that are controversial. Among the things companies should not try to withhold are: production and financial statistics; information on labor disputes, strikes; accidents, wrecks, fires; changes in management; employment figures; pricing information, price changes; and relocation or closing of plants.

On the other hand, editors feel that a company would be justified in refusing the following: to release information that would place it at a competitive disadvantage; prematurely to announce new products and developments; to give personnel information about executive salaries, scandals, or personal matters concerning officers; to release various kinds of confidential financial information, and classified military information.

The Pinkerton article and Opinion Research Corporation study demonstrate the value of paying close attention to the crucial contact between a client organization or a public relations agency and the media whose cooperation is sought. While some general principles help to improve the relationship, these must be supplemented with specific information.

media relations services

Media relations service organizations make it their business to keep posted on what is desired by specific editors, writers, and producers connected with different media. Subject headings, a certain slant, deadlines, and other information are collected. Some services then pass on this information so that public relations men can properly prepare their own materials and submit them; other services may offer to prepare the materials and to get them placed.

One of the services of Public Relations Aids, Inc. is a chatty newsletter called "Party Line" which is distributed to its clients. Here are some examples of its contents:

Oscar Schisgall, free-lance writer, is preparing an article for a national magazine on ways in which American business uses flowers for good-will and other business purposes. If you have statistical data or anecdotes on any clients of yours doing this, send Schisgall a note at 85 East End Avenue, New York 28.

***

Offbeat items on a wide variety of subjects—something kookie, or on the way to popularity—are wanted for LOOK Magazine's feature, "For Women Only" and "For Men Only." Louis Miano, who handles the feature, alternates a general idea page with a theme page. Here is his upcoming schedule:
     Gardens: hints on what to wear while gardening, etc.—deadline March 1 . . .[11]

Another kind of service is provided by such organizations as the North American Precis Syndicate.[12] The story that a client wants told is prepared—either by himself or the service agency—as a feature story in a variety of ways. The features of all the clients are periodically assembled in a collection called *Precis*. A copy is sent to a wide list of editors—including editors of company publications and other often neglected publications. The editors choose whatever features they want by referring to a code symbol. The service then notifies the client to supply the material. *Precis* thus serves a centralized marketing function in bringing clients in contact with editors. The service is suitable for certain kinds of material when the client is willing to leave the choice of media and its implied audience up to others.

Public relations consulting firms will sometimes provide their own specialized media services. Carl Byoir & Associates, Inc., for example, has several departments that serve in a media relations capacity: Business & Financial, Contact & Placement, Magazine, and Radio-Television. These departments not only give advice to account executives but also provide regular news services to media. News concerning a client of Carl Byoir & Associates is included with nonclient-related news. An example of such a service is "People, Spots in the News." Carl Byoir & Associates is willing to provide this weekly news picture mat to editors as long as it does not conflict with any other paper in their area. These mats typically contain four attention-getting pictures and captions. One of the four items will contain client news. Another example is a weekly business news program called "Parade of Business" which is provided without cost to about 360 radio stations. Here again, news about a specific client is included with general business news items.

The military services also provide media relations services in a few major media centers such as New York City and Los Angeles. These offices handle the dual function of servicing the media and communication industries and of providing the military with media contacts. An advertising agency might, for example, request a photograph of a supersonic bomber from the Air Force. In such a case, the account executive would be asked to visit the Air Force's field office and select the photograph that suits his purpose. An Air Force officer would be on hand to answer questions and offer advice. From the viewpoint of military public relations, such services satisfy the requirements that the public be kept informed. Further public relations objectives can, however, be promoted to the extent that initiative is taken in interesting the media in messages of concern to each service.

The key to these various kinds of media relations services is that a point of contact is provided between a source of information and the media of communication. This contact becomes viable to the extent that the needs of the different media are met while at the same time advancing the interests of the source of information.

evaluation of media relations

The difference between satisfactory and unsatisfactory media relations may mean the difference between using somebody else's communication channels and providing one's own. It may also determine whether free or paid space is provided. It comes as no surprise, therefore, that many attempts at evaluating public relations concentrate essentially on media relations measures: the number of contacts made with different media, the number of placed items that appear in different media, and—in the case of more sophisticated approaches—a content analysis of how a particular story was edited or told.

FIVE

evaluation:
comparing
results
with
objectives

20 research as a planning and evaluation tool

Anyone who deliberately selects and prepares designs for persuasive communication automatically engages in research. He does this whenever he consciously sets out to collect information about something in a dependable, systematic way, for that is the basic meaning of research.[1] Guesswork about relevant facts and their interrelationships is replaced as much as possible by provable statements, principles, and theories.

In the physical sciences these scientific statements are highly accurate, exact, and valid. Research techniques are highly refined and of the formal variety. The social sciences try to emulate these standards, but the task of understanding and predicting human behavior in a complex, changing environment is exceedingly difficult. But even imperfect scientific statements are superior to individual guesses.

Communication research is a special application of social science research. The techniques of social research are simply applied to the kinds of problems facing communicators. These are the ones associated with the process of communication as discussed in this book and reflected in the communications model.

Research is a tool for planning and evaluating communications. The focus is on communication objectives, stated in terms of what behavior is ultimately expected from specific individuals or audiences. It also considers all the efforts or steps in the communication process, such as design of the message and choice of media. Evaluation is a comparison of actual effects or results with the intended ones as indicated in the statement of objectives. These factors can be presented as follows:

OBJECTIVES   EFFORTS   EFFECTS

Sender   Message   Media   Audience   Behavior

In the uses discussed below some types of research will refer to several factors while others will concentrate on only one or part of one. The research design must be flexible and study the most critical factors.

DEFINING THE PROBLEM AND OBJECTIVES

The broadest type of study is needed to assess the nature of a communications problem and to decide upon objectives. Such a study is often simply labeled "opinion research" because this technique measures the most important variable with which persuasive communication is concerned. Other terms such as "corporate image study," "communications audit," or "public relations audit" are also used but in more specialized senses.

opinion research

Opinion research is most widely used in public relations applications.[2] Since World War II a sizable number of corporations have tried to determine whether the public was actually friendly or hostile. The public relations professional learned that the opinion survey could be a valuable tool. As stated by Leo Bogart in "Use of Opinion Research":

> It permits him to size up a situation objectively and dispassionately. It gives him a means of singling out the strong and weak points of his company's position; it tells him the arguments used by friends and critics; it shows where the friends and critics are concentrated, what else they believe, and through what media they might best be reached.[3]

Gauging reactions to an existing public issue is not the only function of opinion research; it can "focus management's attention on public relations questions or problems to which it may not normally be sensitive."[4] Robert Carlson refers to the "monitoring function" of opinion research whereby management's positions and views can either be confirmed or reoriented.[5] He also points out that research can clarify questions for management by sensitizing it to the opinions of groups of the population that are not normally articulate or to "spell out some unexpected distortions—either management's or the public's—which creep into the perception of the issues." [6]

Opinion surveys can be repeated at timed intervals so that trends can be established. These trends may be influenced by various current events and public moods, and these should be taken into account when interpreting the findings.

corporate image studies

One kind of specialized opinion survey is a corporate image study.[7] At least three categories of questions are typically included: (1) familiarity or awareness questions which determine to what extent, if any, a corporation is known; (2) favorability questions which measure the direction and intensity of how well people like a corporation; and (3) personality trait questions which try to show how the corporation differs from others in terms of such dimensions as progressiveness, friendliness, and profitability.

While the sample for a corporate image study may be the general population it more frequently is limited to specific publics such as a local community, the corporation's stockholders, security analysts, employees, and opinion leaders. In addition to the above three question areas, special questions probe into the criteria used by each public to judge the corporation.

audience identification studies

The key variable in some communication problems is the identification of the target audience. For example, a marketing program to sell computers or any other specialized industrial product must be aimed at the individuals who make purchase decisions for their organizations; similarly, a lobbying campaign must reach the decision makers as well as those intermediaries who influence these persons. In some areas, particularly politics, the persons or groups who are decision makers and opinion leaders are known because of previous intensive and published studies.[8] But when this information is unavailable a special audience identification study must be undertaken.

A variety of techniques may be employed for this purpose, opinion research being one of them. The basic method, however, is to analyze the process of decision making in whatever area is being investigated. A marketing study of men's underwear might seek to discover what role women play in buying underwear for their husbands or sons; a pharmaceutical company wants to know what doctors will serve as opinion leaders in the adoption of a new drug; a Peace Corps worker tries to identify village leaders who can persuade others to adopt new sanitary practices. Library research dealing with past decisions, sociometric research that shows who talks with whom about what, and survey research that asks questions about who does what and influences whom with regard to a decision are all pertinent methods for the purpose of audience identification.

MESSAGE ANALYSIS

Although messages prepared for persuasive communication are highly creative productions, aspects of them can be analyzed. The main technique used for this purpose is content analysis; another is the study of audience reactions to specific messages. With both techniques attention is focused on variables discussed in earlier chapters: facts, themes, arguments; psychological associations and feeling tone; and appeals to individual and social motives. In short, we are interested in looking for any message variables that the theories and principles of social psychology suggest as critical in persuading people. Content analysis looks for the presence of these variables; audience reaction studies look for people's awareness of these variables.

content analysis

Content analysis is defined by Bernard Berelson as "a research technique for the objective, systematic, and quantitative description of the manifest content of communication." [9] When a journalist describes the content of a newspaper in terms of such subject-matter categories as "domestic affairs," "politics," "labor," "crime," "economic and business news," and so forth, he is using elementary content analysis procedures. If he now extends beyond the use of descriptive categories and provides quantitative facts about the proportion of a newspaper spent on these different subjects, he is making greater use of content analysis techniques. He might go even further by telling us how the stories are slanted.

Three uses of content analysis are of primary interest in persuasive communication. The first is to audit the message content against objectives. [10] For example, a company's new employee communication policy might be to increase the amount of business and company news and to reduce the amount of social news. A simple subject-matter analysis over a time period would serve as a check. A second use of content analysis is to study the presence of propaganda techniques and through the use of expert judgment decide whether their use will enhance the acceptance of the message. A final use of content analysis is the measurement of the readability of messages.

Although readability is sometimes treated as a separate research technique, it is a form of content analysis which examines the factors that distinguish material that is easy or hard to read or comprehend.[11] Early readability tests focused on what words were "easy" or "hard," as indicated by such standard word lists as Thorndike's. Current readability tests, such as Rudolf Flesch's, concentrate on sentence length, use of personal pronouns, and affixes. Readability scores are related to the reader's educational level—that is, as the educational level rises the level of difficulty may also rise. This correlation, however, applies only to general readers and general interest and does not take their special interests and experiences into account.

audience reaction studies

Persons can be shown a message and asked what stands out, what meaning they get from it, and other ways they react to it. In other words, we can pretest a message with a sample of the target audience we want to reach.

One of the most widely used tests of this kind is the Starch Impression Study. It is described as "basically a qualitative service that tells advertisers what meanings people find in advertisements and how much importance they attach to these meanings." [12] The Daniel Starch organization claims that the value of these studies has been demonstrated for answering such important questions as these:

—What image of our company and our product does the advertisement communicate?

—Do illustration and copy work together or clash?

—Do the product features which we are highlighting give us a competitive advantage? Are these features important to readers?

—Do most readers find the same meanings in our advertisement—the meanings we want them to find?

Another useful audience reaction technique is the semantic differential test.[13] It is specifically designed to test the connotative meaning of words—or other distinguishable stimulus such as a picture or sound. The connotative meaning refers to the psychological reaction or "feeling" that a person gets from the word or other stimulus to which he is reacting. The different ways in which a person can humanly react are measured in what is called the "semantical space."

Three major dimensions of this semantical space are typically measured. The first is the evaluative dimension which is roughly the equivalent of what we call attitudes: how favorable or unfavorable something is considered. The second dimension is potency: the concern with power and associated concepts of size, weight, and toughness. The third dimension is activity: the concern with quickness, excitement, warmth, agitation, and the like. Other dimensions such as stability, tautness, novelty, receptivity, and aggressiveness have also been measured, but these account for only a small part of semantic space.

MEDIA RESEARCH

The aim of media research is to measure how well the media perform in conveying messages to intended destinations. We want to know how deeply the arrow representing the media in diagrams of communication models actually penetrate the target audience. The question is not only whether contact is made but how much attention is given to the media and the messages they carry. The compilation of circulation and other media distribution figures is a beginning, but more severe measures must be supplemented.

readership studies

Readership studies are basically concerned with measuring the eye traffic over written materials. Is a particular newspaper or magazine read? Are some pages or sections read more than others? How many people read a copy? And who are these people? In short, readership is a measure of the size and composition of the audience attending to specific written materials.[14] Distinctions must be made among various kinds of readership studies and surveys. Sometimes the circulation figures for newspapers and magazines are used as an approximation of readership. The Audit Bureau of Circulations (A.B.C.), for example, verifies and provides circulation figures of member newspapers and magazines with paid circulations. These figures, however, do not take into account how many persons read a single copy of a magazine; a readership survey conducted by such organizations as Daniel Starch and Staff is needed to ascertain this.

A second distinction is the severity of the test of readership presented to the audience. Taking a person's word that he has read something is different from asking if he remembers anything about the content. Furthermore, the person who can recall something without help from the interviewer (unaided recall) is going through a more severe test than a person who is shown a list from which he can recognize something (aided recall).

broadcast ratings

The equivalent of readership in the field of radio and television are the broadcast ratings.[15] These provide two primary kinds of data: (1) coverage in terms of the total number of households that could be or are reached by particular networks, stations, or channels within each county or group of counties in the United States, and (2) ratings and other related indexes of audience size for a particular program. The second kind of data is the same as the first except that it is applied to a program.

A distinction must be made between potential and actual coverage. Potential coverage is estimated on the basis of total homes in a given area, homes owning one or more radios or one or more television sets, or homes whose occupants report an ability to receive a particular signal within a given audience or market area. Actual coverage is estimated from reports of tuning or listening or viewing behavior. These reports are for specified periods of time: a month, week, day, or parts of a day.

Most of the differences in the various broadcast rating systems— Hooper, Nielsen, ARB, Trendex, Pulse, Singlinger, or Videodex—are based on the modes of measurement or the means of interview used. Reliable information about these differences can be obtained from the federal government in a report entitled *Evaluation of Statistical Methods in Obtaining Broadcast Ratings*.[16] Various levels of severity of testing are involved in the different ratings. The Nielson system, for example, relies chiefly upon a meter installed in the radio and television sets of a sample of households. This meter can only measure whether the set is on and to what channel it is tuned; it cannot determine whether the set is being viewed or listened to.

press clipping and broadcast monitoring services

Because a public relations man has no guarantee that the news releases and other materials he sends to the media will be accepted, he needs some measure of his success. The "clipping book" and figure of the total number of items or column inches that have actually appeared in the various media are a convenient index.

Commercial clippings services provide a convenient and inexpensive means of keeping track of articles in newspapers and magazines that mention a client, a product, or some subject of interest. The three major clipping enterprises are Burrelle in Livingstone, N.J., Luce in Mesa, Arizona, and Bacon in Chicago. Burrelle and Luce are concerned primarily with newspapers and secondarily with trade, technical, and professional publications; with Bacon it is the reverse.

Broadcasts cannot, of course, be picked up in the same manner as written material. Some sort of monitoring system must be established. For items that are expected to appear in specific programs, personal monitoring is possible. It is also possible for an organization with personnel in relevant locations to set up a monitoring schedule. There are, however, companies that provide services in monitoring broadcasts. References such as Alice Shelley's article "Radio and Television Publicity" list these.[17]

MEASURING THE EFFECTS

The ultimate test of the effectiveness of persuasive communication is whether or not audience behavior is influenced. Thus evaluation is the process of comparing actual audience behavior in designated activities with desired behavior as expressed in the communication objectives.

The results of communication activities may have to be measured by opinion research.

Desired behavior should be measured in as concrete and final a form as possible. The following list, for example, suggests some of the ultimate criteria that count in three communication areas:

Marketing communications—increased or at least sustained sales; building of customer loyalty as evidenced, for example, in resistance to price competition.

Employee communications—reduced absenteeism and turnover; better performance as ambassadors for the company; reduction in grievances and days lost through strikes.

Financial communications—maintenance of high price-earnings ratio; ease of floating new issues; high rate of proxy returns in support of management.

To demonstrate the evaluation process, the communications model is sometimes modified into a feedback or "cybernetics" model.[18] The idea of cybernetics is the attainment and maintenance of a given goal—to steer ever closer to the desired objectives so that the ultimate deviation from it is zero.

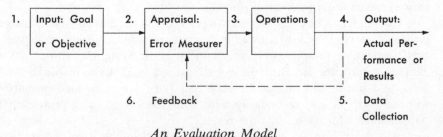

An Evaluation Model

The figure above shows the main elements in this model. The key and characteristic element is the feedback loop. This loop makes evaluation or appraisal possible because the actual performance (4) of operations (3) is somehow measured, summarized, and transmitted (5 and 6) to a point (2) where performance can be compared with objectives (1) and the extent of the error measured.

Whether expressed in such rigid fashion or not, every organization contains many similar control systems so that management can guide its operations. These systems show whether certain operations are justified and whether the greatest return is being obtained for the expenditure of money and other resources. It is an application of this model that Stanley Baar suggests for public relations when he writes it must be able to answer these questions:

1. How much does this activity contribute *specifically* to the attainment of business goals? What specific goals?
2. Are we getting our full money's worth for each of our public relations expenditures?
3. Is the overall cost offset by its accomplishments? Specifically, what accomplishments?
4. All of our public relations expenditures—how much do we really need them *and why*?[19]

No specific answer can be given about the kind of research techniques that are relevant to the process of evaluation. The key problem can, however, be pointed out. Performance must somehow be made measurable so that some data can be collected at point 5 on the figure above. In all areas of management, tremendous efforts are being applied to this problem.[20] These intensified efforts are necessitated by management's need for better control systems as operations become larger and more complex; these efforts are made possible by the revolution taking place in data processing and computerization. Communication cannot remain immune from this process.

CONCLUSIONS

Despite the demonstrated uses of research in planning and evaluating communications, many communicators resist research. Their usual argument is that research cannot displace the creativity and judgment so vital to successful communication.

The intention of research, however, is not to displace human creativity and judgment, but to assist it. After research provides knowledge and insight into the nature of a communication problem, creativity is required to interpret the findings correctly and to discover the practical implications. Judgment is similarly required, for the interpretation of data deals not only with facts that lend themselves to scientific investigation but with values that lie ultimately in the arena of human judgment.

Research certainly does try to replace guesses and hunches with ascertainable facts, but judgment should not be equated with guesswork. Whenever objective data can replace individual impressions, problem solving is enhanced and judgment given a greater opportunity for exercise.

In the final analysis, the value of research must be demonstrated in superior ideas and performance. Does research enable us to generate predictions about behavior? Does it enable us to see relationships between facts and to identify critical facts? Does it support the premises we use in planning or suggest alternative ones? Does it help organize our experience and knowledge into a framework that will be useful for future planning of communication designs?

If these questions can be answered in the affirmative, we shall forever be updating and refining the concepts and approaches discussed in this book.

notes

[1] This approach is used in the introduction to "Persuasion, Expression, and Propaganda," a chapter in Roger Brown's *Words and Things* (Glencoe, Ill.: The Free Press, 1958), pp. 299–341.

[2] Ibid., p. 299.

[3] Herbert A. Simon summarizes this argument in Chapter VII, "Authority," in Conrad M. Arensberg et al., *Research in Industrial Human Relations* (New York: Harper & Brothers, 1957), pp. 103–118.

[4] Kelman, *A Time to Speak: On Human Values and Social Research* (San Francisco: Jossey-Bass, Inc., 1968), see esp. pp. 12–14.

[5] Bauer, "Limits of Persuasion," *Harvard Business Review,* XXXVI (September–October 1958), 105.

[6] Bernays, *Biography of an Idea: Memoirs of Public Relations Counsel Edward L. Bernays* (New York: Simon & Schuster, Inc., 1965), pp. 387, 689.

[7] Berelson and Steiner, *Human Behavior: An Inventory of Scientific Findings* (New York: Harcourt, Brace, & World, Inc., 1964), p. 663, 664.

[8] Bauer, "Our Big Advantage: The Social Sciences," *Harvard Business Review* XXXVI (May–June 1958), 133.

[9] Berelson and Steiner, *Human Behavior,* p. 125.

[10] Vicary's experiment is discussed by Bachrach in "It's Subliminal, But Is It Ethical?" *Best Articles & Stories* (September 1960), pp. 50–53. Also see James V. McConnell, Richard L. Cutler, and Elton B. McNeil, "Subliminal Stimulation: An Overview," *American Psychologist,* XIII (May 1958), 229–42.

[11] Berelson and Steiner, *Human Behavior,* p. 95.

[12] Schramm, *Responsibility in Mass Communication* (New York: Harper & Brothers, 1957), p. 57.

[13] See Mills, *The Power Elite* (New York: Oxford University Press, 1956); Carl R. Rogers and B. F. Skinner, "Some Issues Concerning the Control of Human Behavior," *Science,* 124 (November 1956), 1057–66; Berelson and Steiner, *Human Behavior,* p. 666.

[14] Daniel J. Boorstin, *The Image* (New York: Harper & Row, Harper Colophon Book, 1961), p. 255.

[15] William J. McGuire, "Inducing Resistance to Persuasion: Some Contemporary Approaches," *Advances in Experimental Social Psychology,* I (1964), 192–202. A slightly abridged version appears in Richard V. Wagner and John J. Sherwood, *The Study of Attitude Change* (Belmont, California: Brooks/Cole Publishing Co., 1969), pp. 173–83. Also see Rogers and Skinner, "Some Issues Concerning the Control of Human Behavior," *Science,* 124, 1057–66.

CHAPTER 2

[1] Bernays, *Your Future in Public Relations* (New York: Richards Rosen Press, Inc., 1961), p. 91.

[2] Quote is from editors' introduction to Cox, "Clues for Advertising Strategists," in *People, Society, and Mass Communications,* ed. Lewis A. Dexter and David M. White (New York: The Free Press of Glencoe, 1964), p. 359.

[3] David K. Berlo, *The Process of Communication* (New York: Holt, Rinehart & Winston, Inc., 1960), pp. 23–39.

[4] The following books and articles present various communication models: C. E. Shannon and W. Weaver, *The Mathematical Theory of Communication* (Urbana, Ill.: University of Illinois Press, 1949); Wilbur Schramm, "How Communication Works," in *The Process and Effects of Mass Communication,* ed. Wilbur Schramm (Urbana, Ill.: University of Illinois Press, 1961), pp. 3–26; Wendell Johnson, "The Communication Process and General Semantic Principles," in *Mass Communications,* ed. Wilbur Schramm (Urbana, Ill.: University of Illinois Press, 1960), pp. 301–15; B. H. Westley and M. S. MacLean, Jr., "A Conceptual Model for Communications Research," *Audio Visual Communication Review,* III (Winter 1955), 3–12; G. Gerbner, "Toward a General Model of Communication," *Audio Visual Communication Review,* IV (Summer 1956), 171–99.

[5] As Berlo points out, these three elements agree with the Aristotelian model of: (1) the person who speaks, (2) the speech he produces, and (3) the person who listens. (From *The Process of Communication,* p. 29.)

[6] Schramm, "How Communication Works," p. 4.

[7] B. L. Smith, H. D. Lasswell, and R. D. Casey, *Propaganda, Communication and Public Opinion* (Princeton: Princeton University Press, 1946), p. 121.

[8] Hammond, "Public Relations Counseling," in *Handbook of Public Relations,* 2nd ed., ed. Howard Stephenson (New York: McGraw-Hill Book Company, Inc., 1971), p. 85.

[9] Lippitt, "Dimensions of the Consultant's Job," *The Journal of Social Issues,* XV (1959), 6.

[10] Robert K. Merton, *Social Theory and Social Structure,* rev. ed. (Glencoe, Ill.: The Free Press, 1957), pp. 60–82.

[11] Bernays, ed., *The Engineering of Consent* (Norman, Oklahoma: University of Oklahoma Press, 1956), p. 10.

[12] Howard W. Cutler, "Objectives," in Bernays, *Engineering of Consent,* p. 28.

[13] Ibid., p. 31.

[14] Ibid., p. 34.

[15] Carl Byoir's *Account Executive's Manual* (800 Second Avenue, New York, N.Y.).

CHAPTER 3

[1] For a discussion of the gatekeeper concept, see David M. White, "The 'Gatekeeper': A Case Study in the Selection of News," in *People, Society, and Mass Communications,* ed. Lewis A. Dexter and David M. White (New York: The Free Press of Glencoe, 1964), pp. 160–72.

[2] Walter Lippmann, "The World Outside and the Pictures in Our Heads," in *Mass Communications,* pp. 468-86.

[3] See George A. Borden, Richard B. Gregg, and Theodore G. Grove, *Speech Behavior and Human Interaction* (Englewood Cliffs, N.J.: Prentice-Hall, Inc., 1969), p. 199. Also see Kenneth E. Anderson and Theodore Clevenger, Jr., "A Summary of Experimental Research in Ethos," *Speech Monographs,* XXX (June 1963), 59–78.

[4] Carl I. Hovland, Irving L. Janis, and Harold H. Kelley, *Communication and Persuasion* (New Haven: Yale University Press, 1953), chap. 2.

[5] From Donald E. Payne, ed., *The Obstinate Audience* (Ann Arbor, Mich.: Foundation for Research on Human Behavior, 1965), p. 47.

[6] For an introductory discussion of theoretical approaches to the study of communications, see Alfred G. Smith, *Communication and Culture—Readings in the Codes of Human Interaction* (New York: Holt, Rinehart & Winston, Inc., 1966), pp. 1–10.

[7] Stuart Chase, *The Power of Words* (New York: Harcourt, Brace and Company, 1954); Samuel I. Hayakawa, *Language in Thought and Action* (New York: Harcourt, Brace, 1951); Benjamin L. Whorf, *Language, Thought, and*

Reality (New York: John Wiley & Sons, 1956); Charles Morris, *Signs, Language, and Behavior* (New York: Prentice-Hall, 1946); Roger Brown, *Words and Things* (Glencoe, Ill.: The Free Press, 1958); George A. Miller, *Language and Communication* (New York: McGraw-Hill Book Company, Inc., 1951); C. E. Osgood, G. J. Suci, P. H. Tannenbaum, *The Measurement of Meaning* (Urbana, Ill.: University of Illinois Press, 1957); A. Korzybski, *Science and Sanity: An Introduction to Non-Aristotelian Systems and General Semantics,* rev. ed. (Lancaster, Pa.: Science Press, 1941).

[8] Brown, *Words and Things,* pp. 323–26.

[9] Hammond, "Public Relations Counseling," in *Handbook of Public Relations,* p. 83.

[10] Rogers, *Client-Centered Therapy* (Boston: Houghton Mifflin Co., 1951).

[11] Kahn and Cannell, *The Dynamics of Interviewing* (New York: John Wiley & Sons, 1957).

[12] Ralph G. Nichols and Leonard A. Stevens, *Are You Listening?* (New York: McGraw-Hill, Inc., 1957).

[13] Nichols and Stevens, "Listening to People," *Harvard Business Review,* XXXV (1957), 85–92. Reprinted in Otto Lerbinger and Albert J. Sullivan, eds., *Information, Influence, and Communication* (New York: Basic Books, Inc., 1965), pp. 367–77.

[14] Norman Maier, *Psychology in Industry* (Boston: Houghton Mifflin Co., 1955), p. 600.

[15] Edward T. Hall, *The Silent Language* (Greenwich, Conn.: Fawcett Publications, Inc., 1959).

[16] Burger, "The Crucial Gap in Public Relations," *Public Relations Journal,* XVIII (April 1962), 18–21.

CHAPTER 4

[1] Charles Osgood, "A Behavioristic Analysis of Perception and Language as Cognitive Phenomena," in *Contemporary Approaches to Cognition* (Cambridge: Harvard University Press, 1957), p. 75.

[2] Cherry, *On Human Communication* (New York: John Wiley & Sons, Inc., 1957), pp. 6–7.

[3] Allport, "The Historical Background of Modern Social Psychology," in *Handbook of Social Psychology,* ed. Gardner Lindzey (Cambridge: Addison-Wesley Publishing Co., Inc., 1954), p. 43.

[4] T. M. Newcomb, R. H. Turner, and P. E. Converse, *Social Psychology* (New York: Holt, Rinehart & Winston, Inc., 1965), pp. 41–42.

[5] Allport, "Attitudes," in *A Handbook of Social Psychology,* ed. C. A. Murchison (Worcester, Mass.: Clark University Press, 1935), pp. 798-844.

[6] Krech, Crutchfield, and Ballachey, *Individual in Society* (New York: McGraw-Hill, Inc., 1962), p. 139.

7 William J. McGuire, "The Nature of Attitudes and Attitude Change," in *The Handbook of Social Psychology*, 2nd ed. Vol. III, ed. Gardner Lindzey and Elliot Aronson (Reading, Mass.: Addison-Wesley Publishing Company, Inc., 1969), 148.

8 Ibid., pp. 142–43.

9 Lane and Sears, *Public Opinion* (Englewood Cliffs, N.J.: Prentice-Hall, Inc., 1964), p. 11.

10 McGuire, "The Nature of Attitudes," in *Handbook of Social Psychology*, p. 155.

11 Rosenberg, "A Structural Theory of Attitude Dynamics," in *The Study of Attitude Change*, ed. Richard V. Wagner and John J. Sherwood (Belmont, California: Brooks/Cole Publishing Company, 1969), p. 107.

12 M. B. Smith, J. S. Bruner, and R. W. White, *Opinions and Personality* (New York: John Wiley & Sons, Inc., 1956), p. 39.

13 For a further discussion of canalization, see Paul F. Lazarsfeld and Robert K. Merton, "Mass Communication, Popular Taste and Organized Social Action," in *Mass Culture*, ed. Bernard Rosenberg and David M. White (Glencoe, Ill.: The Free Press, 1957), p. 470 ff.

14 Hovland, Janis, and Kelley, *Communication and Persuasion*, p. 6; and Eugene L. Hartley, Ruth E. Hartley, and Clyde Hart, "Attitudes and Opinions," in *The Process and Effects of Mass Communication*, ed. Wilbur Schramm (Urbana, Ill.: University of Illinois Press, 1961), p. 222.

15 Smith et al., *Opinions and Personality*, p. 47.

16 For an excellent discussion of the implementation step see B. R. Berelson, Paul F. Lazarsfeld, and William N. McPhee, *Voting—A Study of Opinion Formation in a Presidential Campaign* (Chicago: University of Chicago Press, 1954), p. 278.

17 Smith et al., p. 46.

18 Lazarsfeld and Merton, "Mass Communication, Popular Taste and Organized Social Action," in *Mass Culture*, p. 464 ff.

CHAPTER 5

1 Anthony G. Greenwald, Timothy C. Brock, and Thomas M. Ostrom, eds., *Psychological Foundations of Attitudes* (New York: Academic Press, 1968); particularly see Thomas M. Ostrom, "The Emergence of Attitude Theory: 1930–1950," p. 2.

2 McGuire, "The Nature of Attitudes and Attitude Change," in *The Handbook of Social Psychology*, pp. 136–314.

3 Hovland, Janis, and Kelley, *Communication and Persuasion*, p. 15.

4 Much material in this section is drawn from: "Four Fundamentals of Learning," chap. 2 in Neal E. Miller and John Dollard, *Social Learning and Imitation* (New Haven: Yale University Press, 1941), pp. 13–36.

[5] McGuire, *Handbook of Social Psychology*, pp. 167–71.

[6] For a review of the contribution of these individuals see Allport, "The Historical Background of Modern Social Psychology," in *Handbook of Social Psychology*, I, 3–56. Also see John W. Atkinson, *An Introduction to Motivation* (Princeton, N.J.: Van Nostrand, 1964).

[7] Atkinson, *Introduction to Motivation*, pp. 122–23.

[8] Ibid.

[9] Clark L. Hull was a leader among psychologists who emphasized drive reduction as a primary factor in learning. See Hull, *Principles of Behavior* (New York: Appeton-Century-Crofts, 1943).

[10] A good review of these two kinds of motives is in Berelson and Steiner, *Human Behavior: An Inventory of Scientific Findings*, pp. 241–56.

[11] Pierre Martineau, *Motivation in Advertising* (New York: McGraw-Hill Book Company, Inc., 1957).

[12] Abraham H. Maslow, *Motivation and Personality* (New York: Harper & Brothers, 1954).

[13] David McClelland et al., *The Achievement Motive* (New York: Appleton-Century-Crofts, 1953).

[14] David Krech and Richard S. Crutchfield, *Elements of Psychology* (New York: Alfred A. Knopf, 1958), p. 279.

[15] For a review of Ebbinghaus' contribution and a discussion of rote learning see Krech and Crutchfield, *Elements of Psychology*, pp. 409–24.

[16] Miller and Dollard, *Social Learning*, p. 29.

[17] In such a situation a number of parameters of reward may be useful to consider: quantity and quality, delay of reward, changes in amount or quality of reward, derived or secondary reward, and partial or intermittent reward. For a discussion of these see C. N. Cofer and M. H. Appley, *Motivation: Theory and Research* (New York: John Wiley & Sons, Inc., 1964), pp. 539, 560–66.

[18] N. E. Miller, "Learnable Drives and Rewards," in *Handbook of Experimental Psychology*, ed. S. S. Stevens (New York: John Wiley & Sons, Inc., 1951), p. 465. Referred to in Cofer and Appley, *Motivation*, p. 496.

[19] Cofer and Appley, *Motivation*, p. 497.

[20] For a review of Lewin's contribution to cognitive consistency theory see Ostrom, in *Psychological Foundations*, p. 12.

[21] Arthur R. Cohen, *Attitude Change and Social Influence* (New York: Basic Books, Inc., 1964), p. 62.

[22] For a review of the life-space concept see Krech and Crutchfield, *Elements of Psychology*, pp. 210–16; or Atkinson, *Introduction to Motivation*, p. 73 ff.

[23] McGuire, "The Current Status of Cognitive Consistency Theories," in *Cognitive Consistency: Motivational Antecedents and Behavioral Consequents*, ed. Shel Feldman (New York: Academic Press, 1966), p. 28.

[24] Ibid., pp. 10–14; also see R. P. Abelson, "Modes of Resolution of Belief Dilemmas," *Journal of Conflict Resolution,* IV (1959), 343–52.

[25] For a good introduction to Heider see Robert B. Zajonc, "The Concepts of Balance, Congruity, and Dissonance," *Public Opinion Quarterly,* XXIV, No. 2 (Summer 1960), 282–84. For original formulations, see Fritz Heider, *The Psychology of Interpersonal Relations* (New York: John Wiley & Sons, Inc., 1958).

[26] Zajonc, "Concepts of Balance," p. 286.

[27] The example is from Zajonc, "Concepts of Balance," p. 287.

[28] For a simplified introduction, see Festinger, "Cognitive Dissonance," *Scientific American,* 207 (October 1962), 93. For a more complete discussion of cognitive dissonance theory, consult Festinger, *A Theory of Cognitive Dissonance* (Stanford, Calif.: Stanford University Press, 1962); J. W. Brehm and A. R. Cohen, *Explorations in Cognitive Dissonance* (New York: John Wiley & Sons, Inc., 1962); and Festinger, *Conflict, Decision and Dissonance* (Stanford, Calif.: Stanford University Press, 1964).

[29] John J. Sherwood, James W. Barron, and H. Gordon Fitch, "Cognitive Dissonance: Theory and Research," in *The Study of Attitude Change,* ed. Richard V. Wagner and John J. Sherwood (Belmont, Calif.: Brooks/Cole Publishing Co., 1969), p. 58.

[30] Brehm and Cohen, *Explorations in Cognitive Dissonance,* p. 21.

[31] See D. Ehrlich, I. Guttman, P. Schonback, and J. Mills, "Post-Decision Exposure to Relevant Information," *Journal of Abnormal and Social Psychology,* LIV (1957), 98–102.

[32] For a discussion of selective exposure see Sherwood, Barron, and Fitch, in *Study of Attitude Change,* pp. 71–72.

[33] McGuire, in *Nature of Attitude Change,* p. 267; also see p. 149.

[34] Carolyn Sherif, Muzafer Sherif, and Roger Nebergall, *Attitude and Attitude Change: The Social Judgment-Involvement Approach* (Philadelphia: W. B. Saunders Company, 1965), pp. 3, 25.

[35] Katz, "The Functional Approach to the Study of Attitudes," *Public Opinion Quarterly,* XXIV, No. 2 (Summer 1960), 170.

CHAPTER 6

[1] This statement approximates one of the laws of association as stated in Horace B. English and Ava C. English, *A Comprehensive Dictionary of Psychological and Psychoanalytical Terms* (New York: Longmans, Green and Co., 1958), p. 46.

[2] Berelson and Steiner, *Human Behavior: An Inventory of Scientific Findings,* p. 136.

[3] For a typical introductory description of conditioned response learning, see Krech and Crutchfield, *Elements of Psychology,* pp. 401–9.

[4] Ernest R. Hilgard, *Theories of Learning* (New York: Appleton-Century-Crofts, 1948), p. 53.

[5] Krugman, "The Impact of Television Advertising: Learning Without Involvement," *Public Opinion Quarterly,* XXIX (Fall 1965), 349–56. Also see Herbert E. Krugman and Eugene L. Hartley, "Passive Learning from Television," *Public Opinion Quarterly,* XXXIV (Summer 1970), 184–190.

[6] Ibid., p. 353.

[7] Ibid., p. 354.

[8] An excellent treatment of this subject is by Erwin P. Bettinghaus, *Persuasive Communication* (New York: Holt, Rinehart & Winston, Inc., 1968), chap. 6.

[9] Bettinghaus discusses the first two of these methods in *Persuasive Communication,* pp. 139–43.

[10] Ibid., p. 139.

[11] Joseph M. Murtha in *Viewpoint* published by the Public Relations Department, Corn Products Company, 717 Fifth Avenue, New York, n.d.

[12] For a comprehensive treatment of corporate identification see William L. Quirk, "Corporate Image: Projection Through Identity" (Master's thesis, Boston University, 1970).

[13] The RCA illustration is from Quirk, "Corporate Image," pp. 51–57. The Robert W. Sarnoff quote is from "Anatomy of a New Trademark," *Saturday Review,* April 13, 1968, p. 91.

[14] Schladermundt, "Design and the Corporate Image," in *Developing The Corporate Image,* ed. Lee H. Bristol, Jr. (New York: Charles Scribner's Sons, 1960), p. 239.

[15] Goffman, *The Presentation of Self in Everyday Life* (Garden City, New York: Doubleday & Company, Inc., 1959), p. xi.

[16] Quirk, "Corporate Image," p. 59.

[17] From Quirk, in "Corporate Image," p. 36, in a reference to A. J. Spector, "Basic Dimensions of Corporate Image," *Journal of Marketing Research,* October 1961, pp. 47–51.

[18] See English and English, *Psychological and Psychoanalytical Terms,* p. 225. For a discussion of gestalt psychology applied to marketing, see James H. Myers and William H. Reynolds, *Consumer Behavior and Marketing Management* (Boston: Houghton Mifflin, 1967), p. 31.

[19] Gene Wyckoff, *The Image Candidates: American Politics in the Age of Television* (New York: Macmillan Co., 1968).

[20] Ibid., p. 216.

[21] Dan Nimmo, *The Political Persuaders: The Techniques of Modern Election Campaigns* (Englewood Cliffs, N.J.: Prentice-Hall, Inc., 1970), p. 112.

[22] Kurt Lang and Gladys Engel Lang, *Politics and Television* (Chicago: Quadrangle Books, Inc., 1968), p. 189.

[23] Nimmo, *Political Persuaders,* p. 144.

[24] Ibid., p. 151.

[25] Doob, *Public Opinion and Propaganda* (New York: Henry Holt and Co., 1948), p. 317.

[26] Harriet Amster, "Semantic Satiation and Generation: Learning? Adaptation?" *Psychological Bulletin,* LXII (1964), 273–86.

[27] This example and the related discussion is based on an excellent review, "Repetition in Advertising" by Walter Weiss in *Psychology in Media Strategy,* ed. Leo Bogart (New York: American Marketing Association, 1966), pp. 59–65.

[28] Walter Weiss, in *Psychology in Media Strategy,* p. 63. Also see D. E. Berlyne, *Conflict, Arousal, and Curiosity* (New York: McGraw-Hill Book Company, Inc., 1960).

[29] Krech and Crutchfield, *Theory and Problems of Social Psychology* (New York: McGraw-Hill Book Company, Inc., 1948), p. 102.

CHAPTER 7

[1] Katz, "The Functional Approach to the Study of Attitudes," *Public Opinion Quarterly,* XXIV (Summer 1960), 163–204.

[2] Ibid., p. 175.

[3] Irving Sarnoff, Daniel Katz, and Charles McClintock, "Attitude-Change Procedures and Motivating Patterns," in *Public Opinion and Propaganda,* ed. Daniel Katz et al.(New York: The Dryden Press, 1954), p. 306.

[4] See Krech and Crutchfield, *Elements of Psychology,* chap. V.

[5] Halsey, *Training Employees* (New York: Harper and Brothers, 1949), p. 224.

[6] Opinion Research Corporation, "Collectivist Ideology," in *The Public Opinion Index for Industry*(Princeton: Opinion Research Corporation, 1947). Also, for an excellent summary of the conditions under which the "facts approach" works, see Walter Weiss, "Information, Truth, and Opinion Change," *Public Relations Journal* XIII (July 1957), 8–10 ff.

[7] J. S. Bruner, J. J. Goodnow, and G. A. Austin, *A Study of Thinking* (New York: John Wiley & Sons, 1956), p. 79.

[8] S. A. Stouffer et al., *The American Soldier: Adjustment During Army Life* (Princeton: Princeton University Press, 1949), p. 460.

[9] Sarnoff, Katz and McClintock, in *Public Opinion and Propaganda,* p. 305.

[10] For a discussion of rationality in business decision making, see James G. March and Herbert A. Simon, *Organizations* (New York: John Wiley & Sons, Inc., 1958), chap. 6.

[11] Kenneth E. Boulding, *The Image* (Ann Arbor, Mich.: The University of Michigan Press, 1956), pp. 5–6.

12 Ibid., p. 91.

13 George A. Borden, Richard B. Gregg, and Theodore G. Grove, *Speech Behavior and Human Interaction* (Englewood, N.J.: Prentice-Hall, Inc., 1969), pp. 183–84.

14 Erwin P. Bettinghaus, *Message Preparation: The Nature of Proof* (New York: The Bobbs-Merrill Company, Inc., 1966), p. 6.

15 Ibid., p. 5.

16 Ibid., p. 7.

17 Ibid., pp. 102–10.

18 Carl I. Hovland, ed., *The Order of Presentation in Persuasion* (New Haven: Yale University Press, 1957).

19 See Scott M. Cutlip and Allen Center, *Effective Public Relations,* 3rd ed. (Englewood Cliffs, N.J.: Prentice-Hall, Inc., 1964), pp. 282–84.

20 For a discussion of the mass media of publicity, see Cutlip and Center, *Effective Public Relations,* pp. 284–302.

21 For a review of employee communications see Otto Lerbinger, "Employee Communications," in *Handbook of Public Relations,* ed. Howard Stephenson (New York: McGraw-Hill Book Company, Inc., 1960), pp. 439–76.

22 Hovland, Janis, and Kelley, *Communication and Persuasion,* p. 182.

23 Doob, *Public Opinion and Propaganda,* p. 395.

24 See Hovland, Janis, and Kelley, *Communication and Persuasion,* pp. 100–105.

25 Marvin Karlins and Herbert I. Abelson, *Persuasion: How Opinions and Attitudes Are Changed* (New York: Springer Publishing Co., Inc., 1970), p. 13.

26 Hovland, *Communication and Persuasion,* pp. 104–5.

27 Ibid., pp. 57–58.

28 Ibid., p. 58.

29 Ibid., p. 57.

30 Bettinghaus, *Persuasive Communication,* p. 140.

31 Oliver, *The Psychology of Persuasive Speech* (New York: Longmans, Green and Co., 1957), p. 258.

32 Ibid., p. 257.

33 Hovland, *Communication and Persuasion,* pp. 105–11; also Karlins and Abelson, *Persuasion,* pp. 22–26.

34 Doob, *Public Opinion and Propaganda,* pp. 421–22. Also see Hovland, *Communication and Persuasion,* pp. 120–30.

35 Hovland, *Communication and Persuasion,* p. 121.

36 Hovland, *Order of Presentation in Persuasion,* pp. 154–55.

37 Ibid., p. 155.

38 Muzafer Sherif and Carolyn W. Sherif, *An Outline of Social Psychology,* rev. ed. (New York: Harper and Brothers, 1956), p. 47.

[39] See Muzafer Sherif and Carl I. Hovland, *Social Judgment: Assimilation and Contrast Effects in Communication and Attitude Change* (New Haven: Yale University Press, 1961).

[40] Sherif, Sherif, and Nebergall, *Attitude and Attitude Change,* p. 226.

[41] McGuire, "Current Status of Cognitive Consistency Theories," in *Cognitive Consistency,* p. 9.

[42] Lane and Sears, *Public Opinion,* p. 47.

[43] Sherwood, Barron, and Fitch, "Cognitive Dissonance: Theory and Research," in *Study of Attitude Change,* p. 62.

[44] Reviewed in Sherwood et al., "Cognitive Dissonance," p. 67.

[45] Ibid., p. 78.

[46] Milton J. Rosenberg, "An Analysis of Affective-Cognitive Consistency," in *Attitude Organization and Change,* ed. Carl I. Hovland and Milton J. Rosenberg (New Haven: Yale University Press, 1960), p. 52.

[47] Ibid., p. 26.

[48] William J. McGuire, "A Syllogistic Analysis of Cognitive Relationships," in *Attitude Organization and Change,* p. 96.

[49] Ibid., p. 79.

[50] Ibid., p. 79.

[51] McGuire, in *Cognitive Consistency,* p. 16.

CHAPTER 8

[1] Raymond A. Bauer, "The Obstinate Audience: The Influence Process from the Point of View of Social Communication," in *Current Perspectives in Social Psychology,* ed. Edwin P. Hollander and Raymond G. Hunt (New York: Oxford University Press, 1967), pp. 400–408.

[2] Davison, "On the Effects of Communication," *Public Opinion Quarterly,* XXIII (Fall 1959), 360.

[3] Reported in Bauer, "The Communicator and the Audience," in *People, Society, and Mass Communication,* pp. 130–31.

[4] Ibid., p. 136.

[5] For a good introductory discussion of this and other assumptions about people see Harold J. Leavitt, *Managerial Psychology,* rev. ed. (Chicago: University of Chicago Press, 1964), pp. 7–12.

[6] Atkinson, *An Introduction to Motivation,* p. 1.

[7] An excellent review of this model appears in Leonard Berkowitz, "Social Motivation," in *Handbook of Social Psychology,* III, 53–71.

[8] For a discussion of motives and drives, see Miller and Dollard, *Social Learning and Imitation,* pp. 18–21; and Irving Sarnoff, "Psychoanalytic Theory and Social Attitudes," *Public Opinion Quarterly,* XXIV (Summer 1960), 252.

[9] Berkowitz, "Social Motivation," p. 77.

[10] Ibid., p. 77. Also see Janice Loeb, "The Incentive Value of Cartoon Faces to Children," *Journal of Experimental Child Psychology,* I, 99–107.

[11] Berkowitz, "Social Motivation," p. 77.

[12] Ibid.

[13] McGuire, "The Current Status of Cognitive Consistency Theories," in *Cognitive Consistency,* p. 37.

[14] Ibid., p. 37.

[15] Davison, "Effects of Communication," p. 344.

[16] Ibid., p. 359.

[17] Hilgard, *Theories of Learning,* pp. 16, 20. Also see B. F. Skinner, "Operant Behavior," in *Operant Behavior: Areas of Research and Application,* ed. Werner K. Honig (New York: Appleton-Century-Crofts, 1966), pp. 12–32.

[18] See B. F. Skinner, *The Behavior of Organisms* (New York: Appleton-Century-Crofts, Inc., 1938); *Science and Human Behavior* (New York: Macmillan Co., 1953); *Verbal Behavior* (New York: Appleton-Century-Crofts, 1957).

[19] George Caspar Homans, *Social Behavior: Its Elementary Forms* (New York: Harcourt, Brace & World, Inc., 1961), p. 18.

[20] See Eugene Raudsepp, *Managing Creative Scientists and Engineers* (New York: Macmillan Co., 1963).

[21] Martineau, *Motivation in Advertising.*

[22] Vance Packard, *The Hidden Persuaders* (New York: David McKay Company, Inc., 1957).

[23] Alfred Politz, "Motivation Research from a Research Viewpoint," *Public Opinion Quarterly,* XX (Winter 1956–57), 663–73.

[24] F. J. Roethlisberger and W. J. Dickson, *Management and the Worker* (Cambridge: Harvard University Press, 1939).

[25] For a discussion of the philosophy which has come to be known as "Boulwarism," see Lemuel R. Boulware, *The Truth About Boulwarism: Trying to Do Right Voluntarily* (Washington: The Bureau of National Affairs, Inc., 1969).

[26] Delbert C. Miller, *Handbook of Research Design and Social Measurement* (New York: David McKay Company, Inc., 1964), pp. 151, 173–80.

[27] Maslow, *Motivation and Personality.*

[28] Based on the summary by Douglas McGregor, "The Human Side of Enterprise," in *Management of Personnel,* ed. Ramesh C. Goyal and Charles A. Myers (Bombay: Manaktalas, 1967), pp. 274–77.

[29] Douglas McGregor, *The Human Side of Enterprise* (New York: McGraw-Hill Book Company, Inc., 1960).

[30] McGregor, in *Management of Personnel,* p. 272.

[31] Katz, "The Motivational Basis of Organizational Behavior," in *Current Perspectives in Social Psychology,* p. 552.

[32] Ibid., p. 560.

[33] Examples of such specialized books are: Cofer and Appley, *Motivation: Theory and Research;* and Atkinson, *An Introduction to Motivation.*

[34] Books that contain reference to the motives of specific publics are: Raymond W. Peters, *Communication Within Industry* (New York: Harper Brothers, 1950); Joseph A. Livingston, *The American Stockholder* (Philadelphia: J. B. Lippincott, 1958); Louis B. Lundborg, *Public Relations in the Local Community* (New York: Harper Brothers, 1950).

[35] See Robert Ferber and Hugh G. Wales, eds., *Motivation and Market Behavior* (Homewood, Ill.: Richard D. Irwin, Inc., 1958).

[36] Ibid., p. 10.

[37] Hovland, Janis, and Kelley, *Communication and Persuasion,* pp. 120–26.

[38] Lazarsfeld and Merton, "Mass Communication, Popular Taste and Organized Social Action," in *Mass Culture,* p. 470.

CHAPTER 9

[1] Sherif, *The Psychology of Social Norms* (New York: Harper & Brothers, 1936).

[2] Theodore M. Newcomb, *Personality and Social Change* (New York: Dryden Press, 1943). Also see Theodore M. Newcomb, "Attitude Development as a Function of Reference Groups: The Bennington Study," in *Readings in Social Psychology,* rev. ed., ed. Guy E. Swanson, Theodore M. Newcomb, and Eugene L. Hartley (New York: Henry Holt and Company, 1952), pp. 420–30.

[3] Homans, *Social Behavior,* p. 34.

[4] Ibid., p. 45.

[5] For a list of so-called "verbal conditioning" studies, see Berelson and Steiner, *Human Behavior,* p. 144.

[6] Homans, *Social Behavior,* p. 18.

[7] Zajonc, "Social Facilitation," in *Current Perspectives in Social Psychology,* 2nd ed., ed. Edwin P. Hollander and Raymond G. Hunt (New York: Oxford University Press, 1967). Article originally appeared in *Science,* No. 3681 (1965), pp. 269–74.

[8] Ibid., p. 9.

[9] Ibid., p. 11.

[10] Ibid., p. 12.

[11] Festinger, "Informal Social Communication," in *Group Dynamics: Research and Theory,* 3rd ed., ed. Dorwin Cartwright and Alvin Zander (New York: Harper & Row, Publishers, 1968), pp. 182–91.

[12] Ibid., p. 183.

[13] Solomon E. Asch, "Effects of Group Pressure Upon the Modification

and Distortion of Judgments," in Swanson et al., *Readings in Social Psychology*, pp. 2–11.

[14] Ibid., p. 5.

[15] Asch, *Social Psychology* (New York: Prentice-Hall, Inc., 1952), p. 484.

[16] Festinger, "Informal Social Communication," p. 184.

[17] Ibid., p. 190.

[18] Kelman, "Processes of Opinion Change," *Public Opinion Quarterly*, XXV (Spring 1961), 61.

[19] Ibid., pp. 62–65.

[20] For a discussion on source credibility, see Hovland, *Communication and Persuasion*, chap. 2, pp. 19–55.

[21] For a discussion of these films, see Carl I. Hovland, Arthur A. Lumsdaine, and Fred D. Sheffield, *Experiments on Mass Communication*, Vol. III of *Studies in Social Psychology in World War II* (Princeton: Princeton University Press, 1949).

[22] For a review of these studies see Homans, *The Human Group* (New York: Harcourt, Brace & World, Inc., 1950).

[23] Edward Zigler and Irvin L. Child, "Socialization," in *The Handbook of Social Psychology*, 2nd ed., III, ed. Gardner Lindzey and Elliot Aronson (Reading, Mass.: Addison-Wesley Publishing Company, Inc., 1969), 450.

[24] Lee J. Cronbach, *Educational Psychology* (New York: Harcourt, Brace and Company, 1954), p. 310.

[25] White and Lippitt, "Leader Behavior and Member Reaction in Three 'Social Climates,' " in Cartwright and Zander, *Group Dynamics*, pp. 318–35.

[26] Hovland, Janis and Kelley, *Communication and Persuasion*, pp. 157–65.

[27] Stanley Schachter, "Deviation, Rejection, and Communication," in Cartwright and Zander, *Group Dynamics*, p. 166.

[28] See Dorwin Cartwright, "The Nature of Group Cohesiveness," in Cartwright and Zander, *Group Dynamics*, pp. 91–109.

[29] "Adversaries in Steel Fight It Out In Advertisements," *Business Week*, (June 6, 1959), pp. 24–26.

[30] See Asch, "Effects of Group Pressure," pp. 484–92; and Herbert I. Abelson, *Persuasion* (New York: Springer Publishing Co., 1959), p. 26.

[31] Sherif, "Group Influences Upon the Formation of Norms and Attitudes," in *Readings in Social Psychology*, Guy E. Swanson et al., pp. 249–62. Also see Sherif, *The Psychology of Social Norms*.

[32] Gordon W. Allport and Leo Postman, "The Basic Psychology of Rumor," *Public Opinion and Propaganda*, ed. Daniel Katz, Dorwin Cartwright, Samuel Eldersveld, and Alfred McClung Lee (New York: The Dryden Press, 1954), pp. 394–404. Also see James R. Allingham, Lieut. Cmdr., USN, "A Descriptive Study of Communication Networks and Rumor Diffusion Aboard a Navy Ship" (unpublished Master's dissertation, School of Public Communication, Boston University, 1964).

[33] Norman R. F. Maier, *Principles of Human Relations* (New York: John Wiley & Sons, Inc., 1952), chaps. 7 and 8.

[34] Kurt Lewin, "Group Decision and Social Change," in *Readings in Social Psychology,* pp. 459–73.

[35] Ibid., p. 464.

[36] Ibid., chap. 5.

CHAPTER 10

[1] Smith, Bruner, and White, *Opinions and Personality,* p. 36.

[2] Ibid., p. 270.

[3] Ibid., p. 271.

[4] Katz, "The Functional Approach to the Study of Attitudes," *Public Opinion Quarterly,* XXIV (Summer 1960), 163–204.

[5] Ibid., p. 173.

[6] Ibid., p. 172.

[7] Ibid., pp. 184–86.

[8] For a discussion of two of these topics, see Hovland, Janis, and Kelley, *Communication and Persuasion,* pp. 174–214.

[9] For a discussion of the Freudian approach, see Anna Freud, *The Ego and the Mechanisms of Defense* (New York: International Universities Press, Inc., 1946).

[10] Irving Sarnoff, "Psychoanalytic Theory and Social Attitudes," p. 255 ff.

[11] Eunice Cooper and Marie Jahoda, "The Evasion of Propaganda: How Prejudiced People Respond to Anti-Prejudice Propaganda," in *Public Opinion and Propaganda,* ed. Daniel Katz et al. (New York: The Dryden Press, 1954), pp. 313–19.

[12] Ibid., p. 314.

[13] Carl I. Hovland and Irving L. Janis, eds., *Personality and Persuasibility* (New Haven: Yale University Press, 1959), p.v. Also see Hovland, Janis, and Kelley, *Communication and Persuasion,* chap. 6.

[14] Katz, "Functional Approach to Study of Attitudes," p. 204.

[15] Irwin Janis, "Personality as a Factor in Susceptibility to Persuasion," in *The Science of Human Communication,* ed. Wilbur Schramm (New York: Basic Books, Inc., 1963), p. 13.

[16] Ibid., pp. 54–64.

[17] Ibid., p. 62.

[18] Ibid., p. 61.

[19] Hovland and Janis, *Personality and Persuasibility,* p. 230.

[20] Janis, "Personality as a Factor," p. 60.

[21] Ibid., p. 63.

[22] William J. McGuire, "The Nature of Attitudes and Attitude Change," in *The Handbook of Social Psychology*, p. 251.

[23] T. W. Adorno, Else Frenkel-Brunswik, Daniel J. Levinson, and R. Nevitt Sanford, *The Authoritarian Personality* (New York: Harper & Brothers, 1950), p. 228.

[24] Robert F. Bales and Philip E. Slater, "Role Differentiation in Small Decision-Making Groups," in *Family, Socialization and Interaction Process,* ed. Talcott Parsons and Robert Bales (Glencoe, Ill.: The Free Press, 1955), pp. 292–96.

[25] Janis, "Personality as a Factor."

[26] Walter Weiss and Bernard J. Fine, "Opinion Change as a Function of Some Interpersonal Attributes of the Communicatees," *Journal of Abnormal and Social Psychology,* LI (1957), 246–53.

[27] Weiss and Fine, "The Effect of Induced Aggressiveness on Opinion Change," *Journal of Abnormal and Social Psychology,* LII (1956), 180–86.

[28] Milton Rokeach, *The Open and Closed Mind* (New York: Basic Books, Inc., 1960).

[29] Bettinghaus, *Persuasive Communication,* p. 91. Also read pp. 89–92 for an excellent review and interpretation of dogmatism.

[30] Katz, "Functional Approach to Study of Attitudes," p. 190.

[31] Ibid., p. 187.

[32] See Francis X. Sutton, Seymour E. Harris, Carl Kaysen and James Tobin, *The American Business Creed* (Cambridge: Harvard University Press, 1956), p. 57 ff.

[33] See Hadley Cantril, *The Psychology of Social Movements* (New York: John Wiley & Sons, Inc., 1941), pp. 78–122.

[34] Janis, "Personality as a Factor in Susceptibility to Persuasion," p. 57.

[35] Hovland, Janis, and Kelley, *Communication and Persuasion,* chap. 3.

[36] L. Berkowitz and D. R. Cottingham, "The Interest Value and Relevance of Fear Arousing Communication," *Journal of Abnormal and Social Psychology,* LX (1960), 37–43; H. Leventhal and P. A. Niles "A Field Experiment on Fear-Arousal with Data on the Validity of Questionnaire Measures," *Journal of Personality,* XXXII (1964), 459–79. Also see William J. McGuire, "Attitudes and Opinions," in *Annual Review of Psychology,* ed. Paul R. Farnsworth, Olga McNemar, and Quinn McNemar (Palo Alto, Calif.: Annual Reviews, Inc., 1966), pp. 484–85.

[37] Katz, "Functional Approach to Study of Attitudes," pp. 180–87.

[38] Maier, *Principles of Human Relations,* chap. 4.

[39] Katz, "Functional Approach to Study of Attitudes," p. 188.

[40] Abelson, *Persuasion,* p. 65.

CHAPTER 11

[1] Ernest R. Hilgard, *Introduction to Psychology* (New York: Harcourt, Brace & World, 1953), p. 603.

[2] Charles E. Osgood, in particular, uses the term "ports of entry." See "A Behavioristic Analysis of Perception and Language of Cognitive Phenomena," in *Contemporary Approaches to Cognition.*

[3] For an excellent review of the various problems attendant upon subliminal projection, read McConnell, Cutler, and McNeil, "Subliminal Stimulation: An Overview," *American Psychologist*, 13 (May 1958), 229–42.

[4] Charles E. Osgood, *Method and Theory in Experimental Psychology* (New York: Oxford University Press, 1953), p. 194.

[5] Adapted from Wilbur Schramm, "How Communication Works," *The Process and Effects of Mass Communication*, p. 4.

[6] Ibid., p. 3.

[7] For a review of Gestalt theory, see Ernest R. Hilgard, *Theories of Learning*, pp. 222–57.

[8] Ibid., p. 226.

[9] McLuhan, *The Medium Is the Massage: An Inventory of Effects* (New York: Random House, Inc., 1967).

[10] Osgood, in *Method and Theory in Experimental Psychology*, p. 194.

[11] Hilgard, *Introduction to Psychology*, p. 301 ff.

[12] Gibson, *The Senses Considered As Perceptual Systems* (Boston: Houghton Mifflin Company, 1966), p. 319.

[13] Ibid., p. 2.

[14] Ibid., p. 50.

[15] Klapper, "The Comparative Effects of the Various Media," *The Process and Effects of Mass Communication*, ed. Wilbur Schramm (Urbana, Ill.: University of Illinois Press, 1961), pp. 91–105; Travers, *Man's Information System: A Primer for Media Specialists and Educational Technologists* (Scranton, Penn.: Chandler Publishing Company, 1970), pp. 84–93; also see A. Chapanis, *Man-Machine Engineering* (Belmont, Calif.: Wadsworth Publishing Company, Inc., 1965); and W. F. Day and B. R. Beach, *A Survey of the Research Literature Comparing the Visual and Auditory Presentation of Information* (University of Virginia, Contract No. W33–039–ac–21269, E. O. No. 694–37, November 1950).

[16] Travers, "Comparative Effects of Media," p. 86.

[17] Ibid., p. 74.

[18] See Francis Bello, "The Information Theory," *Fortune*, XLVII (December 1953), 136 ff.; and Colin Cherry, *On Human Communication.*

[19] George A. Miller, *The Psychology of Communication: Seven Essays* (New York: Basic Books, Inc., 1967), p. 77.

[20] Ibid., pp. 42–43.

[21] Hilgard, *Introduction to Psychology,* p. 609.

[22] On the general subject of attention see Robert S. Woodworth, *Experimental Psychology* (New York: Henry Holt and Company, 1938), chap. 27. For a communications implication of unity of attention see D. E. Broadbent, "Speaking and Listening Simultaneously," *Journal of Experimental Psychology,* 43 (1952), 267–73.

[23] Jerome S. Bruner, "Social Psychology and Perception," *Readings in Social Psychology,* 3rd ed., ed. Eleanor E. Maccoby, Theodore M. Newcomb, and Eugene L. Hartley (New York: Henry Holt and Company, 1958), p. 86.

[24] Wilbur Schramm, "Information Theory and Mass Communication," in *Communication and Culture: Readings in The Codes of Human Interaction,* ed. Alfred G. Smith (New York: Holt, Rinehart & Winston, 1966), p. 525.

[25] Ibid., p. 525.

[26] Ibid., p. 524.

[27] Ibid., p. 526.

[28] Hilgard, *Introduction to Psychology,* p. 296.

[29] Bruner, "Social Psychology and Perception."

[30] For a discussion of this experiment, see Bruner, "Social Psychology and Perception," p. 88.

[31] Sherif and Sherif, *An Outline of Social Psychology,* p. 96.

[32] Elizabeth C. Winship and Gordon W. Allport, "Do Rosy Headlines Sell Newspapers?" *Public Opinion and Propaganda,* ed. Daniel Katz et al. (New York: The Dryden Press, 1954), pp. 271–74.

[33] Abelson, *Persuasion* (New York: Springer Publishing Co., Inc., 1959), p. 78.

[34] Among the common references to the subject of semantics are: Whorf, *Language, Thought and Reality,* and Hayakawa, *Language in Thought and Action.*

[35] Roger Brown, *Words and Things,* p. 109.

[36] Osgood, Suci, and Tannenbaum, *The Measurement of Meaning.*

[37] See Robert O. Carlson, "The Nature of Corporate Images," *The Corporation and Its Publics,* ed. John Riley, Jr. (New York: John Wiley & Sons, Inc., 1963).

[38] John Millar, "Treatment of Common Issues in General Electric's and IUE's Local 201 Employee Publications" (Master's thesis, Boston University, 1959).

CHAPTER 12

[1] D. E. Broadbent, *Perception and Communication* (New York: Pergamon Press, Inc., 1958).

[2] Travers, *Man's Information System: A Primer for Media Specialists and Educational Technologists,* p. 144.

[3] Ibid., pp. 152–53.

[4] Ibid., p. 160.

[5] H. Ebbinghaus, *Memory: A Contribution to Experimental Psychology,* trans. H. A. Ruger and C. E. Bussenius (New York: Columbia University Press, 1913). Also see Carl I. Hovland, "Human Learning and Retention," in *Handbook of Experimental Psychology,* ed. S. S. Stevens (New York: John Wiley & Sons, Inc., 1951), pp. 613–89.

[6] Norman L. Munn, *Psychology* (Boston: Houghton Mifflin Company, 1946), p. 161.

[7] Hovland, Janis, and Kelley, *Commnunication and Persuasion,* pp. 254–65.

[8] Allport and Postman, "The Basic Psychology of Rumor," in *Public Opinion and Propaganda,* pp. 394–404.

[9] Stanley Schachter and Harvey Burdick, "A Field Experiment on Rumor Transmission and Distortion," in *Communication and Culture: Readings in the Codes of Human Interaction,* ed. Alfred G. Smith (New York: Holt, Rinehart and Winston, Inc., 1966), p. 307.

[10] Allport and Postman, "Basic Psychology of Rumor," p. 398.

[11] Ibid., p. 399.

[12] Travers, *Man's Information System,* p. 148.

[13] Ibid., p. 150.

[14] Ibid., p. 154.

[15] Ibid., p. 156.

[16] B. C. Vickery, *On Retrieval System Theory,* 2nd ed. (London: Butterworth & Co., 1965), chap. 4, pp. 33–71.

[17] Karl W. Deutsch, *The Nerves of Government* (New York: The Free Press, 1966), pp. 98–101.

[18] Tannenbaum, "The Indexing Process in Communication," in Smith, *Communication and Culture,* pp. 480–88.

[19] H. Minami and K. M. Dallenbach, "The Effect of Activity Upon Learning and Retention in the Cockroach," *American Journal of Psychology,* 59 (1946), pp. 1–58.

[20] Ernest R. Hilgard, *Theories of Learning,* 2nd ed. (New York: Appleton-Century-Crofts, 1956), p. 273.

[21] Janis, Lumsdaine, and Gladstone, "Effects of Preparatory Communications on Reactions to a Subsequent News Event," in *Public Opinion and Propaganda,* pp. 347–62.

[22] Referred to in Arthur R. Cohen, *Attitude Change and Social Influence,* p. 122. See William J. McGuire and Demetrios Papageorgis, "Effectiveness of Forewarning in Developing Resistance to Persuasion," *Public Opinion Quarterly,* XXVI (Spring 1962), p. 25.

CHAPTER 13

[1] George M. Beal, Janet S. Payer, and Paul Yarbrough, *Mental Retardation: A Guide to Community Action* (Prepared for and published by Iowa's Comprehensive Plan to Combat Mental Retardation. Des Moines, Iowa, 1965), p. 18.

[2] Adapted from John W. Riley, Jr., and Matilda White Riley, "Mass Communication and the Social System," in *Sociology Today,* ed. Robert K. Merton, Leonard Broom, and Leonard S. Cottrell, Jr. (New York: Basic Books, Inc., 1959), p. 561.

[3] Parsons, *The Social System* (Glencoe, Ill.: The Free Press, 1951), pp. 5–6.

[4] Talcott Parsons and Edward A. Shils, eds., *Toward a General Theory of Action* (Cambridge: Harvard University Press, 1954), p. 7.

[5] Ibid., p. 8.

[6] These social system settings partly follow the outline of the components of a community system in Irwin T. Sanders, *The Community* (New York: The Ronald Press Company, 1958), p. 191. They are also similar to what Howard H. Martin describes as communication settings, "the environment in which communication takes place—the physical and psychological surroundings of the listener or reader" as described in "Communication Settings," in *Speech Communication: Analysis and Readings,* ed. Howard H. Martin and Kenneth E. Anderson (Boston: Allyn and Bacon, Inc., 1968), p. 58.

[7] Heider, *The Psychology of Interpersonal Relations* (New York: John Wiley & Sons, Inc., 1958), p. 1.

[8] The discussion of the functions of interpersonal relations is based on Warren G. Bennis, Edgar H. Schein, David E. Berlew, and Fred I. Steele, *Interpersonal Dynamics: Essays and Readings on Human Interaction* (Homewood, Ill.: The Dorsey Press, 1964), pp. 8 ff.

[9] Paul Watzlawick, *An Anthology of Human Communication* (Palo Alto, California: Science and Behavior Books, Inc., 1964), p. 4.

[10] Ibid., pp. 7–8.

[11] Ibid., p. 9.

[12] Ibid., pp. 11–12.

[13] Ibid., p. 17.

[14] For a further discussion see Paul Watzlawick, Janet H. Beavin, and Don D. Jackson, *Pragmatics of Human Communication: A Study of Interactional Patterns, Pathologies, and Paradoxes* (New York: W. W. Norton & Company, Inc., 1967).

[15] Berne, *Games People Play: The Psychology of Human Relationships* (New York: Grove Press, Inc., 1964), pp. 23–24.

[16] Ibid., p. 29.

[17] Ibid., pp. 31–32.

[18] James Pilditch, *Communication by Design* (New York: McGraw-Hill Book Company, Inc., 1970), p. 35.

[19] The examples that follow are based on Michael Argyle, *Social Interaction* (New York: Atherton Press, 1969), p. 383.

[20] John W. Bennett and Robert K. McKnight, "Social Norms, National Imagery, and Interpersonal Relations," in *Communication and Culture: Readings in the Codes of Human Interaction,* ed. Alfred G. Smith (New York: Holt, Rinehart and Winston, Inc., 1966), p. 600.

[21] Goffman, *Presentation of Self,* p. 2.

[22] Erving Goffman, *Strategic Interaction* (Philadelphia: University of Pennsylvania Press, 1969), p. x.

[23] Ibid., p. 21.

[24] For a discussion of involvement obligations see Erving Goffman, "Alienation from Interaction," in Smith, *Communication and Culture,* pp. 103–20.

[25] Ibid., pp. 106–11.

[26] As reported by Flora Davis, "The Way We Speak 'Body Language,'" *The New York Times Magazine,* VII, May 31, 1970, 9. Also see Randall Harrison, "Nonverbal Communication: Exploration into Time, Space, Action, and Object," in *Dimensions in Communication,* ed. J. H. Campbell and H. W. Hepler (Belmont, Calif.: Wadsworth Publishing Co., Inc., 1965), p. 161

[27] Birdwhistell, *Kinesics and Context: Essays on Body Motion Communication* (Philadelphia: University of Pennsylvania Press, 1970), p. 66.

[28] For a comprehensive review of the literature in nonverbal communication see Michael Argyle, *Social Interaction,* chap. III, pp. 91–126.

[29] Examples from Flora Davis, "The Way We Speak 'Body Language,'" p. 29.

[30] Birdwhistell, *Kinesics and Context,* p. 70.

[31] Ibid., p. 76.

[32] Lawrence K. Frank, "Tactile Communication," in Smith, *Communication and Cultures,* p. 199.

[33] Ibid., p. 208.

[34] Jessie Bernard, *The Sex Game* (Englewood Cliffs, N.J.: Prentice-Hall, Inc., 1968), chap. VI.

[35] Ibid., p. 137.

[36] Ibid., p. 142.

[37] In Argyle, *Social Interaction,* p. 94–96.

[38] Ibid., pp. 97–98.

[39] Ibid., pp. 101–3.

CHAPTER 14

[1] Hare, *Handbook of Small Group Research* (New York: The Free Press of Glencoe, 1962), p. 8.

[2] Robert F. Bales, *Interaction Process Analysis: A Method for the Study of Small Groups* (Reading, Mass.: Addison-Wesley, Inc., 1950), p. 33.

[3] Holm, *Productive Speaking for Business and the Professions* (Boston: Allyn and Bacon, Inc., 1967), pp. 262–63.

[4] Ibid., p. 291.

[5] Hare, *Small Group Research*, pp. 11–12.

[6] Ibid., p. 63.

[7] Robert F. Bales, "Some Uniformities of Behavior in Small Social Systems," in *Readings in Social Psychology*, p. 149.

[8] Robert F. Bales, "The Equilibrium Problem in Small Groups," in *Working Papers in the Theory of Action*, ed. Talcott Parsons, Robert F. Bales, and Edward A. Shils (Glencoe, Ill.: The Free Press, 1953), p. 116.

[9] Robert F. Bales, "In Conference," in *Information, Influence, and Communication: A Reader in Public Relations*, ed. Otto Lerbinger and Albert J. Sullivan (New York: Basic Books, Inc., 1965), p. 346.

[10] Hare, *Small Group Research*, p. 78.

[11] Bales, *Working Papers in the Theory of Action*, p. 126.

[12] Ibid., p. 127.

[13] Ibid., pp. 128–30.

[14] Argyle, *Social Interaction*, p. 230.

[15] For a discussion of these types see Robert F. Bales and Philip E. Slater, "Role Differentiation in Small Decision-Making Groups," in *Family, Socialization and Interaction Process*, pp. 279–99.

[16] Argyle, *Social Interaction*, p. 232.

[17] The articles most readily accessible are Alex Bavelas, "Communication Patterns in Task-Oriented Groups," in *Group Dynamics*, ed. Dorwin Cartwright and Alvin Zander (Evanston, Ill.: Row, Peterson and Company, 1953), pp. 493–506, and Harold J. Leavitt, "Some Effects of Certain Communication Patterns on Group Performance," in *Readings in Social Psychology*, pp. 108–25.

[18] For a discussion of superimposed networks see Colin Cherry, *On Human Communication*, p. 29.

[19] For a discussion of the influence of rank, age, expertness, and prestige in a group, see Harold J. Leavitt, *Managerial Psychology* (Chicago: University of Chicago Press, 1958), p. 221 ff.

[20] Reported in Irwin T. Sanders, *The Community: An Introduction to a Social System* (New York: The Ronald Press, 1958), p. 111.

[21] Moreno's first and classic publication is *Who Shall Survive?* (Washington: Nervous and Mental Disease Monograph, No. 59, 1934).

[22] Kurt Lewin, *Field Theory in Social Science* (New York: Harper & Brothers, 1951), p. 186.

[23] George Caspar Homans, *Social Behavior; Its Elementary Forms*, pp. 349–55.

[24] Ibid., pp. 352–53.

[25] The definition of influence by Edward C. Banfield, *Political Influence* (Glencoe, Ill.: The Free Press, 1961), p. 3.

²⁶ Katz and Lazarsfeld, *Personal Influence—The Part Played by People in the Flow of Mass Communication* (Glencoe, Ill.: The Free Press, 1955), pp. 221, 223.

²⁷ Ibid., p. 324.

²⁸ Ibid., pp. 272–79, 330.

²⁹ Robert K. Merton, *Social Theory and Social Structure*, rev. ed. (Glencoe, Ill.: The Free Press, 1957), p. 414.

³⁰ This discussion is based on Merton, chap. X, pp. 387–420.

³¹ Ibid., p. 407.

CHAPTER 15

¹ See the following books on internal communication: Robert Newcomb and Marg Sammons, *Employee Communications in Action* (New York: Harper & Row, Publishers, 1961); Raymond W. Peters, *Communication Within Industry* (New York: Harper & Row, Publishers, 1950); Paul Pigors, *Effective Communication in Industry* (New York: National Association of Manufacturers, 1949); Charles E. Redfield, *Communication in Management* (Chicago: University of Chicago Press, 1958); and Lee O. Thayer, *Administrative Communication* (Homewood, Ill.: Richard D. Irwin, Inc., 1961).

² Merrill, *Society and Culture: An Introduction to Sociology,* 4th ed. (Englewood Cliffs, N.J.: Prentice-Hall, Inc., 1969), p. 41 ff.

³ R. M. Maciver and Charles H. Page, *Society: An Introductory Analysis* (New York: Holt, Rinehart and Winston, Inc., 1949), p. 12.

⁴ Ibid., pp. 229–30.

⁵ Joseph S. Himes and Wilbert E. Moore, *The Study of Sociology: An Introduction* (Glenview, Ill.: Scott, Foresman and Company), p. 180.

⁶ For data based on two surveys using national samples, see Murray Hausknecht, *The Joiners: A Sociological Description of Voluntary Association Membership in the United States* (New York: Bedminster Press, 1962). One survey, undertaken in 1954 by the American Institute of Public Opinion, showed that 45 percent of the population belonged to no voluntary association. The second survey, undertaken in 1955 by the National Opinion Research Center, showed that 64 percent belonged to no voluntary associations. Based on both surveys, the range of people belonging to one association was from 20 to 30 percent; those belonging to two was from 9 to 16 percent; and those belonging to three or more was from 7 to 9 percent.

⁷ Edward C. Banfield, *Political Influence* (Glencoe: Ill.: The Free Press, 1961), p. 269. Banfield also points out further advantages of being allied with civic associations: receiving their specialized staff assistance, using their mailing lists, and borrowing their leaders. These leaders become "co-opted" insofar as they represent the interests of the organization seeking their support.

⁸ Merrill, *Society and Culture,* p. 48.

[9] George M. Beal, Janet S. Payer, and Paul Yarbrough, *Mental Retardation: A Guide to Community Action,* p. 16.

[10] Wendell Bell, Richard J. Hill, and Charles R. Wright, *Public Leadership: A Critical Review with Special Reference to Adult Education* (San Francisco: Chandler Publishing Company, 1961), p. 6.

[11] Ibid., p. 13.

[12] Floyd Hunter, *The Community Power Structure* (Chapel Hill: The University of North Carolina Press, 1953). For a critique of Hunter's study and a comparison with Robert A. Dahl's study of New Haven, see *Who Governs?* (New Haven: Yale University Press, 1961), consult Morris Janowitz, "Community Power and 'Policy Science' Research," *Public Opinion Quarterly,* XXVI (Fall 1962), 400.

[13] Hunter, *Community Power Structure,* p. 119.

[14] Beal et al., *Mental Retardation,* p. 18.

[15] Robert A. Dahl, *Who Governs?* p. 170.

[16] John M. Foskett, "The Influence of Social Participation on Community Programs and Activities," *Community Structure and Analysis,* ed. Marvin B. Sussman (New York: Thomas Y. Crowell Company, 1959), p. 314.

[17] Wilbur Schramm, "Information Theory and Mass Communication" in *Communication and Culture: Readings in the Codes of Human Interaction,* p. 523.

[18] For review of organizational communication see: Ernest G. Bormann, William S. Howell, Ralph G. Nichols, and George L. Shapiro, *Interpersonal Communication in the Modern Organization* (Englewood Cliffs, N.J.: Prentice-Hall, Inc., 1969), particularly chap. 9, "Barriers to Communication"; and Bernard M. Bass, *Organizational Psychology* (Boston: Allyn and Bacon, Inc., 1965), chap. 8, "Communications in Industrial Organizations."

[19] For one of the best practical treatments of the subject of semantics see William V. Haney, *Communication and Organizational Behavior: Text and Cases,* rev. ed. (Homewood, Ill.: Richard D. Irwin, Inc., 1967).

[20] Holm, *Productive Speaking for Business and the Professions* (Boston: Allyn and Bacon, Inc., 1967), p. 311.

[21] Ibid., p. 337.

[22] These techniques are discussed and illustrated in George M. Beal, Joe M. Bohlen, and J. Neil Raudabaugh, *Leadership and Dynamic Group Action* (Ames, Iowa: The Iowa State University Press, 1962).

[23] Jeppson, "Public Speaking," in *Handbook of Public Relations,* 2nd ed., ed. Howard Stephenson (New York: McGraw-Hill Book Company, Inc., 1971), p. 717.

[24] Wilbur Schramm, *Mass Media and National Development: The Role of Information in the Developing Countries* (Stanford, California: Stanford University Press, 1964), p. 39.

[25] Daniel Lerner, *The Passing of Traditional Society* (Glencoe, Ill.: The Free Press, 1958), p. 60.

[26] Wright, "Functional Analysis and Mass Communication," *Public Opinion Quarterly*, XXIV (Winter 1960), 609.

[27] *Report of the National Advisory Commission on Civil Disorder* (New York: Bantam Books, Inc., 1968), p. 326.

[28] Benjamin D. Singer, "Mass Media and Communication Processes in the Detroit Riot of 1967," *Public Opinion Quarterly*, XXXIV (Summer 1970), 236–45.

[29] A comprehensive attempt to delineate mass communication is by Charles R. Wright, *Mass Communication: A Sociological Perspective* (New York: Random House, Inc., 1959), pp. 12–15.

[30] Another type of definition is used by Carl I. Hovland, "Effects of the Mass Media of Communication," in *Mass Media and Communication*, ed. Charles S. Steinberg (New York: Hastings House, 1966), p. 448.

[31] G. D. Wiebe, "Mass Communication," in *Fundamentals of Social Psychology*, Eugene L. Hartley and Ruth E. Hartley (New York: Alfred A. Knopf, 1952), p. 165.

[32] Ibid., p. 163.

[33] Bernard Berelson and Patricia J. Salter, "An Analysis of Magazine Fiction," in *Mass Culture*, pp. 235–50.

[34] Ibid., p. 246.

[35] Turner and Killian, *Collective Behavior* (Englewood Cliffs, N.J.: Prentice-Hall, Inc., 1957), pp. 165–68.

[36] For a discussion of this War Bond Drive see Robert K. Merton, *Mass Persuasion* (New York: Harper & Brothers, 1946).

[37] Hadley Cantril, *The Invasion from Mars* (Princeton: Princeton University Press, 1940), p. 47.

[38] Maciver and Page, *Society*, p. 434.

[39] For a review of this concept see Leo Bogart, *Strategy in Advertising* (New York: Harcourt Brace Jovanovich, Inc., 1967), chap. 9, pp. 195–218.

[40] Ibid., p. 208.

[41] For a discussion of some dimensions used in market segmentation see Edward C. Bursk and John F. Chapman, *Modern Marketing Strategy* (Cambridge: Harvard University Press, 1964), pp. 172–77.

[42] Peterson, "From Mass Media to Class Media," in *Mass Communications* (Urbana, Ill.: University of Illinois Press, 1960), p. 256.

[43] Ibid., p. 259.

[44] Ralph Lee Smith, "The Wired Nation," *The Nation*, May 18, 1970, p. 583.

CHAPTER 16

[1] Reissman, *Class in American Society* (Glencoe, Ill.: The Free Press, 1959), p. 228.

[2] A good elementary work on social class is Joseph A. Kahl's, *The American Class Structure* (New York: Rinehart & Company, Inc., 1953). The most comprehensive work on social stratification is Bernard Barber, *Social Stratification: A Comparative Analysis of Structure and Process* (New York: Harcourt Brace Jovanovich, 1957). Also see R. Bendix and S. M. Lipset, *Class, Status and Power: A Reader in Social Stratification* (New York: The Free Press, 1953).

[3] W. Lloyd Warner and Paul S. Lunt, *The Social Life of a Modern Community* (New Haven: Yale University Press, 1948).

[4] Kahl, *American Class Structure*, p. 26, based on Warner and Lunt, *Social Life of a Modern Community*, p. 88.

[5] Harry M. Johnson, *Sociology: A Systematic Introduction* (New York: Harcourt, Brace & World, Inc., 1960), pp. 490–91.

[6] Lloyd W. Warner, Marcia Meeker, Kenneth Eells, *Social Class in America* (Chicago: Science Research Associates, Inc., 1949), chap. 8, pp. 121–30.

[7] Reissman, *Class in American Society*, p. vii.

[8] Miller, *Handbook of Research Design*, pp. 98–100.

[9] Ibid., pp. 106–10.

[10] For an excellent review of the conservative-liberal dimension, see John P. Robinson, Jerrold G. Rusk, and Kendra B. Head, *Measures of Political Attitudes* (Ann Arbor, Mich.: Survey Research Center Institute for Social Research, 1968), chap. 3.

[11] Kornhauser, "Analysis of 'Class' Structure of Contemporary American Society—Psychological Bases of Class Divisions," in *Industrial Conflict: A Psychological Interpretation*, ed. G. W. Hartmann and T. Newcomb (New York: Cordon, 1939), pp. 199–264.

[12] Centers, *The Psychology of Social Classes—A Study of Class Consciousness* (Princeton: Princeton University Press, 1949).

[13] Ibid., p. 49.

[14] Ibid., p. 208.

[15] Ibid., p. 28f.

[16] Kornhauser, "Analysis of 'Class' Structure," p. 258, 259.

[17] Ibid., p. 259f.

[18] Paul F. Lazarsfeld, Bernard Berelson, Hazel Gaudet, *The People's Choice* (New York: Duell, Sloan and Pearce, 1944), p. 20.

[19] Mark Abrams, "Social Class and British Politics," *Public Opinion Quarterly*, XXV (Fall 1961), 342–50.

[20] Ibid., p. 344.

[21] Ibid., p. 349–50.

[22] Hamilton, "Skill Level and Politics," *Public Opinion Quarterly*, XXIX (Fall 1965), 390–99.

[23] Ibid., p. 398.

[24] Ibid., p. 399.

25 Reinhard Bendix and Seymour M. Lipset, "The Field of Political Sociology," in *Political Sociology,* ed. Lewis A. Coser (New York: Harper & Row, Publishers, 1966), p. 20.

26 Ibid., p. 31.

27 Alfred Hero, "Public Reaction to Government Policies," in J. Robinson et al., *Measures of Political Attitudes,* chap. 2.

28 Seymour M. Lipset, "Social Stratification and the Analysis of American Society," in *The Behavioral Sciences Today,* ed. Bernard Berelson (New York: Basic Books, 1963), p. 194 f.

29 Robinson et al., *Measures of Political Attitudes,* pp. 267–69.

30 Ibid., pp. 33–34.

31 Angus Campbell, Philip E. Converse, Warren E. Miller, and Donald E. Stokes, *The American Voter* (New York: John Wiley & Sons, 1960), pp. 194–208.

32 William H. Whyte, Jr., and the editors of *Fortune, Is Anybody Listening?* (New York: Simon & Schuster, Inc., 1952), chap. 1.

33 "How Good Is 'Economic Education'?" *Fortune,* July 1951, p. 84.

34 Chamber of Commerce of the United States, "How to Tell Your Business Story in Employee Meetings," *American Opportunity Program* (Washington: Chamber of Commerce of the United States, n.d.), p. 1.

35 For a discussion of programs, see Douglas Williams and Stanley Peterfreund, *The Education of Employees: A Status Report* (New York: American Management Association, 1954).

36 Seymour M. Lipset, Paul F. Lazarsfeld, Allen H. Barton, and Juan Linz, "The Psychology of Voting: An Analysis of Political Behavior," in *Handbook of Social Psychology,* p. 1139.

37 Lipset et al., "Psychology of Voting," p. 1139. Also see Robert K. Merton, *Social Theory and Social Influence,* p. 231, for a discussion of reference group comparisons.

38 Kelley, "Communication in Experimentally Created Hierarchies," *Human Relations,* IV (1951), 39–56.

39 Katona, *The Powerful Consumer* (New York: McGraw-Hill Book Company, Inc., 1960), p. 160.

40 F. Stuart Chapin, *Contemporary American Institutions* (New York: Harper, 1935), pp. 373–97. Also see Reissman, *Class in American Society,* p. 117, and Miller, *Handbook of Research Design,* pp. 114–19.

41 Kahl, *American Class Structure,* p. 45.

42 Martineau, "Social Classes and Spending Behavior," in *Understanding Consumer Behavior,* ed. Martin M. Grossack (Boston: The Christopher Publishing House, 1964), pp. 131–48.

43 Schatzman and Strauss, "Social Class and Modes of Communication," *The American Journal of Sociology,* LX (January 1955), 329.

CHAPTER 17

[1] Klapper, "What We Know About the Effects of Mass Communication: The Brink of Hope," *Public Opinion Quarterly*, XXI (Winter 1957–58), 453–74.

[2] Lazarsfeld and Merton, "Mass Communication, Popular Taste and Organized Social Action," in *Mass Culture*, pp. 457–73.

[3] Lazarsfeld, Berelson, and Gaudet, *The People's Choice*.

[4] Elihu Katz and Paul F. Lazarsfeld, *Personal Influence*.

[5] Ibid., p. 133.

[6] Weiss, "Effects of the Mass Media of Communication," in *Handbook of Social Psychology*, 2nd ed., Vol. V, 147.

[7] Dodd, "Formulas for Spreading Opinions," *Public Opinion Quarterly*, XXII (Winter 1958), 437–554; and Melvin L. DeFleur and Otto N. Larsen, *The Flow of Information: An Experiment in Mass Communication* (New York: Harper & Brothers, 1958).

[8] DeFleur and Larsen, *Flow of Information*, p. xiii.

[9] Everett M. Rogers, *Diffusion of Innovations* (New York: The Free Press of Glencoe, 1962), p. 12.

[10] H. F. Lionberger, *Adoption of New Ideas and Practices* (Ames, Iowa: Iowa State University Press, 1960).

[11] Ibid., p. 213.

[12] The listing is based on Rogers, *Diffusion of Innovations*, pp. 81–86, 98–105.

[13] See Weiss, "Effects of Mass Media," p. 125.

[14] Hovland, Janis, and Kelley, *Communication and Persuasion*.

[15] Rogers, *Diffusion of Innovations*, p. 254.

[16] The same point is made with regard to political propaganda by Alex Inkeles, "The Bolshevik Agitator," in *Public Opinion and Propaganda*, pp. 404–13.

[17] Rogers, *Diffusion of Innovation*, p. 265.

[18] James Coleman, Elihu Katz, and Herbert Menzel, *Medical Innovation: A Diffusion Study* (Indianapolis: Bobbs-Merrill Co., Inc., 1966), p. 53.

[19] Ibid., p. 55.

[20] Ibid.

[21] Ibid., p. 56.

[22] Ibid., p. 57.

[23] Ibid., p. 60.

[24] Elihu Katz, "The Two-Step Flow of Communication," in *Current Perspectives in Social Psychology*, p. 515.

[25] "International Public Relations Case Study: Philippine Farm Marketing Program," NFTC Ref. No. M–6075, August 1, 1966. This case study was pro-

vided by William Baldwin, Director of Public Relations, National Foreign Trade Council, Inc., 10 Rockefeller Plaza, New York.

26 Lester W. Milbrath, *The Washington Lobbyists* (Chicago: Rand McNally & Co., 1963), p. 20.

27 Ibid., p. 249.

28 Ibid., p. 242.

29 Discussed in Harold Brayman, *Corporate Management in a World of Politics* (New York: McGraw-Hill Book Company, Inc., 1967), pp. 83–87, 94–97.

30 Ibid., p. 85.

31 Ibid., p. 86.

CHAPTER 18

1 Marshall McLuhan's most relevant book in this connection is his *Understanding Media: The Extensions of Man* (New York: McGraw-Hill Book Company, Inc., 1964). Perhaps a clearer explanation is in his *The Medium Is the Massage*. Many articles have been written about him. A good collection of readings is Raymond Rosenthal, *McLuhan: Pro and Con* (Baltimore: Penguin Books, Inc., 1968); in it is John M. Culkin's excellent summary article, "A Schoolman's Guide to Marshall McLuhan."

2 Carl I. Hovland, "Effects of the Mass Media of Communication," in *Handbook of Social Psychology*, p. 1082.

3 The Survey Research Center, University of Michigan, *Science, the News and the Public* (New York: New York University Press, 1958), p. 38.

4 See *The Editor and Publisher International Yearbook* (New York: The Editor and Publisher Co., Inc., 1969); *Statistical Abstracts—1970* (Washington: Superintendent of Documents); and Federal Communications Commission, *35th Annual Report—1969* (Washington: Federal Communications Commission).

5 Daniel Starch and Staff, Inc., for example, use these and other variables in their *Demographics, 1969*, the First Primary Plus Secondary and Total Audience Report published by them for clients.

6 Most of the findings are based on the following sources: Wilbur Schramm and David M. White, "Age, Education, and Economic Status as Factors in Newspaper Reading: Conclusions," in *The Process and Effects of Mass Communication*, pp. 71–83; and "The Survey Research Center," in *Science, the News and the Public*, p. 38.

7 Opinion Research Corporation, *The Public Appraises Movies;* Highlights of a Survey Conducted in June and July 1957, for Motion Picture Association of America, Inc. (Princeton, N.J.: Opinion Research Corporation), p. 4.

8 Joseph T. Klapper, "The Comparative Effects of the Various Media," *The Process and Effects of Mass Communication*, p. 104.

9 Erwin P. Bettinghaus, *Persuasive Communication*, p. 169.

[10] Based on a lecture by Nathan Maccoby at the School of Public Communication, Boston University, Boston, Mass., 1956.

[11] For a discussion of this principle as used with film strips, see Carl I. Hovland, Arthur A. Lumsdaine, and Fred D. Sheffield, *Experiments on Mass Communication,* chap. 9, pp. 228–46.

[12] For a discussion of teaching machines and programmed instruction see Wendell I. Smith and J. William Moore, eds., *Programmed Learning: Theory and Research* (Princeton, N.J.: Van Nostrand, 1962); also American Management Association, Personnel Division, *Programed Instruction in Industry* (New York: American Management Association, 1962).

[13] G.D. Wiebe, "Merchandising Commodities and Citizenship on Television," *Public Opinion Quarterly,* XIV (1951), 679–91. Also see a discussion of his point in Elihu Katz and Paul F. Lazarsfeld, *Personal Influence,* p. 29.

CHAPTER 19

[1] O'Hara, *Media for the Millions* (New York: Random House, Inc., 1961). See chap. 6, "Forms of the Media."

[2] For Further References See Karl E. Ettinger, "Fact-Finding for Public Relations Work," in *Public Relations Handbook,* ed. Philip Lesly (Englewood Cliffs, N.J.: Prentice-Hall, Inc., 1962), pp. 664–95.

[3] For a review of this progress in the field of electronic data processing and mathematical models, see: William N. McPhee, *Formal Theories of Mass Behavior* (Glencoe, Ill.: The Free Press, Inc., 1963); "New Tool, New World," *Business Week,* February 29, 1964, pp. 70–71 ff.; Harold Guetzkow, ed., *Simulation in Social Science: Readings* (Englewood Cliffs, N.J.: Prentice-Hall, Inc., 1962); "Proceedings of the Seventeenth Annual Conference of the American Association for Public Opinion Research," *Public Opinion Quarterly,* XXVI (Fall 1962), 457–60.

[4] From "A Summary of the Services Provided by PR Aids," Public Relations Aids, 305 East 46th St., New York, N.Y. 10017.

[5] "Can Mathematics Pick a Good Media Schedule?" *Printers' Ink,* May 11, 1962.

[6] Ithiel de Sola Pool, "The New Technology and the Public," a speech given at the 15th National Public Relations Conference, Boston, Mass., November 14, 1962.

[7] For a theoretical discusison of this point, see B.H. Westley and M.S. MacLean, Jr., "A Conceptual Model for Communications Research," *Audio-Visual Communication Review* (Winter 1955), pp. 3–12.

[8] Warren Breed, "Social Control in the News Room," in Schramm, *Mass Communications,* p. 170.

[9] William M. Pinkerton, "Businessmen and the Press," *Harvard Business Review,* XXVIII (May 1959), 25–32.

[10] Opinion Research Corporation, "The Press and Business," *The Public Opinion Index for Industry*, XX, No. 7 (July 1962).

[11] From "Party Line" issue of January 14, 1960, No. 3 (Public Relations Aids, Inc.).

[12] North American Precis Syndicate, Inc.

CHAPTER 20

[1] Ralph O. Nafziger and David M. White, *Introduction to Mass Communications Research*, rev. ed. (Baton Rouge: Louisiana State University Press, 1963), p. 238.

[2] Edward J. Robinson, *Public Relations and Survey Research* (New York: Appleton-Century-Crofts, 1969), p. x.

[3] Bogart, "Use of Opinion Research," *Harvard Business Review*, XXIX (March 1951), 113.

[4] Ibid.

[5] Robert O. Carlson, "The Use of Public Relations Research by Large Corporations," *Public Opinion Quarterly*, XXI (Fall 1957), 341–49.

[6] Ibid., p. 344.

[7] For a discussion of the corporate image see John W. Riley, ed., *The Corporation and Its Publics*, particularly the chapter by Robert O. Carlson, "The Nature of Corporate Images," pp. 24–47.

[8] For example, see the study of political decisions by Lipset, Lazarsfeld, Barten, and Linz in "The Psychology of Voting: An Analysis of Political Behavior," in *Handbook of Social Psychology*, pp. 1124–75.

[9] Berelson, "Content Analysis," *Handbook of Social Psychology*, p. 489. Other major references dealing with content analysis are: Berelson, *Content Analysis in Communication Research* (Glencoe, Ill.: The Free Press, 1952); Ithiel de Sola Pool, *Trends in Content Analysis* (Urbana, Ill.: University of Illinois Press, 1959); Richard W. Budd and Robert K. Thorp, *An Introduction to Content Analysis* (Iowa: State University of Iowa, 1963).

[10] For a discussion of this and other uses of content analysis, see Berelson, *Content Analysis*, pp. 490–507.

[11] Berelson, "Content Analysis," p. 496. For further information about readability tests see George R. Klare, *The Measurement of Readability* (Ames, Iowa: Iowa State University Press, 1963); and Rudolf Flesch, *The Art of Plain Talk* (New York: Harper & Brothers, 1946).

[12] This description and the questions listed below are extracted from the standard explanation as printed in a confidential client report.

[13] For a description of the semantic differential, see Osgood, Suci, and Tannenbaum, *The Measurement of Meaning*.

[14] For a list of further kinds of questions that might be asked in reader-

ship surveys, see: Russell N. Baird and A. T. Turnbull, *Industrial and Business Journalism* (New York: Chilton Co., 1961), p. 221.

[15] For an introductory discussion, see: Martin Mayer, *The Intelligent Man's Guide to Broadcast Ratings* (New York: Advertising Research Foundation, Inc., 3 East 54th St., 1962).

[16] U. S. House of Representatives, *Evaluation of Statistical Methods Used in Obtaining Broadcast Ratings,* Report of the Committee on Interstate and Foreign Commerce, Report No. 193, 87th Congress, 1st Session, March 23, 1961.

[17] In *Public Relations Handbook,* 2nd ed., ed. Philip Lesly (Englewood Cliffs, N.J.: Prentice-Hall, Inc., 1962), pp. 540–58.

[18] For a review of cybernetics see: Norbert Wiener, *The Human Use of Human Beings* (Boston: Houghton Mifflin Company, 1950).

[19] Baar, "Yardsticks for Public Relations," *Public Relations Journal,* XIII (April 1957), 19.

[20] Some recent literature dealing with management evaluation methods is: Raymond F. Valentine, *Performance Objectives for Managers* (New York: American Management Association, 1966); Ernest C. Miller, *Objectives and Standards,* AMA Research Study 74 (New York: American Management Association, 1966).

index

Cognitive dissonance (*see also* Cognitive consistency theory):
  justification for discrepant behavior, 76
  theory, 48–50
Cognitive maps, 66
  form of stored information, 118
Cognitive strain, avoidance of, 123–24
Cognitive structure, in memory, 136
Cohen, Arthur R., 242, 243, 255
  cognitive dissonance theory, 49
Cohesiveness, in social design, 96
Coleman, James, 264
Collective bargaining:
  economic education programs, 188
  public relations aspects, 97
  strikes, 149
Collective behavior, 177
Commitment, 76, 99
Communication (*see also* Mass communication and Interpersonal communication):
  conditions of viewing, 208–9, 211
  influence of social class, 189–92
  meaning, 31
  nature, 117
  networks:
    communities and organization, 172–173
    four small group patterns, 161–63
    single vs. multiple, 162
  research, 227–36
  setting:
    classification, 145
    conferences and meetings, 156
    psychiatric, 147–48
    structure, 147–48
Communicator, *ego state* of, 148 (*see also* Source)
Community:
  communication in, 172–74
  leadership, 199
  power structure, 171–72
Compliance:
  forced, 49
  process of social influence, 92
Conclusion-drawing, explicit vs. implicit, 71
Conferences, suggestions for running, 159
Connotative meaning, 27–28, 57–58, 117 (*see also* Expressive language)
Consistency:
  attitudes and behavior, 38–39
  human need for, 47
  theory (*see* Cognitive consistency theory)
Constancy, in perception, 118

Consumer demand, stimulation of, 83–84
Content analysis, 107, 176, 230–32
Context, of message, 23, 119 (*see also* Frame of reference)
Control:
  behavior, 7–8
  employee environment, 25
  message and media, 23
  persuasive situation, 37
Converse, Philip E., 240, 263
Cooper, Eunice, 251
Corn Products Company, 244
Corporate identification programs, 59–60
Corporate image:
  programs, 59–60
  studies, 229
Correlation, as mass communication function, 175
Coser, Lewis A., 263
Cottingham, D. R., 252
Cottrell, Leonard S., Jr., 256
Counseling, 15, 26
Counter-propaganda:
  related to one-sided vs. two-sided approach, 73
  use of retroactive inhibition, 139
Cox, Donald F., 238
  advertising, 10
Credibility, of medium, 211 (*see also* Source credibility)
Creel, George, 6
Cronbach, Lee J., 250
  teacher as identification figure, 94
Crowds, 202
Crutchfield, Richard S., 240, 242, 243, 245
  definition of attitudes, 32
  listing of motives, 44
Culkin, John M., 265
Culture:
  small groups, 155
  system, 145
  transmission of, 175
Cutler, Howard, 239
  setting of objectives, 15
Cutler, Richard L., 237, 253
Cutlip, Scott M., 246
Cybernetics:
  model of man, 115
  use as evaluation model, 234

Dahl, Robert A., 260
Dallenbach, K. M., 255
Daniel Starch and Staff, Inc., 265
Darwin, Charles, on human instincts, 43

Fine, Bernard J., 252
  authoritarian personality, 105–6
Fitch, H. Gordon, 243, 247
Flesch, Rudolf, 267
  readability formula, 231
Fluoridation, as public health issue, 96, 108
Forgetting curve, 131–32
Foskett, John M., 260
Frame of reference (*see also* Field of experience):
  field of experience, 117
  making of judgments, 74
  perceptual theory, 50
Frank, Lawrence K., 257
  tactile communication, 151
Freud, Anna, 251
Freud, Sigmund:
  ego defense mechanisms, 102
  life and death instincts, 43
Functional theory:
  attitude change, 41
  cognitive design, 65
  four functions of attitudes, 51, 101
Fundraising, 82

Gatekeeper:
  change agent, 197
  defined, 21, 164
Gaudet, Hazel, 262, 264
  two-step flow, 194
Gebbie's House Magazine Directory, 217
Gerbner, George, 238
Gestalt psychology:
  applied to corporate image, 60
  "figure and ground," 23, 135
  need to explore, 66
  sensations vs. percepts, 117–18
Gibson, James J., 253
  perceptual systems, 120
Gladstone, Arthur, 255
  preparatory communications, 139
Goffman, Erving, 244, 257
  impression management, 59, 149
  kinesics, 152
  strategic interactions, 150
Goodnow, J. J., 245
Goyal, Ramesh C., 248
Greenwald, Anthony G., 241
Gregg, Richard B., 239, 246
Grossack, Martin M., 263
Groups:
  buzz sessions, 174
  decision-making, 98
  equilibrium, 159

Groups (*cont.*)
  locomotion, 91
  secondary, 169
  substitutes for mass media, 203
Grove, Theodore G., 239, 246
Guetzkow, Harold, 266
Guthrie, Edwin R.:
  law of association, 56
  value of practice, 137
Guttman, I., 243

Hacker, Andrew, predictable man, 9
Hall, Edward T., 240
  degrees of proximity, 152
Halsey, George D., 245
  employee information, 66
Hamilton, Richard F., 262
  political attitudes, 185–86
Hammond, George, 239, 240
  public relations counseling, 26
  research of client's problems, 13
Haney, William V., 260
Hare, A. Paul, 257, 258
Harris, Seymour, 252
Harrison, Randall, 257
Hart, Clyde, 241
Hartley, Eugene L., 241, 249, 261
Hartley, Ruth E., 241, 261
Hartmann, G. W., 262
  rational vs. emotional leaflet, 72
Hatt, Paul K., occupational prestige ratings, 182
Hausknecht, Murray, 259
Hayakawa, Samuel I., 23, 239, 254
Head, Kendra B., 262
Heider, Fritz, 243, 252
  interpersonal relationships, 146
Hepler, H. W., 257
Hero, Alfred, 263
  international affairs issues, 186–87
Hilgard, Ernest R., 244, 248, 253, 254, 255
Hill, Richard J., 260
Himes, Joseph S., 259
  social institution, 170
Hollander, Edwin P., 247, 249
Holm, James N., 258, 260
  conferences vs. meetings, 156
  public speaking, 173
Homans, George Caspar, 248, 249, 250, 258
  effect of status, 165
  operant conditioning, 82
  social approval, 89
Honig, Werner K., 248

Hovland, Carl I., 239, 241, 246, 247, 249, 250, 251, 252, 255, 261, 264, 265, 266
  learning theory, 42
  mass media, 205–6
Howell, William S., 260
Hull, Clark L., 242
Hunt, Raymond G., 247, 249
Hunter, Floyd, 260

Identification:
  personal, 101
  process of social influence, 92
  teacher as identification figure, 94
Ideology:
  attitudes toward free enterprise, 37
  business creed, 187–88
  economic education programs, 188
Immediacy, as media characteristic, 208–9
Impression management, 59, 149, 150
Indexing, as memory aid, 136
Information game, in impression management, 149
Information storage, 131–37
Information theory, 122, 124
Inhibition, as defense mechanism, 102
Inkeles, Alex, 264
Innovations:
  diffusion process, 198
  small groups, 164–65
Instrumental function, of attitudes, 51
Intelligence:
  explicit conclusion-drawing, 71
  one-sided vs. two-sided approach, 72–73
  susceptibility to propaganda, 71
  three components of, 71
Interaction analysis, in small groups, 156–60
Intercultural communications, 149, 151
Internalization, process of social influence, 92–93
International affairs, attitudes toward, 186
Interpersonal communication:
  blending with mass communication, 193–204
  diffusion process, 198
  media selection, 214
  nonverbal, 147
  small groups, 154–67
  social relationship, 146–53
Interpersonal relations:
  defined, 146

Interpersonal relations (cont.)
  in drug adoption, 198
  instrumental functions, 147
Interviewing skills, 26
"Invasion from Mars," 177
Investment promotion campaign, 215–16
Issues, description of, 17–19

Jack Tinker & Associates, 61
Jackson, Don D., 256
Jahoda, Marie, 251
Janis, Irving L., 239, 241, 246, 249, 250, 251, 252, 255, 264
  authoritarian personality, 105
  preparatory communications, 139
  public health issues, 109
  self-esteem, 104
Janowitz, Morris, 260
Jeppson, Lawrence S., 260
  speaker's bureaus, 174
Johnson, Harry M., 262
Johnson, Wendell, 238

Kahl, Joseph A., 262, 263
  social class, 181, 190
Kahn, Robert L., 240
  controlled nondirective interview, 26–27
Karlins, Marvin, 246
Katona, George, 263
Katz, Daniel, 243, 245, 248, 250, 251, 252, 254, 259, 264
  functional theory, 51, 101
  general persuasibility, 103
  knowledge function, 65
  voting behavior, 106–7
Katz, Elihu, 264, 266
  opinion leadership, 166
  two-step flow, 194
Kaysen, Carl, 252
Kelley, Harold H., 239, 241, 246, 249, 250, 251, 252, 255, 263, 264
  effect of status on communications, 189–90
Kelman, Herbert C.:
  ethics of social science, 6
  processes of social influence, 92
Kerner report (see Report of the National Advisory Commission on Civil Disorder)
Killian, Lewis M., 261
  collective behavior, 176–77

Parsons, Talcott, 252, 256
  social systems, 145
Participants, in social action programs, 171–72
Pavlov:
  captive audience, 63
  classical conditioning, 45, 55–56
Payer, Janet S., 245, 260
Payne, Donald E., 239
Perception:
  classical approach, 115–19
  defined, 115
  external and internal factors, 118–19
  man's perceptual system, 115
  perceptual barriers, 116
  subliminal, 116
  technical aids to, 121
Perceptual theory:
  attitude change, 41
  cognitive design, 66
  credibility, 50
  television advertising, 57
Personality:
  authoritarian, 105
  dogmatism, 106
  in marketing, 83
  system, 145
Persuasion:
  defined, 3
  limits of, 6
  nature of communication problems in, 12
  related to authority, force, and freedom, 4–5
  vulnerability to, 102
Persuasive monopoly (see also Monopolization):
  "total institution," 43
  totalitarian societies, 24, 97
Peterfreund, Stanley, 263
Peters, Raymond W., 249, 259
Peterson, Theodore, 261
  magazines, 179
Pharmaceuticals, and diffusion process, 197–98
Pigors, Paul, 259
Pilditch, James, 256
  corporate communications, 149
Pinkerton, William M., 266
  business press, 220–21
Planning, use of research, 227
Pluralistic ignorance, defined, 177
Pluralistic society, 9
Political attitudes:
  college students, 89
  interest theory, 186
  social class, 183–87

Political attitudes (cont.)
  socialization process, 37
Political campaigns:
  advertising agencies, 60–61
  image-building, 60
  inducing action, 40, 138
  Nixon-Kennedy debates, 60
  television commercials, 61
  use of mass media, 202
  voting behavior, 95, 106–7
Political sociology, 183–87
Politz, Alfred, 248
Pool, Ithiel de Sola, 266, 267
  simulation, 219
Postman, Leo J., 250, 255
  rumor transmission, 134–35
Prejudice:
  anti-prejudice propaganda, 103
  anti-Semitism, 33, 127
  effect of social status, 187
  Nazi Germany, 107
  personality design, 100
Preparatory communications, 138
Press clipping services, 233–34
Pressure group communications, 200–202
Prestige, of medium, 211
Primacy, law of, 73
Primary group, 144 (see also Small groups)
Print media, 209–10 (see also Billboards, Magazines, and Newspapers)
Printers Ink, 218
Proactive inhibition, 139
Projection, as defense mechanism, 103
Projective techniques, 36, 87, 119
Proof, Toulmin model of, 69
Propaganda:
  compared to persuasion, 3
  evasion of, 103
  "innoculation" against, 139
  sociopolitical programs, 187–89
Pseudo-environment, 9, 21
Psychological formula, S-O-R related to learning theory, 42
Public health and safety:
  cranberry case, 108
  personality design, 107–9
Public information programs, 69–70
Public relations:
  collective bargaining, 97
  counseling, 13, 26
  dealer relations, 199
  expenditures, 6
  ideological campaigns, 107
  media relations, 219–20
  media services, 222
  personality design, 100

Social status (*cont.*)
  in shopping, 190–91
  socioeconomic basis, 182
Social stratification, 180 (*see also* Social
    Status)
Social sub-system, defined, 145, 146
Social system:
  communication in large social systems,
    168–79
  defined, 144–45
  importance in communication, 144
Sociograms, 162–64
"Socratic method," arousing inconsis-
    tency, 77
Source (*see also* Objectives):
  in communication model, 11
  as employer or client, 12–16
Source credibility:
  ethos, 21
  expertise vs. trustworthiness, 21, 93
  likability and prestige, 22
  local vs. cosmopolitan, 167
  loss of, 25
  and perceptual barriers, 116
Spector, A. J., 244
  corporate image categories, 60
Speech:
  and cognitive design, 68–69
  in communities, 173–74
  conferences vs. meetings, 156
  conversations, 146, 150
  study of audience, 79
Speed of transmission, as media char-
    acteristic, 215
Standard Rates and Data Service, 217
Starch impression study, 231
Steele, Fred I., 256
Steinberg, Charles S., 261
Steiner, Gary A., 237, 238, 242, 243, 249
  classical conditioning defined, 56
  hypnosis, 7
  image of man, 7, 9
  subliminal projection, 8
Stephenson, Howard, 239, 246, 260
Stereotypes, 65, 146
Stevens, Leonard A., 240
  retention of speech, 131
Stevens, S. S., 242, 255
Stimulus:
  intense, 116
  internal, 79–80
  learning theory, 42
  motive arousal, 87–88
  part of S-O-R formula, 30
  unpleasant, 80–81
Stimulus situation:
  ambiguity in, 97

Stimulus situation (*cont.*)
  defined, 20–21
  defining of, 38–39
  design of, 20–26
Stokes, Donald E., 263
Storage, of information, 121
Stouffer, S. A., 245
Strategy:
  defined, 10
  execution of, 28–29
  master plan, 10
  in social relationships, 149–50
  steps in design of, 11–26
  strategic interactions, 150
Strauss, Anselm, 263
  social class and language, 191
Subliminal perception, 116
Subliminal projection, 8
Suci, G. J., 240, 254, 267
Sullivan, Albert J., 240
Supplementation, of mass media, 193–200
Surveillance, as mass communication
    function, 175
Survey Research Center, 265
  media usage study, 206
Sussman, Marvin B., 260
Sutton, Francis X., 252
Swanson, Guy E., 249, 250

Tactile communication, 151
Tannenbaum, Percy H., 240, 254, 255,
    267
  incongruity principle, 75
  indexing, 136–37
Target audience (*see* Audience)
Taylor, Wilson, "cloze" readability test,
    125
Teaching machines, 211
Television:
  advertising in, 57
  characteristics, 208, 209, 212
  news dissemination, 195
  in political campaigns, 60
  in riots, 175
Tension, 47, 80, 81
Thayer, Lee O., 259
Theories:
  of attitude change, 41
  balance, 40
  cognitive consistency, 46–50
  cognitive dissonance, 48
  congruity, 48
Theory, usefulness in counseling, 14
Thorndike, Edward L., law of effect, 82
Thorp, Robert K., 267